Corsair

Books by Andrew Sinclair

Prohibition: The Era of Excess
The Emancipation of the American Woman
The Available Man: The Life Behind the Masks of
Warren Gamaliel Harding
Dylan Thomas
Jack: A Biography of Jack London
John Ford

NOVELS

The Breaking of Bumbo
My Friend Judas
The Raker
Gog
Magog
The Facts in the Case of E. A. Poe

Corsair

The Life of J. Pierpont Morgan

ANDREW SINCLAIR

Little, Brown and Company — Boston – Toronto

FIRST EDITION

LIBRARY OF CONGRESS CATALOGING IN PUBLICATION DATA

Sinclair, Andrew.
Corsair: the life of J. Pierpont Morgan.

Bibliography: p.
1. Morgan, John Pierpont, 1837–1913. 2. Bankers—United States—Biography. I. Title.
HG2463.M6S56 332.1'092'4 [B] 80-22525
ISBN 0-316-79240-3

MV
Designed by Susan Windheim

Published simultaneously in Canada by Little, Brown & Company (Canada) Limited

PRINTED IN THE UNITED STATES OF AMERICA

Acknowledgments

I am most grateful for the help of the staff of the Widener Library at Harvard University and of the J. Pierpont Morgan Library in New York City. I am further indebted to Mr. Henry Morgan and Mr. Herbert Calhoun for making available to me the papers on J. Pierpont Morgan held in his library. The editorial assistance of Robert Emmett Ginna, Jr., has been invaluable.

I am also grateful for permission to quote from the following works:

Excerpts from *The Story of a Varied Life* by W. S. Rainsford, reprinted by permission of Christina Rainsford.

Excerpts from *Memories of a Happy Life* by Bishop William Lawrence, reprinted by permission of the copyright holder.

Excerpts from *J. Pierpont Morgan: An Intimate Portrait* by Herbert L. Satterlee, copyright 1939 by H. L. Satterlee, renewed 1967 by Mabel Satterlee Ingalls, reprinted by permission of Macmillan Publishing Co., Inc.

Excerpts from *Lady Sackville: A Biography* by Susan Mary Alsop, copyright © 1979 by Susan Mary Alsop, reprinted by permission of Doubleday & Company, Inc.

Contents

An Accounting xi

1. The Balance Sheet of Youth 3
2. Guns, Gold and No Glory 15
3. Robbery Among the Barons 27
4. Cure by Acquisition 39
5. A System for Society 50
6. Blackmail, Water and Order 58
7. Trust, or a Gentlemen's Agreement 70
8. The Enemy of the West 80
9. The Gold Bugs and the Government 91
10. The Grand Style 105
11. Steel, Rails, Raids and Murder 124
12. An Uncrowned Monarch 140
13. Adversaries in Harness 159
14. Panic, 1907 174
15. A Discriminating Collector 192
16. Going Down and Going Up 209
17. Death in Rome 219
18. The Rich Are Different . . . 230

Chapter Notes 241

A Select Bibliography 251

Index 257

Illustrations

Between pages 146 and 147

Pierpont Morgan at sixteen
Junius Spencer Morgan
Cragston, Pierpont Morgan's summer home
Mrs. Junius Spencer Morgan
The J. Pierpont Morgan home on Madison Avenue
J. Pierpont Morgan, 1868
Mrs. J. Pierpont Morgan, 1902
A gallery of some of Morgan's friends and foes
Morgan satirized in a cartoon
As commodore and yachtsman
Morgan's yacht *Corsair*
The Morgan family's home at Prince's Gate in London
With King Edward VII at Nuneham Park
Maxine Elliott
Morgan defends his privacy
Wall Street in the panic of 1907
The Morgan Library
The West Room of the Library
Morgan at the Pujo Committee Hearings
With his daughter, Louisa Satterlea and his son, J. P. Morgan, Jr.
The Harvard Club of Khargeh
The Morgan Bank building at Wall and Broad streets

An Accounting

THE heavy old man with the huge ruby nose sat in the committee room. He was seventy-five years old, and he had been called to testify about what he had done in his life. He was believed to be the head of a Money Trust, which could create and avert panics on Wall Street. He was said to have saved the gold standard of the United States. He was known to be the most powerful financier in America and perhaps in the world. His name was J. Pierpont Morgan.

Yet that December morning of 1912, the self-promoting chief counsel of the congressional committee did not call Morgan to be a witness. For Samuel Untermyer had a canny sense of what was news. He knew the value of the late-afternoon sensation that would become the headlines at tomorrow's breakfast table. So he did not call Morgan to be examined at once, but left him to doze at the back of the room. Occasionally the old man woke to glare with his piercing eyes at anyone unwise enough to disturb him.

Untermyer had helped to publicize the concept of a Money Trust so that he could prosecute it for his own glory. An ambitious man who wanted to become a legend was trying to destroy an aged man because he was already a legend. It was not so much David against Goliath, but the ass braying against King Midas. A public spectacle was being made of a great figure, who feared nothing except ridicule and muckraking.

Morgan was bored and weary to death of his expensive attorneys who kept on advising him on what he should say. He would not listen to them. He had always looked out for himself. Even if he moved slowly now and his memory was intermittent, he knew what he had done and was proud of it. He also knew that he would give Samuel Untermyer nothing at all. There would be no sensation and no disclosures.

When he was finally called to the dais where the investigating committee was sitting, he tried to stick to his famous taciturnity. He would only say "Yes" and "No" in answer to the questions. Then his sense of theater and his need to dominate asserted themselves. He began banging on the table and barbing his answers. He refused to admit that anything wrong had ever been done by the house of Morgan. There was no

Money Trust. He had never been the head of one. The whole idea was a political invention. The committee was chasing the chimera it had created.

He was right in his way. The days of his youth were forever gone. Then a few speculators could drive up the price of gold or create a shortfall in the Treasury of the United States. But now there was an international currency market, and New York was only a small part of it. By incredible willpower and self-assertion, he had saved the gold standard in America for Grover Cleveland as later he had saved the credit of Wall Street for Theodore Roosevelt. But he was too old now for such grand gestures. In his arrogance, he believed that nobody else could have done it, that nobody else could take his place, and that everybody should know that he had done it all for the good of his country.

He did not display this arrogance in the public show being made of him. He chose to deny the character he had assumed since his father's death twenty-two years before. He said he did not have vast power. He said he did not run his own firm, J. P. Morgan and Company. He said he was not the final authority in it. He had never been. In fact, he was unconscious of any power he was meant to have.

The spectators were amused. Morgan was refusing to admit what everybody knew, that he was a financial behemoth who still bestrode the earth. He denied all the sharp practices of the companies he was deemed to control, the stock-watering and the price-fixing and the voting trusts. He did state that he preferred combination to competition, but even then, he said he liked a little competition. His chief hate was manipulation of the market. And his second hate was explanation. When asked why he had bought control of a large insurance company, he would only say, "For the very reason that I thought it was the thing to do."

He declared that he always distinguished between his own interest and the public interest. He knew the difference between what was good for him and what was good for his country. He had always done what he believed to be right in the circumstances. As for a Money Trust run by a few of his men, whom Untermyer claimed to be holding 341 directorships in 112 corporations capitalized at more than $22 billion, that was untrue. There were no plots in his business. Everything depended on who you were and were known to be.

MORGAN: The question of control, in this country, at least, is personal. That is in money.

UNTERMYER. How about credit?

MORGAN: In credit also.

UNTERMYER: Personal to whom — the man who controls?
MORGAN: No, no. He never has it. He cannot buy it.

Above all men, he knew that it was impossible to control the money power of the United States. The only check in a time of panic was the authority of one man, himself. And yet, what he said was true for him alone. His personality dominated the other bankers and managers of credit. He had no need for written or illegal agreements. A word in his mouth was an order elsewhere. He had stamped his mark on national and international finance. His name on a list was enough to make up a syndicate. Morgan meant reliability, millions, credit, trust.

Untermyer returned to the attack:

UNTERMYER: Is not commercial credit based primarily upon money or property?
MORGAN: No, sir. The first thing is character.
UNTERMYER: Before money or property?
MORGAN: Before money or anything else. Money cannot buy it.
UNTERMYER: So that a man with character, without anything at all behind it can get all the credit he wants, and a man with the property cannot get it?
MORGAN: That is very often the case.
UNTERMYER: But that is the rule of business?
MORGAN: That is the rule of business, sir.[1]

By saying that the first thing in credit was character, Morgan stole the headlines from Untermyer. He was certainly the first character in international commerce at that time, also the second very rich man who was as sure as Andrew Carnegie that he had earned his passage through the eye of the needle. He was the last symbol of an era when never before had so few been allowed to make so much at the expense of so many. It could not last, it was not lasting. That was why he was being examined on the dais in the congressional committee room.

Yet he won his final victory. Nobody could prove that there was or had been a Money Trust. He was exhausted now. Even though he left the room with his enemies baffled and his reputation of flawed greatness intact, he had used up his resources. He had to believe his legend, that he had saved America time and again; but he was being everywhere reviled for ruining his country. He had lived too long into contradictory times.

Even if the New World was ungrateful, there was still the Old. He was tired unto death. He would sail away to the worldly wisdom of London, the ancient wisdom of Egypt, the ultimate wisdom of Rome. These were fit places for the end of a man who had always served a nation that had once trusted him too much and now had turned on him. There must be other judgments on what he had done.

At one time, he had been reproached for the secrecy of his dealings.

"You would not show your books to anyone," his friend and confessor W. S. Rainsford had said to him.

"Well, Rector," Morgan had replied, "the time is coming when all business will have to be done with glass pockets."[2]

The time had already come for Morgan to be open about his business, to look back clearly, to balance the books of his life. Even when a boy, he had been taught to cast up his accounts, a penny here, a few cents there, and to go to church regularly. There was a calculus in business just as there was surely a final judgment. That is what his grandfathers and his father had taught him in those simpler days in Connecticut long ago.

Corsair

1

The Balance Sheet of Youth

> The whole composition of our society is arithmetical; each gentleman ranking according to the numerical index of his property.
>
> — Francis J. Grund, *Aristocracy in America* (1839)

The year of John Pierpont Morgan's birth, 1837, was a year of panic for the infant economy of the United States. God, greed and inexperience seemed to conspire against the new nation. The crash had its withered roots in a crop failure two years before. The heavens had blighted the grain on the prairies. The farmers of the West had become dependent on the spreading web of early canals and railroads to send their produce to the factory cities of England. Without those shipments, the European money that had financed the new transport systems could not be serviced. This was the ominous act of God.

Greed had driven on the speculation in western lands. There was "a mighty spreading and shifting" in the virgin territories on either side of the Mississippi — "good land, dog-cheap everywhere, or for nothing, if you will go for it."[1] The result was an insane exchange of title deeds and a price spiral as tens of millions of acres were bought from the government and sold more dearly for drafts on unsteady local banks. Paper empires covered the wilderness, discounting invisible farms where buffalo still roamed over the red grass.

The towns of the East, like Hartford, Connecticut, where the Morgan child was born on April 17 of the panic year, had been emptied of the restless and the enterprising and the failures. Home ground had been abandoned to the canny ones who stayed behind, men of the nature of the child's grandfather Joseph Morgan. He preferred to run a hotel rather than build a sod house, to deal in town lots not in virgin lands, and to sell insurance against the natural disasters he did not care to undergo. His fortune was, indeed, based on the great Wall Street fire of December,

1835, when he had made his Aetna Fire Insurance Company pay up promptly in order to attract more business at triple rates.

The inexperience of the people's President, Andrew Jackson, had hastened the crash. He had particularly represented the back country and the South because he seemed a self-made and self-sufficient man, Old Hickory, someone who dared to do. In a time of expansion and ferment, when fortune favored the rough and resolute, Jackson was its ideal. His successes and failures in his eight years in the White House had been part and parcel of his belief, not in the common man, but in the uncommon man who could make himself rich through hard work, without a government to stop him.

In the name of free competition and opportunity, Jackson had attacked the Second Bank of the United States because its policy of currency control and tight credit denied western farmers and small businessmen the loans they needed to expand. He had destroyed the bank's hold on the economy just as he had destroyed the British at New Orleans. "The Bank," he had declared to his Vice-President and successor, Van Buren, "is trying to kill me, but I will kill it."

In killing it, he killed off restraint on the money supply in the United States. The income from federal customs duties and land sales had already paid off the national debt and was now deposited in favored state banks, which lent more and more money to land speculators. Credit was stretched beyond its outer limits, debt piled on top of debt, as paper acres spread from hand to hand. And when some mercantile houses failed in London in 1836 because of American defaulters, Jackson moved too late to dam the flood. A Specie Circular now required payment in gold or silver for government lands; a Deposit Act limited federal funds at the favored banks. The result was a draining of bullion and a calling in of loans. Cotton brokers collapsed in New Orleans, land companies went bankrupt in their thousands. Within the first month of the Morgan child's life, the Hartford banks had to suspend payment in silver and gold.

The age of Jackson and the financial crisis actually created more opportunity for the Morgan family. Encouragement of speculation led to a flood of foreign investment, handled by new eastern bankers. One of them, the thrifty and charitable merchant and railroad pioneer George Peabody, had set up two years before the panic a banking house in London to compete with the Barings and the Rothschilds in selling American securities to English investors reaching out to tap the resources of the colonies they had lost. "We did not care three straws for that separation — " an Englishman told Francis Grund in Jackson's time, "for our annual commercial balances against you are now greater than they ever were before the revolution. . . . As for your *independence*, it's all my eye and Betty Martin, as the saying goes, as long as you borrow money, and we are the ones that lend it you. A man in debt has lost his freedom, and the same holds of a nation."[2]

Yet the middleman, who stands between the debtor and the investor, gains freedom and power from his intervention. The Morgan family in the town of Hartford, growing on its fledgling insurance industry, stood between the urgent needs of the bursting West and the long reach of the exploiting British Empire. The panic of 1837 had already shown how international America's economy had become. The new merchant banking houses like George Peabody and Company might come under severe pressure because of default by many American states and companies on the interest payments on their securities. But with a man like Peabody, who had foreseen the panic and had advised his associates "to keep everything *snug*, and be prepared for the emergency," foreign confidence in the United States would soon revive, especially as he himself bought in depreciated state bonds to preserve his country's credit and wait for their rise once the panic was over.[3] The year after the panic, he arranged in London a loan of $8 million for the bankrupt state of Maryland. He knew, as Edward Everett said, how to perform the miracle by which an honest man turns paper into gold.

The future, as smaller merchants like the Morgans of Hartford knew, belonged to the brokers operating between the American interior and the London market. They would become the conduits of capital for the development of the nation's prosperity — and their own. Since they were largely untaxed and unregulated, they would be able to grab spoils beyond the dreams of Midas, and international financial power beyond the reach of Washington. Their strength would grow in the absence of government. And more certainly than the British statesman George Canning, they would call the New World into existence to redress the bank balance of the Old.

Stories of the youth of tycoons suffer from the golden hindsight of their later success. Precocious smartness is found in the cradle and on the playground. But in John Pierpont Morgan's case, it was found in the family. He was no Horatio Alger boy, beginning his rise from rags to riches by saving pennies or picking up pins from the street. He rose from respectability to aristocracy, from pews to power. His Morgan grandfather was a shrewd Hartford trader, politician and dealer in real estate, while his father, Junius, would make the big jump from storekeeper to international banker.

His mother, however, represented his father's one act of folly allied with social advancement. Juliet Morgan was the daughter of the Reverend John Pierpont, the outspoken preacher of the Old Hollis Street Congregational Church in Boston. Zealous in opposing slavery and strong drink, he offended his flock, who tried to oust him from his pulpit. He would not go, for he was a man of principle who had written the famous poem about Dr. Joseph Warren's address to the militia as the redcoats were advancing uphill from Boston at the start of the American Revolution:

> Stand! The ground's your own, my braves;
> Will ye give it up to slaves?

So John Pierpont Morgan was born with one foot in Connecticut trade and the other in a Boston pulpit. He had two serious illnesses in his infancy, but survived with a weakened constitution to play with his three sisters, born in succession after him. The strongest early influence on him seems to have come from his Morgan grandfather, who spent much of the day in church on Sundays at morning and afternoon and evening services, and much of the week entertaining Whig politicians and businessmen. Jacksonian Democrats and freethinkers were damned; good order was praised in state and church and heaven. In the diaries of his youth, John Pierpont Morgan would always note the hymns that were sung and even the verses omitted from them. In religion, he was taught to be exact.

In 1844, the railroad was completed linking Hartford to Worcester and Springfield and Boston. Grandfather Morgan abandoned his interests in stagecoaches and became a director of the new company. He took his grandson on a first trip by rail, something which was never forgotten. The next year, the boy was sent alone on the cars to stay a week in Boston with his mother's father. The aging radical preacher was giving up the fight against the Proper Bostonians and soon accepted a call from a church in Troy, New York. Near there, the causes and fads of the time had found their theater and battleground. Spiritualism, magnetism, cold-water cures and phrenology were smoking alongside temperance, antislavery and woman's rights in the brush fires of reform and revivalism of this "Burned-Over" District of frequent change.

With the removal of the firebrand preacher as an influence, the young

Pierpont Morgan lived out the years of his childhood in Connecticut. Once he went fishing with two older boys, fell in the river, and was saved only by catching hold of the fish pole as he was going under for the last time. As yet, he showed none of the shrewdness of Tom Sawyer, who took in trade while his friends whitewashed the board fence for him. And he seems to have had little more formal education than Huckleberry Finn at the start. He was nine before he went to his first "dame school," and after a brief stay at an Episcopalian academy the same year, was brought back to be with his Morgan grandfather in the old man's last six months of life.

The slow deaths of relations at home gave a melancholy and necessary understanding to children in the nineteenth century. The young Pierpont Morgan spent many months watching his grandfather pass away. This sad perception was counterbalanced by a boisterous and close friendship with his two Goodwin cousins, who went to the local Pavilion Family School. There Pierpont was sent to board at the age of ten and to start on the study of the classics, French, German, arithmetic and decent handwriting. He was large for his age and dominant among the other boys, forming the partnerships among children that are now called gangs. In those days, his group was called a society; young Pierpont's training made him become its secretary and treasurer with an account book which he had checked at his father's store.

His first business venture was with Jim Goodwin at the age of twelve. The boys made and exhibited a diorama of the landing of Columbus. Young Pierpont was the senior partner and kept the accounts, recording the purchase of materials, the sale of tickets to view, and the final balance sheet. He was already trained at home to reduce the discovery of the New World to a ledger entry. It was a New England system of education that Bostonians found praiseworthy. The city's rich men were mostly self-taught country boys in origin, "possessed of no other learning than the art of making dollars in a neat, handsome, clean manner." Their proficiency gave them a higher standing in society than if they had known all the philosophy in the world and made them fit husbands for the old families' daughters.

It was to Boston that Junius Morgan went in 1851 to set up a dry goods store with a partner called Beebe. He was following the trail that George Peabody had blazed from local merchant through seaport trade toward international finance. The year before, he had visited England to see the sights and set up contacts with Baring Brothers and other banking firms. While in London, he had received a letter from the young Pierpont, the first in a long transatlantic correspondence. Junius had praised the boy for sending him political intelligence he had not known.[4]

As young Pierpont showed little will to work at the high school in Hartford, he was sent to a boarding school in Cheshire, Connecticut. His father wrote to him to be careful about making friends, "not to get intimate with any but such as are of the right stamp." Pierpont followed his father's advice, becoming friendly with Joseph Wheeler, later a Confederate cavalry commander and a major general in the Cuban campaign at the end of the century. He agreed with Junius's words: "*Now* is the time for you to form your character and as it is formed now so it will be likely to remain."[5]

Character formation had to do with keeping money and accounting for it. In a revealing letter, Junius reproached the thirteen-year-old for losing a small sum from his pocket. "You were very foolish carrying it with you," Junius wrote, "and should not have done so, and trust you will be wiser the next time. I enclose you one dollar towards your allowance as I suppose your loss will put you entirely out of money. Hope you will put this in safe place, and not spend it foolishly — keep a correct account of the money you receive and spend."[6]

When his father moved the family to a modest house in Boston, young Pierpont was soon enrolled in the English High School on Bedford Street, an institution his preacher grandfather had helped to found. Boston was then a city under tight Yankee control. The Irish and German and Italian immigrants were kept to their ghettos and the dock areas, while the good high schools were reserved for the older emigrants from England. There was no question of young Pierpont's mixing with the new Americans who were to become the industrial masses of the eastern seaboard. His separate education gave him no chance to meet the poor or the alien. Their problems were no part of his rearing. Early his mind was formed to separate business from the irrelevant lives of those who toiled in its factories. He might have to see poor people unavoidably in the packed streets of Boston, still so small in the 1850s, but he never had contact with them or chose to enter their lives.

The quirky and acute Francis Grund noted the impossibility of a northern aristocracy in early American society. There was a monied movable group of people who thought themselves superior, distinguished by their greater display of wealth and waste. But the mark of aristocracy was stability, and the moguls of the mid-nineteenth century depended on luck and the business cycle. The particular genius of the American people, Grund claimed, was its ability to create an instant aristocracy, "cheap, and plenty as bank-bills and credit, and equally subject to fluctuation. Today it is worth so much,—tomorrow more or less,—and, in a month, no one will take it on any terms. We have, in fact, at all times, a *vast deal* of aristocracy; the only difficulty consists in retaining it."[7]

Yet times were changing, international finance growing, the first great American fortunes of the Astors and the Vanderbilts purchasing the physical separation between rich and poor, impossible in the squash and hurly-burly of the young Atlantic cities. After the Civil War, Junius Morgan and his son would enjoy a gilded age and create a family so monied and stable and set apart in its style of life that it could be called aristocratic as the generations passed. But in the young Pierpont's boyhood, the ambitious had to be content with pretensions and "the incessant craving after artificial distinctions."[8]

Even at the time of the small fortunes of Jacksonian democracy, when to be rich in Boston meant to have a hundred thousand dollars, Grund noted the thrift and caution that ruled business there. It was opposed to the wild genius of the New York merchants, who, "if every other resource were to fail them, would not hesitate one moment, instead of payment, to take and offer drafts payable in the moon." The chief defect of the Bostonians seemed to be their overpraise of common sense. "All the rest we consider as moonshine," a Bostonian said to him. "You must know that a young man learns as much in six months in a counting-room as in four years at college [which] only made poor gentlemen, and spoiled clever tradesmen." Particularly repellent to Grund was the local teaching method of paying students for getting good grades. "No stimulus to learning," the Bostonian continued, "can be half as great as when a boy can figure it out on his slate how many dollars and cents his geography, grammar, spelling, reading and good conduct comes to *per annum*."[9]

Young Pierpont was taught common sense and how to measure out his life in dollars and cents. If he was exposed to the Brahmin culture of Whittier and Emerson and Oliver Wendell Holmes, his school notebooks showed no sign of anything but an ordered arithmetical mind, which preferred statistics to descriptions, even classifying the Holy Land in square miles, and by longitude and latitude. He kept up his business partnership with Jim Goodwin by letter, accounting for purchases in each other's cities, and describing their relationship as "Goodwin, Morgan & Co." Perhaps he was only the earnest monkey of his father's acts, but already he was showing a taste as well as a head for business. At the back of his diary he even kept a cash account, showing his weekly quarter divided cent by cent into candy and pencils.

He was doing better at school, rising near the top of his class before illness struck him down when he was fifteen. He developed rheumatic fever in hip and knee. He tried to go on with his education, but he had to take to his bed for months. It was the turning point of his life because he was forced to consider the nature of illness and death. He was also conscious of missing many of the pleasures of youth — the lounging and the flirting, the jokes and the camaraderie. A prolonged early illness is a factor in the lives of many great men, a forced period of isolation and introspection, out of which they appear to rise more decisive and aggressive, as if compelled to seize the satisfactions and years they have lost.

A picture of Pierpont at sixteen shows a strong-jawed boy with a low forehead, thick dark hair, small eyes and a prominent nose as yet unmarked by the disfiguring red blight inherited from his mother and her father. The strength of the features is softened by a sensitive and sensual mouth; suffering from illness seems to have aged the face. There is a seriousness in the expression not only due to holding a pose in front of an early camera lens.

Worried about his son's health, Junius Morgan sent him on the barque *Io* to the Azores for a long convalescence. One of Pierpont's legs was now shorter than the other, and he was so weak that he had to be carried on board. But a winter in Fayal, watched over by the American consul, who was a family friend, restored the invalid's health. He rode a donkey until he could walk again, and he enjoyed the relaxed Portuguese pace of the island. The coming and going of ships was the lazy barometer of his excitement; the mail and newspapers from America were his chief delight. Storms sometimes drove battered ships ashore, and he dutifully noted down the insurance value for his father. But his sense of melancholy and isolation was increased with the death by tuberculosis of his best friend on the island, Dr. Cole, whose grave he would visit fifty years later.

In April, the young man sailed to England to meet his father and mother, who had come over on a business trip. He climbed up the dome of St. Paul's Cathedral and held a million pounds in notes in his hand in the Bank of England. His parents had a significant dinner with George Peabody, already a power in the City of London. Then he was taken on his first European tour through Belgium, Germany and France before returning to see Queen Victoria and the Prince Consort review the military maneuvers in Surrey. The grandeur and order of British life did not fail to impress him, for he visited Windsor Castle, tried to get into the House of Lords, and listened to a sermon by the Archbishop of Canterbury. His trip ended with brief excursions to Scotland and Ireland before the return voyage across the Atlantic. It was a pattern for travel that the young man would not forget.

Recovered now, he began working in the various departments of his father's store until high school opened again. He had lost a year's education, but soon caught up and stood near the head of his class. When school was over, he often visited his father's office, as though commerce were already in his blood. He played few games, gave little offense, and made no great effect. But his graduation composition was, predictably, on Napoleon.

It was an ordinary boyhood. Young Pierpont was his father's child. His opportunity was the same as that of Junius Morgan, whose own father had invested shrewdly enough in Hartford to set up his son in business. The one special circumstance was Pierpont's long illness, in which he developed a secret strength and taciturnity, hardly yet evident among the silent awkwardnesses of adolescence. But there was nothing else to distinguish him from ten thousand other Yankee merchants' sons, no indication that he would succeed triumphantly on the failures of so many of his contemporaries. His boyhood lacked the materials of myth. He had a practical upbringing in an expanding country, where equality meant the opportunity to become richer than other people.

George Peabody was an aging and wealthy bachelor. His generosity and his charity were famous, his politics eccentric for a man who had made a fortune of twenty million dollars. He was a friend of the utopian socialist and businessman Robert Dale Owen, and he gave half a million pounds to build Peabody homes for the working poor of London — so well built that many still survive. He remained a republican all his life, even refusing a knighthood from Queen Victoria. He was praised as a champion of the poor by such radicals as Louis Blanc and Victor Hugo. Yet he and Joshua Bates of Baring Brothers, and August Belmont, who represented the Rothschilds in New York, were the three hard creators of the financial links between London and the United States before the Civil War. Through them, the capital flowed that allowed the American railroads to increase their length seventeen times over in the twenty years after 1837, until foreign investors were holding one seventh of all American stocks and bonds.

The business was proving too much for Peabody on his own. He wanted a partner and an heir. Junius Morgan had impressed him in London and was rising by the same path he had taken through Boston.

In 1854, Peabody offered the younger man a partnership if he would cross the Atlantic and settle in London. Junius accepted, knowing how rich and respected Peabody had become from his small offices at 22 Old Broad Street. This was an extraordinary opportunity and chance of inheritance.

Before he transferred his family to London, Junius sent off young Pierpont with his cousin Jim Goodwin on a tour upcountry. They went to Buffalo on the new Erie Railroad, soon to become infamous from its financial mismanagement by Jacob Little and Daniel Drew. Then they proceeded to Niagara Falls and Saratoga, taking the network of tiny rival railroads, struggling to survive. Short of money, they caught the boat back from Portland, Maine, and arrived home without a cent. So young Pierpont knew of the inefficiency of the competing tracks sprawling toward the West — and of what it was like to be dead broke.

His father enrolled him in a popular finishing school for American boys on Lake Geneva, the Institute Sillig. Like the young Byron fleeing his country, Pierpont could enjoy the sight of the high peaks rising above the lucid lake. He grew in strength toward the tall and burly man he would become, over 200 pounds and capable of carrying for miles one of his comrades who had sprained an ankle. He did well in French and mathematics; a later legend claimed that he was a prodigy in calculating decimals. He certainly relaxed enough to show the impulsive good nature he had inherited from his mother, except for a month of surliness during another illness.

Only the first frightful outbreaks of his hereditary skin disease marred his confidence and his face, although he could boast to Jim Goodwin that he pursued beautiful girls through a series of private subscription balls got up with the young men of Vevey. He was particularly struck by a Swiss Miss Hoffmann; his letters disguised the self-consciousness and shyness caused by his temporary disfigurement. He sounded like an aged relative when he cautioned his cousin not to fall for an opera singer in Hartford, because both of them would become merchants and should select wives who would suit their homes and duty.

In April, 1856, young Pierpont left his Swiss academy to spend more than a year at the University of Göttingen, famous in New England from its connections with Franklin and Bancroft and Longfellow. Although he hardly spoke a word of German, he enrolled in courses of lectures on trigonometry and chemistry. He also became a member of the Hannovera, one of the German student corps that specialized in drinking and dueling, and had been led by Otto von Bismarck. Not wishing to add to his facial scars, young Pierpont refused to fight with sabers, but kept his green corps cap with pride.

He returned to London in the summer to work as an assistant to George Peabody, trying to put the old man's papers in order. He was bored and found himself acting as a guide to visiting American friends of his father's. Even Miss Hoffmann's visit did not distract him from his pledge to marry a good American wife, although he wrote to Jim Goodwin that he would never meet her equal. But back at Göttingen, he plunged into the study of German and mathematics, again creating a legend that if he had stayed there, he would have become a professor, such was his gift for figures. He and his father, however, had no intention of taking the low pay of the high road to learning. So when Junius negotiated a place for his son in the New York office of his friend Alexander Duncan of Duncan, Sherman and Company, young Pierpont left Göttingen in 1857. His final toast to the other German students mistakenly wished them long and lasting sorrow.

Pierpont Morgan had been born in a year of panic, and he began business in a year of panic. But then, as the New York *Herald* noted, "a little panic now and again in Wall Street has only a momentary effect — it merely serves to give the fashionable and monied classes a short breathing time — and off they start again in the race of enjoyment and extravagance, with renewed ardor."[10] Brought up in thrifty households in Connecticut and Massachusetts, young Pierpont had never seen people approved for wasting so much, "a reckless system of expenditure . . . prodigal of other people's money."[11] In this movable aristocracy that was swamping the old Knickerbocker families by its lavish living on credit, he was one of the few businessmen who came from two generations of wealthy men and whose ancestors had reached the New World soon after the arrival of the *Mayflower*. In American terms, young Pierpont was already an aristocrat and would remain so if his family could keep their money.

The causes of the new panic were much the same as the previous one, although acts of God and inexperience had less to do with it. It was begun by the collapse of the grain market when the Crimean War ended and there were no more armies waiting for bread in bulk. The Gold Rush to California and the hope of an inexhaustible flow of bullion had encouraged the same wildcat issue of bank drafts as in the age of Jackson. Moreover, the acquisition of the American Southwest after the war with Mexico had meant more land to exploit, more railroads to build. As one commentator noted, premature railroads had fostered premature cities, teeming with premature traffic for a premature population.[12] The only things that matured were payments on the bonds used to finance the future: this "Western Blizzard" snowed Wall Street under in the year that Pierpont Morgan came there at the age of twenty.

The panic was signaled by the failure of the Ohio Life and Trust Company for five million dollars. Nine hundred other companies failed in its wake. Even the steady house of Peabody was in trouble, unable to collect from its American creditors because payments in specie were again stopped by the banks. The Bank of England itself had to save Peabody's firm by lending it a million pounds on the strength of the old financier's prestige. The negotiation of the loan was Peabody's last service to Junius Morgan before he began to prepare for his retirement. Even young Pierpont had to admit to his father that going to the Bank of England for a loan was "rather mortifying to the pride."

The survival of the Peabody house meant the survival of Duncan, Sherman and Company. Pierpont Morgan had observed his first major crisis, which had nearly destroyed the firm in which he worked and his father's fortune; at one low point, Junius confessed to his son that he felt as if all he had collected in twenty-two years was gone.[13] One message was clear: gold was the only stability in a world of paper dreams. Without that security in reserve, young Pierpont might have joined the ruined thousands in the street and fulfilled his father's doubts about him. For Junius, like most fathers, was known to express the fear that his son would not be able to take his place. He said on occasion, "I don't know what in the world I am going to do with Pierpont."[14] Of course, Pierpont knew.

2

Guns, Gold and No Glory

I am never satisfied unless I either do everything myself or personally superintend everything done even to an entry in the books. This I cannot help.

— J. Pierpont Morgan (1862)

In the years before the Civil War, New York was a small city of some half-million people clustering on the tip of Manhattan Island, where the business was done. Uptown began at the smart houses around Washington Square, and the blocks soon petered out beyond Seventeenth Street, where young Pierpont shared rooms with a young Peabody. He was following his father's advice after the crash of 1857, not to set up a separate establishment. "These times call upon all of us to use great *economy*," Junius had written, and so young Pierpont would walk or ride to work downtown at 11 Pine Street, where he was learning bookkeeping from Charles H. Dabney, another friend of his father's.[1] He showed his usual flair for keeping accounts. He had kept them all his life.

He was unpaid, as if he were serving an apprenticeship. His father kept him dependent by giving him an allowance. His real job was to act as Junius's eyes and ears in New York. He knew the sailing times of the steamers to England, and he would get on each of them a long letter to his father in London, explaining the progress of American business in general and Peabody and Company's in particular. These outspoken and confidential letters were bound by Junius in volume form and kept until his death in 1890. They were an autobiographical record of thirty-three years of business activity. Pierpont destroyed nearly all of them at the end of his life, when he feared for his later reputation and decided that the taciturnity which was his trademark should extend from beyond the grave.

Another aspect of Pierpont's life has been forgotten. Like his contemporary Edward, Prince of Wales, who had to linger until old age before he might succeed his mother on the British throne, Pierpont existed in his father's shadow until he was nearly fifty years old. Although he was to show his independence in his American dealings, he was always accountable to the London office. He was his father's agent and weekly reporter, never his own man. He was also, in effect, an only son; his younger brother had died in March, 1858, seven weeks before Pierpont's twenty-first birthday. Junius had lost the love of this gentle, affectionate boy. Now he put all his hopes and strictures on his surviving son, who had come of age. "Do not let the desire of success or of accumulating," Junius wrote, "induce you ever to do a single action which will cause you regret. Self-approbation and a feeling that God approves will bring a far greater happiness than all the wealth the world can give."[2]

Yet Junius Morgan let his young dog run on a long leash in New York. With his sense of the proper order of people and things, Pierpont could be trusted to move with the right people in the right circles. The friends of his own age bore old names, Charles Lanier and George Bowdoin. He was joining St. George's Episcopal Church, where the Reverend Tyng was the shepherd of a well-born flock with fleeces of gold. He sought out his father's friends, the Babcocks and the Ketchums, who noticed the young man's liking on Sunday evenings for singing hymns strenuously by the piano.

He also met the Sturges family, long established in Manhattan. They attracted him through their cultivation of the genteel arts and through the refinement of their daughter Amelia, called Mimi. Older than Pierpont, she was almost Quakerish in the severe style of her parted hair and prim dresses; but there was a sweetness and understanding in her that attracted the protective and reserved young man, whose silence was often unnerving. In fact, he was dropped from the board of a railroad company, where his father had placed him, because he never opened his mouth at meetings and stared fixedly at the other directors.

On a visit to New York, Junius Morgan approved of his son's courtship of Mimi Sturges and asked his wife to take her back to London in 1859. Pierpont was left to go down to Cuba to learn about sugar and shipping there, and to acquire a fine taste in cigars. Then he sailed back to study the cotton business in New Orleans. He spent much of his time on the levee, examining the boats as he always had since his convalescence in the Azores. With the arrogance of a rich man's son, he made his first speculative killing. He bought up a cargo of coffee with a sight draft drawn on Duncan, Sherman and Company, then sold the coffee in small lots and cleared several thousand dollars. By the time his firm had telegraphed their protest, he was able to reply that he had made a profit. Even if he had lost, he knew that Junius Morgan would have honored the sight draft. To him whose father hath shall it be given.

Partly because of this act of independence, Duncan, Sherman and Company refused Junius Morgan's demand for a partnership for his son, even though the Peabody house had just saved the firm during the panic. Pierpont sailed to London for the summer to see his parents and Mimi Sturges, then returned with her to New York for the winter. She was frail in the romantic style popular in mid-Victorian times, and he too, despite his powerful body, was subject to strange fainting fits, probably nervous in origin. Yet when his skin erupted and disfigured him, his strength would return, as though the blight drew off the mysterious weakness in his system. He also bolted his food and suffered from stomach attacks. "You are altogether too rapid in disposing of your meals," his father wrote to him from London. "You can have no health if you go on in this way."[3]

Pierpont also dealt privately and as his father's agent in New York, particularly in the cotton market. Business at home was booming as the nation lurched toward civil war. The government needed loan after loan to build up its armed forces, and Pierpont was a pipeline to those Europeans who feared a civil war and needed to stockpile raw materials such as cotton. When the first shots were fired on Fort Sumter, Pierpont decided to serve the Union by doing what he did best: arranging loans on the London market and looking out for his own interests.

If the New York market was raffish in the last years of the peace, when the fortune of the shipping and railroad magnate Cornelius Vanderbilt was being seized in the teeth of other greedy men, it was vicious and malignant during the war. Speculators follow armies as sharks follow wrecks. The Union military machine had a thousand wants, and tens of thousands of manipulators tore at each other to profiteer from their country's needs. The worst of them, the wizened and sanctimonious Daniel Drew, had made his first money by selling himself for a hundred dollars as a draft substitute in the War of 1812; but now, he gave up "wiggle-waggling" Erie Railroad stock and led those fattening on Union blood.

"It's good fishing in troubled waters," he said. "We fellows in Wall Street have the fortunes of war to speculate about."[4] One of the minor speculators was J. Pierpont Morgan. He had had "rather a serious year" financially in 1860, as his father pointed out to him.[5] He needed to recoup.

To this day, the Hall Carbine Affair discredits the name of Morgan. The muck has been raked, the mud thrown. The facts are indisputable. In the spring of 1861, the chief of ordnance in Washington agreed to sell some six thousand army carbines at $3.50 each, as they were. The buyer was an obscure gun dealer from New Hampshire called Arthur M. Eastman. His only recommendation was a letter of introduction from a home senator. He did not have the capital to pay for the weapons.

The smoothbore carbines were out-of-date breechloaders. They had been popular in the Black Hawk and Mexican wars, but they had to be converted from flintlock to percussion. They had been superseded by the Sharps and Burnside rifles; but five thousand of them, delivered in 1852, still lay unused in their packing cases on Governors Island off Manhattan, while another thousand were scattered across other government armories. With their steel barrels and loading levers, these weapons were the best of their make. Eastman knew the facts and hoped to profit from them, should the South begin to win the war.

The rout of the Union troops at Bull Run provoked a scramble to equip the new forces raised by the North. Eastman saw his opportunity. He approached a leading Republican politician in New York called Simon Stevens, a vain, plausible and tricky man of some social standing. Stevens agreed to buy the carbines on condition that Eastman have the barrels rifled and the breeches enlarged to meet minimal army standards. He contracted to pay $20,000 in five days for the five thousand improved carbines against a final purchase price of $12.50 each. He knew of Major General Frémont's desperate need for arms to equip his troops in the West. The carbines were offered at $22 apiece. Frémont accepted. He had used the weapons on his old campaigns. They had worked well and were now available. Nothing else was.

Yet Stevens had no more capital than Eastman did. Both were middlemen without resources. However, Stevens had long-standing connections with Pierpont Morgan. His sister Sophia had taught the boy at the Hartford High School — history, grammar and arithmetic. His brother Henry was a book buyer for the Smithsonian Institution in London, and a friend of George Peabody's and Junius Morgan's. So Stevens approached Pierpont Morgan in New York for a loan of $20,000 secured on the five thousand carbines. Young Morgan advanced the money on condition that all receipts from their sale should first go to him, so that he could repay himself for his loan and collect interest, his expenses and a commission.

Morgan took a personal and canny interest in his loan. He went with Eastman and Stevens to Governors Island to pay the captain in command $17,500 for the five thousand carbines at $3.50 apiece. The balance of the $20,000 was paid to Eastman. Probably at Morgan's request, Stevens confirmed his deal with Frémont by cable. The general wanted the weapons improved and shipped to him in St. Louis as soon as possible.

The rifling of the smoothbore barrels took weeks. Morgan lost patience and began to press Stevens for repayment of his loan. He refused to allow the shipment of the second half of the carbines until he had received full payment for the first half. It was the act of a good financier and a poor patriot.

Stevens was still committed to pay the rest of the purchase price to Eastman, who otherwise could repossess the guns. Morgan refused to advance him any more money. So he approached the private bank of Ketchum, Son and Company. The senior partner, Morris Ketchum, was a close confidential friend of Morgan and his father. He advanced Stevens enough to pay off Eastman a few days before Stevens's agent in St. Louis used his influence on Frémont's captain of ordnance, who spent most of his meager funds to settle in full for the first twenty-five hundred Hall carbines. This draft, for some $55,000, reached Morgan a week after the Ketchum loan to Stevens and five weeks after his own loan to buy the guns. He deducted interest at 7 percent, his expenses, and a commission of a dollar a carbine, thereby clearing nearly $6,500 for his help to the beleaguered Union.

That was the end of Pierpont Morgan's direct involvement in the matter, but not of his connection with the scandal. Frémont proved unlucky and incompetent; he lost his command. Rumors of war profiteering led to the creation of a select committee of the House of Representatives to examine government contracts. Frémont's purchase of the Hall carbines at more than six times the price the army had sold them to Eastman seemed a scandal. "The arm had been rejected from the public service as practically worthless years ago . . ." the committee found. "If so, the re-purchase of the arm is without any possible excuse; if otherwise, the original sale of the arm is utterly indefensible."

The committee did not censure Pierpont Morgan at all. It only accused the chief of ordnance in Washington and Frémont in St. Louis of blundering and failing to communicate. Eastman was condemned for speculating on the misfortunes of his country; Stevens was suspected of acting as Frémont's agent and doubling the price to sweeten his own pocket. "To seize upon the pressing necessities of a nation, when the welfare of the whole people is in imminent peril, and the more patriotic are sacrificing life and fortune in the common cause, to gratify a voracious cupidity and coin money out of the common grief, is a crime against the public safety, which a sound public policy must condemn."

An ordnance commission was set up to settle war claims against the government. In the Morgan case, it followed the congressional committee's findings and sought to settle with Ketchum and Stevens for a fraction of the sum they still claimed from the sale of the Hall carbines, having only received half the sum agreed by Frémont. The matter finally went to the Court of Claims and was judged in favor of Ketchum six years after the scandal. The U.S. government ended by paying with interest more than six times what it had received for the sale of its own weapons.

The discovery of this shoddy business was a boon to the muckrakers in the Progressive era and to the Marxists in the Depression years. Even during Morgan's life, a biased version of the Hall Carbine Affair was used by Gustavus Myers to condemn the financier's ethics and patriotism in his *History of the Great American Fortunes*. His findings were overused by the enemies of capitalism for the next thirty years. Then a vice-president of J. P. Morgan and Company devoted a whole monograph to the scandal in an attempt to clear the founder's name.

Yet the excuser accused. Whitewash spreads the dirt. Although such distinguished historians as Allan Nevins praised the monograph for completely exploding an old fiction by a dubious author, the bank vice-president printed damaging facts, until then ignored. He stated that Morgan personally went to Governors Island to check the carbines and pay the government for them; it was no arm's-length transaction. He showed the family connection between J. P. Morgan and Simon Stevens and allowed the possibility of collusion. And he demonstrated Morgan's ruthlessness in witholding the shipment of half the carbines to Frémont until payment had been made, despite Frémont's telegram: GOOD MEN ARE LOSING THEIR LIVES WHILE THE MEN WHOM THEY DEFEND ARE DEBATING TERMS.

Most damning of all, a facsimile of Ketchum's account with Stevens, taken from the banker's evidence given to the House investigating committee, was reprinted without comment. Ketchum stated that not only did Morgan receive $26,343.54 to settle his original loan, his commission, his expenses and interest, *but also that a certain J.P.M. received a further check for $3,797 two days after Ketchum's first loan to Stevens.*[6]

The House committee did not ask for an explanation of this added payment. Ketchum did not volunteer one. The Court of Claims upheld it. The government paid for it. The only plausible explanation is that J. P. Morgan took another brokerage fee of 7 percent on the first Frémont draft of $55,000 for introducing the business to Ketchum, although he was pressing Stevens at the same time for immediate repayment of his advance money. At any rate, his profit from his brief loan was more than 50 percent at 10 percent a week. It was usury at a time of national emergency.

A remarkable fact of the affair was that J. P. Morgan was never summoned to give evidence before the House select committee or the ordnance commission, even though he was the payee for the carbines when Frémont bought them. His sudden marriage to the sick Mimi Sturges in October, 1861, and his seven months' stay afterwards in Europe removed him from America during most of the investigation by Congress and the commission. If he did not mean to escape giving evidence, yet he was overseas.

J. Pierpont Morgan had a Puritan conscience and an Episcopalian sense of sin. The first pricked at him persistently, the second was excused through public piety. Unlike many of his friends, he did not volunteer to fight in the Civil War. He was fit and strong, even if liable to an occasional fainting spell. He simply did not choose to go.

Yet he knew perfectly well than tens of thousands of men were being butchered to defend his privileged life in New York. Moreover, he had made a large profit from selling the hard-pressed federal army its own weapons, and Congress was angry at war profiteering. He was young and proud — and now under scrutiny from himself, the state and his God. He resolved on an act of expiation.

It was romantic and quixotic, a tribute to his impulsive heart and contradictory generosity. He decided to marry Mimi Sturges, although she was weakened by tuberculosis and probably doomed. The urge to save her was confused with his need to avoid the problems of the Civil War. When he was a youth, flight had built up his powers after his physical collapse. Now, going away to battle death for his love might cure his moral collapse. In saving one life abroad, he might forget the sacrifice of so many lives at home. And he might recover his sense of self-approbation and the feeling of God's approval.

He gave his cousin Jim Goodman power of attorney to run his affairs in his absence from his small office at 54 Exchange Place. He insisted on a quick marriage against his father's objections and those of Mimi's father. He won his way. Mimi was already so weak that the ceremony took place in the Sturges town house. None of the groom's family were present, only the bride's. Morgan's new rector, the Reverend Tyng from St. George's Church, married the couple, with the strong husband holding his wife upright during the short service. The wedding guests watched through open folding doors. Mimi was too ill even to attend the wedding breakfast, and Morgan had to carry her out to a carriage, which took them to the pier and their escape across the Atlantic.

Another generation, another choice. While the young Morgan for personal reasons left the United States in its time of travail, his grandfather went to war to bring consolation to the troops. At the age of seventy-six, the Reverend John Pierpont lived up to his radical principles. He enlisted as a chaplain with the Twenty-sixth Massachusetts Regiment and served in its camp on the Potomac until he was transferred to Washington because of his age and poor health. After the victory of the Union, his eightieth birthday would serve as a celebration for those who had finally abolished slavery. He would see little or nothing of the Morgan family for the rest of his life and die in poverty.

Meanwhile, Pierpont and Mimi were sailing to Liverpool on the *Persia*. They visited his family in the London house at Prince's Gate before going on to winter in Algiers and then in Nice. Junius Morgan took "a gloomy view" of Mimi's case and was proved right. The rest and the sun in those leisurely Mediterranean cities could not save her. Mrs. Sturges sailed to Nice to be present at her daughter's deathbed in February, 1862. She stayed with the inconsolable husband for two months after Mimi's burial, then returned with him to the United States at the beginning of May. A photograph taken of him at that time shows his suffering. He is wearing a black suit and a tie over a stiff white collar. His features are set with pain, his hair and mustache are unkempt, his eyes tortured and luminous.

He threw himself into business again to forget his personal loss. With Jim Goodwin, he founded his own firm, J. P. Morgan and Company. He found he could delegate little, even to his closest friend. "The wear and tear upon me does not arise from deficiency in help," he wrote to his father in September, "the fault is with myself and myself only. It is my nature and I cannot help it. When I have responsibilities laid upon me I cannot throw it upon anyone else."[7]

Morgan still did not equate his sense of responsibility and his private tragedy with the national cause. He continued to be able to live in compartments. His heart had nothing to do with his business mind. His feelings were irrelevant to his economic actions. He could strongly support the Union and declare that the United States would become the richest and most powerful country in the world, but he would also speculate against Abraham Lincoln's treasury policy in order to make a killing in the market. As yet, his mind was so curiously organized that he seemed blind to the relation between the public good and his private gain. His profit meant more to him in the end than his patriotism.

On some occasions he did help the Union cause through his connections with the Peabody house. When the financier Jay Cooke disposed of his three great government loans through the New York market to subsidize the Union armies, young Morgan passed on the information to London, where his father's firm subscribed heavily to the loans. It was also the Peabody house which paid the million pounds in gold demanded by the British government as a compensation fund against claims by the Confederacy before it would embargo the building of privateers in British shipyards.

Although after the war the Peabody firm was accused of acting as a funk hole for American capital flowing out from the hazards of the fighting, and even of supporting the blockade runners that brought the essential cotton through to the English mills, there is no question that old George Peabody himself was a republican and Union supporter. Yet business was business for him, too, and Junius Morgan was not as scrupulous as he. The impossible choices forced on him by the Civil War finally persuaded Peabody to hand over his firm totally, so that he could devote himself to his many charities. Junius liked to tell the story of the old man standing with a bad cold in the rain to save a penny on bus fare while on his way to contribute one hundred thousand pounds to the London poor. But he was not so charitable himself when he took control. He changed the company's name to his own, J. S. Morgan and Company, leaving Peabody to be remembered by his good works and a statue put up by the grateful City of London.

If Junius Morgan was growing even richer from transferring funds from the North of America to England and back again, his son was once again involved in dubious speculations. He formed an association with Morris Ketchum's son Edward and had installed in his office the first telegraph wire in Wall Street, so that he could receive immediate news from the battlefronts. With this advance knowledge, he and Edward Ketchum could operate successfully in the most fevered commodity of dangerous times — gold.

For patriotic reasons, the New York Stock Exchange discouraged gold speculation by those profiteers whom Jay Cooke called "evil geniuses." They were driven to a dingy back area where a certain Gallagher ran a "gold room" that stayed open when the official one had closed. The scenes of dealing often seemed like a Roman circus:

> In the days of the war an unexpected victory converted the gold arena into a den of wild beasts. The bulls fought against the inevitable decline with the ferocity of gladiators. The chaos of voices and the stamping of feet shook the building as in an earthquake, and boomed out of the open windows into the street below like the discharge of artillery. . . . The gloom or the gladness over success or defeat of the national flag mingled with individual passions. Men leapt upon chairs, waved their hands, or clenched their fists; shrieked, shouted; the bulls whistled "Dixie," and the bears sang "John Brown"; the crowd swayed feverishly from door to door, and, as the fury mounted to white heat, and the tide of gold fluctuated up and down in rapid sequence, brokers seemed animated with the impulses of demons, hand-to-hand combats took place, and bystanders, peering through the smoke and dust, could liken the wild turmoil only to the revels of maniacs.[8]

With their advance information from the telegraph, young Morgan and Edward Ketchum joined the battle and secretly acquired some two million dollars' worth of gold in small quantities. Ostentatiously, they then shipped to Junius Morgan in England half of their hoard to raise the price. They kept enough reserves to buy in more gold from other speculators who were trying to break their corner in the bullion market. Finally, they unloaded their treasure at a profit of $160,000. They ignored Abraham Lincoln's desire to shoot off the devilish heads of all the Wall Street gold gamblers, who played games with the currency during a national emergency.

Such actions pushed Congress to pass a gold bill in 1864 to end the speculation. Young Morgan was secretary of a bankers' association that denounced the lawlessness of Congress in trying to cut down their profits. The measure proved ineffective, driving up the price of gold still higher on the black market until the bubble burst with the Union victory and Edward Ketchum was ruined, turned to forgery, and ended in jail.

Young Morgan had left that dangerous game in good time, although he lost all the profits from his transactions through the forged gold certificates of his partner. It was the second of his discreditable actions during the war. That thousands of other businessmen in New York were behaving just as badly does not excuse his behavior, nor does it excuse his avoidance of the draft of 1863, which was called after the Battle of Gettysburg. He paid for a substitute to serve in the army instead of himself, a normal practice at the time for young men who thought themselves rich, superior or important. The list of later financial magnates who avoided fighting was a dishonor roll that included Jay Gould, Jim Fisk, the elder John D. Rockefeller, William H. Vanderbilt, Andrew Carnegie, Philip Armour and the young Mellon. "It is only greenhorns who enlist," Judge Thomas Mellon assured his son. "In time you will understand and believe that a man may be a patriot without risking his own life or sacrificing his health. There are plenty of other lives less valuable or others ready to serve for the love of serving."[9]

It is true that Pierpont Morgan was no hypocrite, running away to the West to speculate in pork contracts or pretending pacifism. He simply took advantage of the law and hired "the other Pierpont Morgan" to take his place in the ranks. He could plead that he had been ill enough from a sort of smallpox the previous winter to make his mother come across from London to nurse him. But by July, 1863, he was in very good health; even his skin disease and fainting fits had left him. He was in better shape than tens of thousands of Union soldiers slogging toward Lee's guns. It was the act of an arrogant young man who felt himself richer and better than most other people. He salved his conscience, however, by renting a pew in St. George's Church, selling government bonds, and helping charities for the wounded and war widows.

Junius Morgan might approve his son's avoidance of the war, but he was unhappy in general with his behavior. If he set the Hall Carbine Affair and the Gold Room disaster with Edward Ketchum alongside the doomed marriage to Mimi Sturges, he could only have seen a mixture of questionable dealing and romantic instability. Although his son had efficiently seen to the affairs of the new J. S. Morgan and Company in America, he decided to curb Pierpont's independence. He arranged for the brilliant and trusted accountant from his son's first firm, Charles H. Dabney, to join his son as the senior partner in his New York house. Pierpont was forced to agree to take on this mentor, guide and watchdog.

By 1864, Pierpont Morgan's personal income had reached more than fifty thousand dollars a year. He was leading the social life of a wealthy young widower, sharing a small house with his other partner, Jim Goodwin. He was always being asked out to dinner, and thrifty about time, he learned to dress in a white tie and tails in a matter of minutes. He was not a man to waste hours on trivialities, although he loved playing games with small boys and girls, organizing the church's business, and moving the Young Men's Christian Association to better premises to bring in more members. The war hardly affected him at all.

He did not mourn Mimi Sturges publicly for too long, even if the memory of her dying always marked him with a secret sorrow. He met the six handsome daughters of a leading New York lawyer, Charles Tracy, a man of political astuteness who was also prominent in the affairs of St. George's Church. He was particularly attracted by the cameo loveliness of Frances, who responded to his loneliness and longing for family life. After a short engagement, he married her with his father's warm approval at the end of May, 1865, and took her to Europe to meet his parents. They approved his choice, happy to see their son happy. A short trip to Paris and to Pierpont's old school in Switzerland followed, and then the young couple returned to set up house on Madison Avenue. There, every Sunday evening, Pierpont sang his favorite hymns vigorously with his friends, especially "The Church's One Foundation."

The years of civil war that had unsettled the nation had settled Pierpont Morgan. The impulsive, awkward youth who had worked without pay for his father's friends had avoided the scandal which had affected some of his associates and had emerged as clean as a ledger entry, as promising as a deposit account. He had married well the second time and was soon elected to the vestry of the leading Episcopal church in Manhattan. Little was known about his ventures in Hall carbines or the Gold Room, and these hardly mattered in a society that respected sharp business as long as it was kept out of the drawing room for which it had paid. The ethics of the money changer must have nothing to do with the temple of the home.

The young Pierpont Morgan was respected and respectable. He had sowed no wild oats, only a few tares among the wheat of the golden harvest that would follow the war.

3

Robbery Among the Barons

> No one could yet guess which of his contemporaries was most likely to play a part in the great world. A shrewd prophet in Wall Street might perhaps have set a mark on Pierpont Morgan, but hardly on the Rockefellers. . . . Out of any score of names and reputations that should reach beyond the century, the thirty-years-old who were starting in the year 1867 could show none that was so far in advance as to warrant odds in its favor.
>
> — Henry Adams, *The Education of Henry Adams* (1918)

When the war ended, another war began. It was still the war of the North against the South, but fought by different means.

Lincoln's assassination began the other war. To finance the old one, he had allowed the new profiteers and millionaires to begin the corruption of the Republican party into that of big business and high tariffs. Three railroad companies had been given seventy million acres outright, in return for laying tracks to the West. National banking acts had been passed to remove power from the states to Washington and deny Jackson's assault on central financial control. A huge federal debt had been incurred, which made the government vulnerable to eastern and foreign bondholders. A westerner himself, Lincoln could not have raised the money for the Union without mortgaging his own people to the Atlantic manipulators. And his death prevented any mercy to the defeated South. The good he did was interred with his bones. The evil his party did lived after him.

The radical Republicans inflicted an odious and corrupt government on the South and reduced it to poverty for generations. They disenfranchised the southern Democrats, thus turning their own party into a majority one. The plutocrats who had made fortunes from supplying war needs captured the party and used it against northern factory workers and western farmers. Both the national and the states' governments showered favors on industrialists and speculators, and politics often seemed a mere greasy wrestle in a full pork barrel.

What was curious was the acquiescence of the American people in the open corruption at the top. War weariness was one reason, the dream of individual wealth another. The myth of rags to riches inspired most Americans. It was true of Wall Street's worst plunderers, Daniel Drew and Jay Gould. As a farmboy, Drew had fed cows with salt to make them blow out with water before a sale, and he still watered stock in the Erie Railroad to make his millions. Country tricks worked in the big city. The backwoods trail still seemed the high road to Fifth Avenue.

Those who had licensed themselves to loot society did not find it hard to explain their self-interest as the national interest. Samuel J. Tilden was to put it well to the assembled magnates at a dinner for Junius Morgan: "While you are scheming for your own selfish ends, here is an over-ruling and wise Providence directing that the most of all you do should inure to the benefit of the people. Men of colossal fortunes are in effect, if not in fact, trustees for the public."[1] Thus, vast wealth was justified, great greed confused with public service, and vile methods of accumulation called good for the nation.

This comfortable doctrine suited a political system that became corrupt and exploiting after the Republicans waved the bloody shirt in 1868 and put General Grant in the White House. He was unable to influence the House of Representatives, which was described by a former congressman as an "auction room where more valuable considerations were disposed of under the speaker's hammer than in any other place on earth."[2]

With graft in government and social restraint for sale, Wall Street was given over to the most audacious gang of pirates in American history. The old speculators like Commodore Cornelius Vanderbilt were unscrupulous bullies, prepared to bribe legislatures and judges, but the Commodore's practices stopped short of outright fraud. He would defy the law, but not deny it until he had bought its change. And he would keep all he seized. "To hear to 'em," he said of the few radicals who dared to point at his plundering, "ye might think a feller didn't have a right to what was his'n."[3]

Yet when he tried to take over the Erie Railroad to add to his three lines already running to New York, he had to fight Drew and his allies: Jay Gould, "the corsair," and fat Jim Fisk, "the supreme mountebank of fortune." Even he went down before their barefaced skulduggery. He was defeated by a flood of false stock, by a deluge of bought injunctions, by largesse to the legislature beyond the dreams of El Dorado, and by open warfare from thugs and "Erie specials." He had to settle for a loss and withdraw, partially paid off by Drew and Fisk and Gould's plundering the Erie Railroad still more than they had already done. In all, they increased the swollen capitalization of their company by some $60 million in eight years. It was a story "of fearsome speculation, of revolting dishonesty, of superlative profiteering."[4] And these were the people Pierpont Morgan intended to challenge and defeat in open warfare.

Until his struggle against Fisk and Gould, the life of Pierpont Morgan had been domestic, profitable and calm. His wife Frances bore him two children, Louisa Pierpont and another John Pierpont Morgan. He followed fashion and moved his family higher up Madison Avenue, where the rich were emigrating from Washington Square. And he rented a summer house upstate at Buttermilk Falls. On the commuter train back to New York, he struck up a friendship with Samuel Sloan, who had been president of the Hudson River Railroad before Vanderbilt snatched it, and who now headed the Delaware, Lackawanna & Western. He encouraged Morgan's interest in railroads at the time when the wars of consolidation were beginning with Vanderbilt's defeat in the Erie affair.

Dabney, Morgan and Company was already heavily engaged in dealing in railroad securities for the international market founded by George Peabody and developed by Junius Morgan. When Vanderbilt wanted British iron rails to improve his tracks, he used Pierpont Morgan to arrange and finance their import. Although ranked only sixteenth among the leading New York banking houses in 1870, Dabney, Morgan was known as a firm of high repute that dealt largely in railroad stocks. "In London," a contemporary wrote, "it has been very popular with railroad men and railroad contractors. It has been able to control an immense trade."[5]

The control actually lay in the hands of Junius Morgan, now the most important American banker in London. The Victorians' confidence in the railway system at home led them to suppose, wrongly, that the same stability might be found in investing in American railroads. So Junius Morgan was able to sell on the London market even such dubious offerings as $4 million worth of 6 percent Erie bonds, watered by Daniel Drew thinner than workhouse gruel.

Andrew Carnegie, then hustling the beginnings of his own colossal fortune, also managed to sell Junius Morgan another $5 million worth of Allegheny Valley Railroad bonds, although he had been unable to unload them in New York or on the Barings. He had already impressed the elder Morgan by selling him bonds to pay for the building of a bridge over the Mississippi at St. Louis and gave the London banker the first refusal on all his schemes. Junius Morgan rarely turned down the young man, recognizing in him a similar righteous ambition to be rich, and when he was asked unblushingly by Carnegie to pay him a quarter of the profit made by the use of any of his ideas, he agreed.[6] By 1869, Europeans owned one third of all American government bonds, a billion dollars' worth, with another half billion invested in American companies; and two years later, Junius Morgan would sell the greater part of $110 million worth of American stock dumped in London that year.

So powerful did the lure of the railroads become that conservative financiers, once repelled by the notorious example of the Erie Railroad, now competed for the different stock offerings. Junius Morgan made a connection with Philadelphia house of Drexel and Company through the Allegheny Valley bonds, because the Drexels had been sucked into the affairs of the guarantor of the bonds, the Pennsylvania Railroad. Even the great Jay Cooke, who had spurned an offer to finance the Northern Pacific Railroad, was seduced on a western trip by the possibilities of Minnesota and changed his mind, committing his resources and prestige to laying tracks across the prairies.

Pierpont Morgan was not immune to the contagion. In the spring and summer of 1869, he took his wife, a sister-in-law and a girl cousin by rail to the Far West so that he could examine the terminals in Chicago and reach the railhead in Utah. In Salt Lake City, he visited Brigham Young and later claimed he nearly lost his sister-in-law to the Mormon leader as his twenty-first wife. Stagecoaches took the party on to California to meet the Central Pacific Railroad, which would take them to San Francisco. During their long California holiday, the last spike connecting the Central Pacific with the Union Pacific was driven home at Ogden, Utah, so that Pierpont Morgan could take one of George Pullman's newfangled "gorgeous traveling hotel" cars all the way back across the continent. He had time to brood in private state about the huge sums needed to send other such tracks spinning the length and breadth of America until they might bind the markets of West and South and North in an iron web.

On his return, Dabney, Morgan and Company floated an issue of $6.5 million worth of Kansas Pacific Railroad bonds to help open up the prairies to the ports. And Morgan was given the chance to get into the railroad game close to home. His friend Samuel Sloan told him of the war on the Albany & Susquehanna Railroad, only 142 miles long, but a vital link between three other rival railroads, all competing for contracts to carry coal. Jay Gould had begun to buy up stock in the line and to secure injunctions from the judge used against him by Vanderbilt. These prevented the board of the Albany & Susquehanna from issuing new stock to protect itself and forced the suspension of the railroad's president, Joseph Ramsey; the judge even appointed Jim Fisk as a receiver until the ownership of the railroad could be settled.

Ramsey fought back and found another judge, who confirmed his rights and gave him an injunction against the Fisk receivership. Fisk and his men then seized some of the rolling stock and one end of the line, while Ramsey seized the rest of the cars and the other end. Each side hired gangs to do battle, which finally broke out at the Harpursville tunnel. There the Ramsey men captured a Fisk locomotive, which was then rammed by another enemy engine, causing a fracas with knives and revolvers and bottles between the two drunken mobs. At one moment, twelve thousand men were facing each other in the rival camps, and the governor of New York State threatened to call out the militia to keep the peace. Of course, nobody thought of the passengers wanting to use the line.

The split of the railroad was paralleled by the split of the law. Ramsey's judge set aside the injunctions of Gould's judge, and Gould's judge returned the compliment. But Ramsey had made an error: he and his supporters had bought their additional stock in the company on the security of the company's bonds, putting down only 10 percent in cash. This trickiness made him vulnerable. He had no money left for bribing the legislature. Hearing this, Samuel Sloan, who hated the open robbery by the Erie bandits, advised Ramsey to consult Pierpont Morgan because he was backed by the vast reserves of his father in London.

Morgan wanted to fight. He knew that railroads were the future of the nineteenth century. He was also the opposite of Drew, Gould and Fisk, the Speculative Director and the Corsair and the Mountebank. Although he was proud of bearing the same name as the pirate Henry Morgan, and though he was to call each of his four black-hulled yachts *Corsair*, he was a gentleman buccaneer who wanted to organize and consolidate, exactly as his namesake had done when he had united all the pirates and led them to sack Panama for the British Crown. Both Morgans wanted to eliminate competition and opposition in order to rule, while primitives like Drew and Gould and Fisk wanted to obliterate their rivals and each other for the sake of becoming personally richer. Morgan's way was the way leading to the trusts and cartels that would provoke the intervention of the federal government; the Erie directors were merely grander cutthroats than those seen by Grund in Jackson's day, divided into as many different castes as there were ways of getting rich, without a rallying point "because everyone makes money for himself, and not for his neighbor."[7]

Morgan also disapproved of the Erie directors. They were self-made, vulgar men who devalued the worth of serious financiers. Even in that permissive age, Jim Fisk's flamboyant life with chorus girls in the gilt-and-plush Pike's Opera House, which he had converted into the Erie offices, and Drew's blatant frauds behind his mask of piety, and Gould's stealthy and submarine assaults on every principle said to be dear to businessmen — these offended the young banker with his Puritan descent, his Episcopalian faith, his new membership in the Union Club, and his closeness to his family. He wanted an end to the indiscreet debauchery and financial saturnalia that tarred all with the black excesses of the few.

He engaged his father-in-law Charles Tracy as his attorney and was advised to retain a tough Albany lawyer, Samuel Hand, in order to resist the political pressure of Boss Tweed, who was working for Fisk and Gould. Dabney, Morgan and Company bought six hundred Albany & Susquehanna shares to give itself an interest. The judge in the pocket of the Erie immediately issued an injunction against the sale by Ramsey. But Morgan checked the legal position with Tracy and Hand at Albany, and he had a stockholders' meeting called there. A later legend states that Morgan and Ramsey personally threw Fisk and some of his Bowery Boys downstairs to keep them from attending. Whether the story was true or false, Fisk did not disrupt the meeting and held a rival one of his own. Each side claimed control of the little railroad and peppered the enemy with injunctions thicker than buckshot.

Then the Erie directors fell into Morgan's trap and sent a letter to the governor of New York, requesting him to supply a nominee to run the railroad until there was a legal solution. Before the governor had time to consider, Morgan, now a director of the company, held a board meeting and persuaded Ramsey and his supporters to lease to him the railroad through the Delaware & Hudson Canal Company. He had the lease drawn up and signed at Albany before the Erie forces had time to stop him with an injunction. Later, the state supreme court confirmed the lease and Ramsey's legitimacy. The company stock rose six times over. Morgan had won his first triumph in the railroad wars.

It was as astonishing a victory for the young Morgan as Gould's had been against Vanderbilt. An organizing genius had blocked the slippery and the fraudulent, who had defeated the most unscrupulous bully of them all. It was a prophetic win, foretelling the triumph of the trusts to come, and showing how ephemeral the fortunes of the scandalous speculators might prove to be. Wealth needed combinations to endure for generations. Gould and Fisk and Drew could well have asked with Brecht's Macheath: What is robbing a bank compared with founding a bank? But they were thieves without honor who could not understand that a little credibility might make a rich man able to hand his gains on to his heirs through the institutions he had made.

In one way, Morgan only won a Pyrrhic victory in the Albany & Susquehanna affair. He had learned the dirty tricks of his enemies, the stock-watering and the forging of share certificates, the blackmail of rival lines, and venal legal devices. He knew the worst methods and could apply them to his own use. It was dangerous knowledge. For he had the one thing the Erie gang lacked: the backing of international finance through Junius Morgan. Gould was so impressed with that resource that he was to ask Junius to join the Erie board just before he was ousted himself.

Perhaps Jay Gould would have beaten Pierpont Morgan if he had given his full attention to the little railroad war. But he was already setting up his most audacious coup, a conspiracy that would make Morgan's exploits in the Gold Room during the Civil War seem like a penny dreadful. For Gould aimed to corner the whole bullion market of the United States with the connivance of the Treasury Department.

Normally in New York there was less than $20 million worth of gold in circulation, while the Treasury in Washington held some $90 million worth to back the currency. Two million dollars' worth of this hoard was sold each month. Gould's plot was simple. If Grant's government could be persuaded not to sell any gold for some months, and if a corner could be made in the gold in circulation, he would make the killing of all time from those who had sold short. In 1868, Drew and Fisk had engineered a bear market by twice locking up most of the greenbacks in the city. The following year, Gould reckoned to do better by locking up bullion, although a contemporary compared his operation to pumping out New York Bay with a grand combination of steam engines.[8]

In the manner of the time, Gould gave a patriotic reason for wishing to drive up the price of gold. It would stimulate the sale of western products, increase the profits of railroads like the Erie that were "starving to death," and aid the repayment of the foreign debt incurred in the Civil War. All the Secretary of the Treasury needed to do was to suspend government gold sales for two or three months. Gould and the Gold Room would do the rest.

First, President Grant had to be won over. He was no friend of the gold speculators, who had been called "General Lee's left wing" in the Civil War; but his brother-in-law Abel Corbin was easily influenced by Gould and brought the President of the United States to sit in a box at the opera with the Erie directors. Until the meeting, the President had wanted a low price for gold, but afterwards he seems to have accepted Gould's theory that a high price would benefit grain sales and the western farmers. He certainly wrote back to Washington asking the Treasury Department not to sell gold in large amounts until the crops were moved. Abel Corbin now had evidence for Gould that he could get the Treasury Department to do what he wanted.

These were Gould's cards, but it was a shaky hand. Grant had given no definite commitment to stop gold sales, and Corbin might be misrepresenting his power over the President. The strong New York firms with international connections, such as J. and W. Seligman and Duncan, Sherman and even Dabney, Morgan, did not believe the Erie directors could corner the bullion market. But, using certified checks from a bank they controlled, the Tenth National, Gould and Fisk terrified the Gold Room by instructing their brokers to buy phantom gold to the amount of nearly $100 million — more than the total held in the Treasury in Washington. When this gold was called, all of it would not exist, and the sellers would have to buy some of it back at any price to cover their shortfall. Of course, the phantom gold had been bought by phantom deposits in the Tenth National Bank, but nobody could prove that in the days before Black Friday, September 24, 1869.

On the Wednesday, however, Grant had learned about the feverish speculation. His wife wrote to Mrs. Corbin, telling her in the President's name that her husband had to disengage himself from his Erie friends and the gold business. Abel Corbin had to go to Gould and confess that his influence over the President was gone. Gould now knew that the Treasury would probably break his corner, but he did not tell his partner Fisk. He had to sell the gold he had while pretending to buy. His nervousness showed. "When Gould found himself loaded down to the gunnels and likely to go under," Fisk said, "the cussed fellow never said a word — he's too proud for that — but I saw him tearing up bits of paper. When Gould snips off corners of newspapers and tears 'em up in bits, I know that there's trouble."[8]

Fisk did not know that the trouble was intended for him. He began Black Friday by leaving the Opera House, now called Castle Erie, with two beautiful actresses in his carriage. He was dressed magnificently, scented and oiled and curled like an Assyrian Bull. He went around to the offices of a gold-broking firm and began to bid in the Gold Room through the red-eyed, neurotic Albert Speyers, who was to go insane in the course of the day. Speyers was known to be representing Fisk and Gould through Belden and Company, and as the tension grew, he bid up the gold price from 143½ to 162½, committing $60 million on the deals. While some of the Americans who had sold short broke and ran to Gould to buy gold at any price, the foreign banking houses held firm, knowing that they could import gold from Europe to meet their commitments. What nobody knew was that Gould was secretly selling off his hoarded gold through a dozen brokers — and not to Speyers.

Something had to break. Fisk and Gould now apparently owned twice the gold supply of the whole East Coast of the United States, including the Treasury. Those who had sold short had to cover or go under. "The agony of Wellington awaiting Blucher," one observer wrote, "was in the souls of the bears."[10] But the international financiers still held. And Gould's fear became a fact. The news came from Washington that the Treasury was selling $4 million worth of gold to break the speculation. The market collapsed thirty points. Speyers had to be pulled out of the Gold Room, babbling, in the hands of his friends. Gould and Fisk barricaded themselves in Castle Erie, protected by their thugs from a furious mob. And Fisk soon learned that Gould had sold him out, making about $11 million while he was apparently bankrupt.

Naturally Fisk was too much of a rogue to go down. He even admired Gould for his shrewdness in making a fortune from the debacle. Speyers was left to fail, and so was Belden and Company, for $70 million. The Erie legal machine spewed out injunctions to protect their bosses from paying their debts. Fisk and Gould only demanded payment when they won and repudiated their commitments when they lost. After all, they would even betray each other. And so the gold conspiracy failed, bringing down hundreds of financiers and letting the plotters escape. As a contemporary wrote:

> But ten days before, and Wall Street had been waving with banners of pride and fortune; on Saturday, the 25th, it was a Golgotha — a place of skulls. . . . Night fell, but brought no rest. A crowd of well-dressed barbarians thronged the halls of the Fifth Avenue Hotel. Men sat on chairs, speechless and stupefied by their fall in an hour, from affluence to beggary. Others sought to drown recollection in deep drinking. One man stood leaning against a column, feebly gesticulating, and moaning, "Lost, lost!" . . . But the worst was not yet. The darkness which had fallen upon the

market about noon on Friday, that day of financial wrath and doom, still brooded over it — thunderings, lightnings and thick darkness. Monday brought no relief. Firms failing by the score, wild faces, painted by ruin a dead white, were flitting about the market. Human scorpions seemed to have been bred in an hour, who turned and stung those who but lately were their dearest friends.[11]

This was the instability and orgy of greed which men like the young Morgan were rising to control. Black Friday was the worst display of it, but not the last. International financiers and the United States government had finally moved to prick Gould's glittering bubble, just in time, nearly too late. Their combination did stop the looting by the Erie gang, which was soon eliminated from the leadership of the railroad. Drew was ousted by his two confederates, Fisk was shot and killed in the Grand Central Hotel, while Gould was sold out in turn by the other Erie directors to a reform group prepared to bribe the board in order to remove corruption from the company.

Pierpont Morgan's bad experience in the Gold Room in the Civil War kept him out of the disaster on Black Friday. Many of his friends were ruined, but he was not involved. He had even defeated Fisk and Gould in a minor railroad war. Impressed by these proofs of his son's new strength and discretion, Junius Morgan delivered him from his watchdog and partner, Dabney, who wanted to retire, and encouraged him to join with the great Philadelphia house of the Drexels as its New York representative. In 1871, Drexel, Morgan and Company was formed, ready to replace the gaudy pirates of the postwar speculation with the combinations of international finance.

The larcenous antics of Gould and Fisk may have worried the rising mercantile aristocracy of Morgans and Drexels, who aimed to eliminate them; but they scandalized the old American aristocracy, which they had displaced. Charles Francis Adams, Jr., and his brother Henry (whose education always made him feel more unwanted) were descended from two Presidents of the United States, and they were disgusted by what they saw. In a series of articles about the Erie scandal, Charles Francis showed the contempt and courage to call Gould and Fisk the crooks they were. His words also revealed the despair of those who felt born to rule their country, but not in the time of its corruption. America no longer seemed to revere Founding Fathers, but financial predators. The two Erie bandits "walked erect and proud of their infamy through the streets of our great cities . . . and, by exposing their portraits in public conveyances, converted noble steamers into branch galleries of a police office."[12]

Worse than that, their notoriety bred emulation and destroyed the old values of America. "It speaks ominously for the future. It may be that our society is only passing through a period of ugly transition, but the present evil has its root deep down in the social organization, and springs from a diseased public opinion. Failure seems to be regarded as the one unpardonable crime, success as the all-redeeming virtue, the acquisition of wealth as the single worthy aim of life. Ten years ago such revelations as these of the Erie Railway would have sent a shudder through the community, and would have placed a stigma on every man who had had to do with them. Now they merely incite others to surpass them by yet bolder outrages and more corrupt combinations."[13]

Charles Francis Adams saw clearly in 1871 that postwar conditions encouraged the rise of organizing financiers like Pierpont Morgan. Only a decade before, a Vanderbilt corporation worth a few million dollars was thought suspicious and dangerous. Now corporations worth hundreds of millions of dollars were controlling state legislatures. So far, only in New York had the Vanderbilt and Erie groups shown how great was the corrupt power of ambitious, reckless men. Yet they were the forerunners of what must come. Like Count Frankenstein, modern society had created a class of artificial beings which would soon be the masters of their creator.

> The system of corporate life and corporate power, as applied to industrial development, is yet in its infancy. It tends always to development,— always to consolidation,—it is ever grasping new powers, or insidiously exercising covert influence. Even now the system threatens the central government. . . . We shall see these great corporations spanning the continent from ocean to ocean,—single, consolidated lines, not connecting Albany with Buffalo, or Lake Erie with the Hudson, but uniting the Atlantic and the Pacific, and bringing New York nearer to San Francisco than Albany once was to Buffalo. Already the disconnected members of these future leviathans have built up States in the wilderness, and chosen their attorneys senators of the United States. Now their power is in its infancy; in a very few years they will re-enact, in a larger theater and on a grander scale, with every feature magnified, the scenes which were lately witnessed on the narrow stage of a single State. The public corruption is the foundation on which corporations always depend for their political power.[14]

Charles Francis Adams was right about the future, which would exclude him and his brother Henry from the levers of power. Wealth would replace birth as the key to government. Yet he left out the chief resource of the new masters, the international strength of those few financiers whose connections were crossing the Atlantic as well as the continental divide. The designated heirs of George Peabody of Boston would displace the aristocratic Adamses, whose forefathers had been in the White House while Peabody was born in poverty or had worked as a clerk in a store.

The old man had died in London in November, 1869. Queen Victoria had wanted this benefactor of the English people buried in Westminster Abbey, but his will required that he be buried in his birthplace, the village of Danvers, Massachusetts. A British ironclad, the *Monarch*, brought his body back to Portland, Maine, where it was met by Admiral Farragut's squadron. In charge of the funeral arrangements was Pierpont Morgan. He suggested that British and American sailors and marines should march together behind the coffin. So he staged a symbolic Atlantic alliance at the burial of one of its founders, whose heir was the Morgan house, already linking both sides of the ocean like the new cable that sent telegrams across in minutes.

Junius Morgan was, indeed, about to show the resources of the Anglo-American connection by intervening like a Rothschild in the affairs of Europe. In 1870, Bismarck's German armies captured Napoleon III and swept on to besiege Paris. The provisional French government at Tours sent for Junius Morgan and asked him to raise fifty million dollars to finance the war. Junius consented on harsh financial terms and laid off the discounted bonds in England and in America through one of the first syndicates ever formed. When peace was agreed and the French government returned to Paris, he and his associates cleared five million dollars on the sale of the bonds. They had helped France in its hour of trial, but their terms were hardly a repayment for Lafayette.

The success of the Morgan syndicate with the French loan foretold even more certainly the future of finance. The lone wolves were doomed, the packs of international dealers inevitable. Pierpont Morgan was the hinge between his father's associates in Europe and great American houses like the Drexels. He could grow rich as the necessary link, if he would. But at this moment of opportunity, he was overcome by a curious nervous lassitude. He had wanted too much and worked too hard. And now that he was offered his desire, he found he did not want it. There had to be something more than simply making money.

4

Cure by Acquisition

As for us — I mean the higher classes of Americans, — we are everywhere at home — except in the United States.

— Francis J. Grund, *Aristocracy in America* (1839)

Pierpont Morgan had to make himself distinct from his father, who had arranged his new partnership. It was Junius who had written to him, "It is possible that Drexel may want to see you about a certain matter."[1] It was Junius who had agreed with Drexel that Pierpont should be given a year's sabbatical to recover from his fatigue and come to Europe so that he could learn more about his father's business. And it was to Junius that Pierpont and his family would report first after leaving America.

The son never revealed his resentment of his dominant father. He was one of the old school before the age of Freud. He could not admit to any hidden antagonism to his parents. Such a feeling would have been shocking and almost blasphemous; an attack on the holiness of the family would be a sin from somebody who believed in the Holy Family. Even at the age of thirty-four, Pierpont could not show his rebellion against authority. He could only disguise it as a minor breakdown and a wish to give up business altogether.

When he and his wife and three children arrived at his father's home at 13 Prince's Gate, Junius did not press Pierpont about the future, suffering as he was from skin eruptions and insomnia. Seeing his father in London did not improve Pierpont's health. After a fortnight, he took his family to stay in Paris at the Hotel Bristol, managed by one of Junius's previous butlers. Doubtless he was told to report back to London on conditions in France, because of the Morgan loan to the embattled French government. After the bloody work of the suppression of the Commune, the French capital was anything but soothing, more a wreck than a rest home. So the Morgan family soon fled to the French countryside, then over the border to Carlsbad.

On their way across France, they passed the German occupation forces. They saw a military order imposed on a ravaged land. Pierpont's restlessness and discomfort increased. He did not like to see society unsettled. He seemed only happy on the move. But at the baths in a fashionable spa that ranked with Baden-Baden and Marienbad and Bad Homburg, he began to relax. War was far away. He had found a style of life which attracted him and denied the lessons of his upbringing.

Carlsbad was Pierpont's introduction to the rituals and raffishness of European aristocratic ways. Edward, Prince of Wales, regularly took the cure in Germany, and once a year old Kaiser Wilhelm I made his court go down to Baden-Baden for the sake of his health — and he was to reign until the age of ninety-one. The royal example inspired a cult for spa life more compelling than even the Prince Regent had inspired at the time of Beau Brummel's Bath. The aristocrats followed the Prince of Wales and the Kaiser, who had taken the title after his victory over France; and the diplomats and the businessmen, the spies and the adventuresses, followed the wellborn and the wealthy as they always had in Europe.

For the puritans in royal circles, life at Baden-Baden or Carlsbad in 1871 was as the English Crown Princess Victoria of Prussia described it in a letter to her mother, Queen Victoria: "Swarms of people and a very uninteresting society. More fatiguing than Paris during the Exhibition, more tiring than the London Season — an excessive bore besides."[2] But to ambitious people outside royal circles, like the Morgans, the German spas were an introduction to ruling society in that last aristocratic age of the grandees, so alluring to conservative Americans because of their power, exclusiveness and stability. Pierpont relaxed in such an ordered and respectful ambience, where republicanism was only a disease of the defeated French or of the other side of the Atlantic Ocean.

He also enjoyed the undercurrent of diplomatic and financial intrigue as well as the presence of the actresses and demimondaines who joined the wealthy men in the casinos for the paid liaisons of their "cures" away from their homes. It was like a grand Pike's Opera House licensed by high society on holiday; Castle Erie translated into a genuine Gothic castle; "Colonel" and "Admiral" Fisk become Count Eulenburg or Field Marshal von Moltke. The great and the famous were seen discreetly with many of the famous courtesans of Europe. And the atmosphere was enticing. As the notorious Marie Colombier wrote, the spa season in Germany re-created "the fantasy, the irresponsible madness of the *kermesses* of olden times."[3]

The official cure of the baths and the unofficial sights of the bathers were new to the Morgan experience. Pierpont recovered his health and zest at Carlsbad and later in the Austrian Tyrol, mountain climbing with young English army officers as if he were still a young man in Switzerland. He could not escape his father, however, as Junius brought his family out to Innsbruck, traveling through Paris to see the French government and to inquire into the state of his bonds. At the end of a summer all together, Pierpont took his household on to Vienna, where the court of the Habsburg Emperor had formed a most rigid and hierarchical society, a social summit in Pierpont's ordered mind.

As the weather became colder, the Morgans moved toward the sun, first to Rome and then on to the Nile. The impulses that drove Pierpont to Egypt were the urge toward the unknown, the remnants of the romanticism he had shown by his first marriage, and the need to be distinct by what he chose to do. He took a Cook's steamer up the great river as far as the first cataract, saw all the antiquities he could, flourished in the dry desert air, and returned to Cairo. On the way, he bought ancient and modern souvenirs without much care or selection.

Pierpont had always been a collector. His early account books did not satisfy all of his magpie instinct. His first collections were the petty hoards of most small boys — stamps and coins and autographs. But at Vevey and Göttingen he had begun to amass fragments of stained glass that had fallen on the ground from the windows of old European cathedrals. He loved their jeweled colors and filled a barrel with glass bits found on his walking expeditions; they were eventually to be used in the West Room of his Library. What Europe ignored, Pierpont picked up, particularly when it was for free. And unconsciously, his early taste was formed.

His aesthetic judgment was still uncertain and conformist. The drawing room of his new house at 6 East Fortieth Street had been furnished in the usual overstuffed Victorian way, with silk sofas dripping their fringes onto the Persian carpet, lace antimacassars crowning the carved chairs, poor pictures of common panoramas in thick gilt frames cramming the patterned paper on the high narrow walls. The clutter suggested opulence without choice, accumulation without discrimination. It was the house of a young New York financier at that time.

Yet Pierpont was learning to know better. Before going to Europe, he had become one of the first fifty Patrons of the Metropolitan Museum of Art. He had carefully looked at all the objects the new museum was acquiring, and he was instructing himself. He had also joined a committee of the American Museum of Natural History, although the only beasts of prey he knew well were on the board of the Erie Railroad. He was beginning to feel that avid discontent which is the gut of the true collector, the restless search after the possession of perfect things that is so often the last refuge of an imperfect man tired of making the money he can never see.

The origins of great art collections differ, in Joseph Alsop's opinion, from patronage and the gathering of treasure. The mighty temples and tombs of ancient Egypt, which Pierpont Morgan had visited, had been constructed for the honor and ritual burial of the divine pharaohs. The temples of Greece had been built by public treasuries or private donors to commemorate the gods. The works of art amassed in these special places were not collections in the modern sense of the word. For art collecting depends on an aesthetic and controlling perception, on a comparative history of art capable of describing the merits and values of individual artists, and on competitive rich people who are prepared to embellish their palaces. King Attalos I of Pergamon was the first recorded collector who was neither a patron nor a worshipper. He had nothing to do with the creation of works of art, only with their buying and storage and arrangement. His collection ended with his grandson's bequest of it to the Roman Senate and tax authorities. Later, another Greek named Damasippos played the role of art dealer to the Roman plutocrats exactly as Duveen was to do with the American plutocrats led by Pierpont Morgan.[4]

Thus in ancient times the technique was invented of enriching the new masters with the culture of the old by possession rather than education. A thing — money — could buy other things, which added to the owners a polish and luster not their own. To have the beautiful was to appreciate the beautiful if not to be the beautiful. The museum at home was to deny its source in the office downtown, while the acquisition of the rare was to give its possessor an absolute distinction. Any unique object set its owner apart from all others. The man who could not commission a statue of himself from Praxiteles or a bust from Bernini could buy one and say, "This is mine."

The European royalty and aristocracy, which Pierpont Morgan had admired at Carlsbad, had long owned personal collections, sometimes acquired, usually inherited from the plunder of the past. They had adorned their private palaces with the most prized art of history in order to impress their peers with their grandeur and good taste. Until the late eighteenth century, few commoners outside international banking families like the Rothschilds or the Venetian merchant princes had possessed the resources or the gall to compete for the masterworks pried loose by war, bankruptcy or revolution. The remarkable collection of Charles I of England, for instance, was dispersed by Cromwell, but most of it fell into royal hands in Europe.

By the time of the French Revolution, however, the nabobs and moguls of the East and West Indies trade did have the pride and wealth to compete for the spoils of the Orleans collection when it was sold in London. The greater part of the buyers were commoners, outnumbering the noble lords by nearly three to one.[5] A leveling and a spreading was taking place in the art world. In the nineteenth century, rich men ousted titled ones, from the fruits of the first Industrial Revolution. Factories were the pillars of the private museum.

Pierpont Morgan became aware of the opportunity to buy distinction on his tour of Europe and Egypt. He came from a New England family that had accumulated its capital through caution and saving. Junius Morgan could not spend money like a Maecenas; it takes two generations to forget a grandfather's wisdom. Joseph and Junius Morgan had founded a family fortune by refusing to compete with the European peerage. Unlike the rich Americans whom Grund had found trying to imitate the English aristocrats, they did not want to risk ruin or feel "very much in the position of a sailor on horseback."[6]

Not so Pierpont Morgan. He had been schooled in Europe and was being educated in the ways of New York society and in art appreciation. Times were changing from the Age of Getting to the Gilded Age. And even his father knew how to hold his son through the hook of possessions. A man had to work hard to have a great deal. So when Pierpont, back for a second "cure" at Carlsbad in the summer of 1872, telegraphed the London offices of J. S. Morgan and Company that he wanted to make an offer for a large Victorian house on the Hudson River called Cragston at Highland Falls, Junius telegraphed the New York office to buy the place at any price. Once Pierpont had his Cragston, he would work for Junius in New York to pay for it and to justify it. And that is what he did.

Not only Cragston was waiting for Pierpont's return to the United States, but also the white marble halls of the new Drexel block on the corner of Broad and Wall streets. It rose six stories in ornate ribbing to a hexagonal cupola at the top, rather in the French imperial style, which would become so popular in New York that the first skyscrapers would be crowned by aerial châteaux. There Pierpont Morgan had his office, for Junius Morgan had contributed nearly $750,000 as his son's share of the capitalization of Drexel, Morgan and Company. Back from Europe, Pierpont could work in a place that brought Europe close to home.

As the junior partner of his father and the Drexels, his role was to observe and to report, not to decide. He still had to suppress the aggressive and commanding parts of his nature outside his social life at Cragston or trips down the Nile, which he ran like military expeditions. In the next incursion of Junius Morgan and the Drexels into the preserves of American high finance, Pierpont would hardly open his mouth. One of the roots of his famous taciturnity was a refusal to speak out as his father's messenger.

Jay Cooke and his associates, chiefly the Rothschilds and the German banking houses of Frankfurt, had taken up the huge bond issues of the American government during the Civil War. The United States Treasury had tried to sell its bonds directly in 1871 and had failed; the great banking houses had made their profits as middlemen, not buyers; and Jay Cooke had finally picked up the issue as a whole and had disposed of it. Two years later, Cooke again proposed to handle the whole of a government borrowing of $300 million, but he was bitterly opposed by a syndicate formed by the London bank of the Barings, by the Drexels and the Morgans, and by one of Junius's old partners in his Boston firm, Levi P. Morton, who had also risen to become a power in international commerce. The fight extended to the Ways and Means Committee of the House of Representatives, where the large profits derived from the Cooke monopoly were questioned. One New York congressman supporting the rival group called the Cooke syndicate a devilfish clasping human forms in its slimy claws, "an animal peculiar to Pennsylvania, with a head of iron, eyes of nickel, legs of copper, and a heart of stone. It consumes every green thing outside of its own state." The New York *World* was even more ironical, writing of Cooke's proposal for his single syndicate:

Say, is it a corner,
Where Jay Cooke as Horner
Can pull out a very big plum?[7]

In his testimony before the House committee, Levi Morton was more temperate. If he wanted to end Cooke's monopoly, he also wanted syndicate control and a share in the profits, not direct bond sales to the public. He insisted that large government loans could only be negotiated through private bankers, who could spread the risk. He asked that the present bond issue be split between the two rival syndicates. This would end monopoly and allow limited competition and prevent the mistakes of the previous bond issue. Pierpont Morgan sat and heard Morton's testimony without giving evidence himself. He was learning to despise the political process, which was later to call him out and stain his reputation.

The bond issue was finally split between the two syndicates, although a financial crisis made their rivalry futile. A third great panic, even worse than those of Pierpont Morgan's birth and young manhood, destroyed Jay Cooke utterly. The underlying causes were much the same. There was a slump in wheat prices after the end of the Franco-German war just as there had been a slump after the Crimean War. The farmers' failure led to a western speculators' failure and thus to the failure of the new railroads, dependent upon their freight charges to service the dividends on their watered stock. Cooke's Northern Pacific line defaulted, his far-flung empire collapsed. More than five thousand other companies went down with him. There could be little financial confidence during the end of Grant's regime, tainted by the gold scandal of Black Friday and even more by the notoriety of the Crédit Mobilier bribery. In time of boom, corruption may seem the grease in the engine. In slump, it is the spanner in the works.

Six years of recession followed the panic of 1873. Only the cautious and the international banking firms did any business. European investors were even more badly burned than in previous crises, and American stocks were hard to sell at any price. Pierpont's chief task was to sail regularly across the Atlantic to meet his father's investors and to reassure them that business would revive and that American Treasury bonds would eventually be redeemed in gold, despite the agitation of the Greenbackers and the silver lobby of the western states. He was a transatlantic Gabriel in golden armor, bringing glad tidings of good news to come. In one of his biographer's words, it was a kind of missionary work, if sending European capital to develop America can be called a mission.[8]

Andrew Carnegie related a revealing story of Pierpont Morgan's minor but important role at the time. Carnegie had given Junius Morgan in London the opportunity to plunge heavily in Allegheny Valley Railroad stock, and now Junius wanted to buy him out during the panic. He instructed Pierpont to be his agent and offer Carnegie sixty thousand dollars for his interests. "In these days," Carnegie replied, "I will sell anything for money." Pierpont then added another check for ten thousand dollars, saying that there had been a mistake and that his father's firm owed Carnegie the difference. Carnegie tried to return the second check, but

Pierpont would not accept it on his father's behalf. "I cannot do that," he said.

Carnegie's comments were significant. After that incident, he became a firm friend of the Morgans, father and son. "Not the letter of the law, but the spirit," he wrote, "must be the rule." Stock gambling was incompatible with proper business. In his opinion, old-fashioned bankers like Junius Morgan were becoming rare; he did not give his opinion of Pierpont. Yet despite this trust, Carnegie would not let the Morgans do what they normally did with friends, putting down favored names willy-nilly as partners in any syndicate they wished to form. He refused to join in the funding of the new Texas Pacific Railroad, which soon went down, leaving the Drexels and the Morgans as losers. His independence, for once, did not cost him their friendship, for he was proved right. His reason, as he told a Drexel, was that he would not endorse commercial paper if he did not have the cash in reserve. As the western saying went, Never go in where you can't wade.[9]

Although Pierpont Morgan worked in the shadow of his father and the Drexels, he was becoming richer in his own right. During the depression years between 1873 and 1875, he took all the money he needed for his style of life in New York and at Highland Falls, yet he had enough left over to plow back into Drexel, Morgan and Company between two hundred thousand and three hundred thousand dollars annually. As most partners were taking out half their share of the profits, Pierpont's income was great in a time without income tax. He spent it like a patriarch who was dominated by another patriarch, who in turn was influenced by the ultimate matriarch of them all. For Junius Morgan had adopted what most of English society had adopted, the taste and habits of Queen Victoria. She had elevated a good family life into a royal example, bringing comfort into the cold English country house, preferring a multitude of rambling rooms at places like Osborne to the large drafty ones of Buckingham Palace, and stuffing every space with horsehair, cushions and charming bric-a-brac. She had turned palaces into country homes, and she was the model of her age.

When not at Prince's Gate, Junius Morgan lived at his Georgian estate of ninety-two acres, Dover House, at Roehampton, where rolling lawns led down to the Thames River and prize herds distantly grazed and leading members of the clergy were invited to take their ease among the Anglo-American business families of their host's acquaintance. Pierpont's Cragston was a transatlantic version of his father's style of home life: a lawn sloped from the south side of a large adapted farmhouse toward the Hudson River, herds of prize Alderneys and Guernseys chewed the cud far away, while Episcopalian bishops were invited to join the Morgan business friends and family friends. Like a pyramid, the Queen's crowning example spread down past Roehampton to Highland Falls, making a solid triangle of wealth, church and home.

The church was more and more important in Pierpont's life, as if he needed a sanction for what he did, a consolation for how he lived. Every Sunday he would put his wife, son and three daughters into a huge wagonette, which he would personally drive to the church gate of Highland Falls, and in the evening he would sing his favorite hymns at home. His sisters said that he sang out of tune, but he sang loud enough to drown their voices. He even became a financial backer of Moody and Sankey's huge revival meetings at the city railroad terminus, which was to become Madison Square Garden, and he would go there most nights for months on end, sitting in the front row on the platform and singing the hymns as lustily as possible.

He liked to demonstrate his faith. He began his practice, never to be interrupted, of attending the major conventions of the Episcopal Church. As in the public dealings of Drexel, Morgan and Company, Pierpont said nothing at first among the divines, but watched the way things were done and made important friends, who only saw in his home the autocracy he did not yet want to display elsewhere. When a local train was not available to take the future bishop Henry C. Potter back from Cragston to New York in time for evensong, Potter saw Morgan himself break into the local railroad station and flag down an express to put his guest on board.[10] Divine service seemed more important than a train schedule to a financier who used the railroad often enough as a commuter to believe he should own it. One day, he would.

Pierpont's piety was genuine, but it had an element of social hypocrisy. He was one of the founders of the New York Society for the Suppression of Vice. Its agent, Anthony Comstock, was to be the Bowdler of America, giving his name to prurient interference in the mild eroticism of the day. He did not attack social evil, he drew a fig leaf or a doily over it. The new rich of midtown Manhattan did not want to see any evidence of degrading poverty when they drove to their downtown offices or their upcountry estates. Comstock's job was to clean up appearances so that the New York plutocrats could ignore the foul conditions of the slums and the back streets, where half the babies were dying in infancy and men and women had to struggle like beasts to survive. Not until a less comfortable priest than the Reverend Tyng took Tyng's place at St. George's would Pierpont Morgan's conscience be pricked into helping to cure social evils, which Wall Street perpetuated by its jobbing and indifference.

Segregation of rich and poor had been almost impossible in Jackson's day, but it became more usual in Grant's Gilded Age. The few millionaires had become many. Thrift was now called meanness, wealth was to be consumed openly. The careful habits of the old Knickerbocker families were being overlaid by the lavish spending of the new social arbiters, the second generation of Astors and Vanderbilts, who had inherited their wealth. In a new nation, to appear to be an aristocrat was only a matter of one generation.

In spite of his happy domestic life, his growing riches and his secure place on earth and in heaven, Pierpont was still dissatisfied. He had not escaped the bondage of his father's wishes. He still had to conceal his vaunting ambitions. His nervous attacks returned, particularly the disease that made his nose a small volcano, acne rosacea. This mutilation hurt his pride and made him depressed. He was too young at thirty-nine to turn his affliction into a weapon against society. It only made him feel more unnecessary and inferior.

He was certainly not indispensable in the dealings of Drexel, Morgan and Company. In June, 1876, he set off with his family for another whole year of convalescence. In later life, even at the height of his powers, he would regularly take off three months a year, saying that he could do a year's work in nine months, but not in twelve.[11] Yet by that future time, he would have brilliant and subservient partners, who would do what he had decided should be done in his absence.

At this time, he was still his father's son, superfluous in the last resort, replaceable by a Drexel. So he was recalled again to London, where he could work in his father's office and live in his father's home. This time, Junius took him into the City of London every morning in spite of his son's nervous illness. He himself was very fat now, like "the ponderous figure of an East Indian merchant prince in an old English play."[12] At the age of sixty-four he was beginning to train his heir and replacement, slowly, slowly, nothing of King Lear in him, not giving up his power too soon.

Pierpont fled with his family again to Paris and Venice and on to Egypt. He did not recover his health or spirits until he had organized his own special expedition up the Nile, answerable to nobody but himself. He was richer and could charter a whole steamer for his party, the *Beni Souef*, and take a personal French doctor to look after his ailments and his family's. At Luxor, the party visited the ruins of Karnak and was photographed among the mighty temple pillars. In their topees and veils and fezzes, their knickerbockers and trailing skirts and high bootees, they looked like the British imperialists they were largely to replace.

Pierpont began collecting antiquities in earnest, determined on a special hoard and a particular knowledge of his own. He cultivated the friendship of archaeologists like Lord Lindsay and studied how to distinguish between the ancient and the forged artifact. He remained restless, only happy to be moving along the Nile or across the desert, or organizing an expedition or a firework display. Even when a fugitive in Egypt, he knew that he would have to return to London and New York and the long reach of his father's control.

At the end of his life, Pierpont Morgan was to flee obsessively to Egypt every year until his death. Then he had to escape his country's judgment, not his dead father's. He had had a steamer built just for cruising up and down the Nile; it was called the *Khargeh* after the great oasis southwest of Cairo, where Egyptian and Roman remains littered the site. And when asked which places he favored most in his regular wanderings, he would reply, "New York, because it is my home; London, because it is my second home; Rome and Khargeh."[13]

He insisted he meant it, although he would not say why. It was because he had always fled from the restrictions and opinions of his country, his home and his father to where he could most feel powerful and free and unaccountable. Contemplating in Rome the site of the mightiest military power in history and of the greatest church on earth, he could sense the limitless boundaries of a great ambition. Drifting down the Nile on the boat called *Khargeh*, he could feel free of the grand irrelevance of power, which had finally to end in ruin. In either refuge, he stood alone, his own man.

Abroad, he was often most at home with himself.

5

A System for Society

> When, in one of our Atlantic cities, it is once known that a man is rich, that "he is very rich," that he is "amazingly rich," that he is "one of the richest men in the country" . . . the whole vocabulary of praise is exhausted; and the individual in question is as effectually canonized as the best Catholic saint.
>
> — Francis J. Grund, *Aristocracy in America* (1839)

Pierpont Morgan returned to a country of forced reconciliation and unwilling combination. The presidential election of 1876 could have led to another civil war. The Republican party had fixed the votes in the Electoral College to give their candidate, the preaching Rutherford Hayes, the victory by one vote over the reforming Tilden from New York, even though he had a clear popular majority. Tilden acquiesced in the injustice, preferring peace to victory. And in the two houses of Congress, conservative southern Democrats now joined with conservative Republican financiers against the restive western representatives. Each group conceded the other the wrong dearest to its heart. The rich Republicans abandoned the cause of the freed blacks and allowed the southern whites to exclude them from the political system, while the southerners permitted the eastern moneymen to set up their rail and industrial combines, unchecked by federal regulation. So Jim Crow lay down with the Golden Eagle, and the rationale of secession was replaced by the rationale of reunion.

There had been too much plundering, too much notoriety. It was time to organize both business and society. If politics was being stabilized for a generation, the same could be done for finance, leadership and the law. The Supreme Court was dutifully to follow the election returns, declaring the Civil Rights Act unconstitutional and giving large corporations the inalienable right of every American individual to take all he or it could. A natural controller like Pierpont Morgan was being given power by his father at the right place and at the right time. His genius lay in ordering and consolidation.

It was fitting that his major act of 1877 was to guarantee the army's pay while it was fighting one of the last Indian wars on the last unsettled frontiers. During the electoral crisis over the presidency, the southerners in Congress blocked an appropriation for the army, which was then pursuing the Nez Percés under the remarkable Chief Joseph through the Far West. The government had no pay for the soldiers. In this impasse, Pierpont Morgan wrote to the Secretary of War that Drexel, Morgan and Company could not lend the government money for the soldiers, but it would cash the pay vouchers of the troops at a minimum handling charge. The government could settle when the appropriation finally passed. So Drexel, Morgan paid out $2.5 million to the soldiers over the next five months. To them, Morgan was a friend in need.

This was a brilliant coup for the prestige of the young financier. It wiped out any memory of his inglorious performance during the Civil War. He and his father and the Drexels, now working with August Belmont and the Rothschilds as well as Levi. P. Morton and the Seligmans, also took over the government bond market, selling $235 million worth of Treasury stock at a profit of $25 million, which was split in fifths between the five partners of the syndicate. With the fall of Jay Cooke, the Morgans had induced his old European backers to join with them. And within two years, their pressure on the White House forced redemption of government bonds in gold, despite the opposition of the West. A fortunate rise in grain prices made the return to the gold standard appear a blessing and the Morgan–Rothschild syndicate seem to be correct in insisting on restoring America's international credit after the losses of the depression years. Large imports of gold were also arranged from Europe to ease any shortage in the United States.

After aiding the army and the Treasury, Morgan and his partners now moved toward the great rationalization, the need to make sense out of the inefficient and competitive railroad systems snaking across the land. Sometimes they seemed no more than coils of vipers, ruining each other in venomous freight wars and biting their investors to death. Confidence had to be restored in them; during the six years after the crash of 1873, European investors had lost some $600 million, mainly in railroad stocks. This task would occupy Pierpont Morgan until the end of the century. In the absence of government control, some man had to elect the role of bringing order out of chaos. If he did it for his own interest and his partners' profits, yet he was also doing something that had to be done for his country, until his country would do it through federal authority.

The minor victory in the war with Fisk and Gould over the Albany & Susquehanna Railroad was followed by a small acquisition in 1878, when Drexel, Morgan and Company picked up part of the Long Island Railroad after its entrepreneur had gone bankrupt through overexpansion. But during the next year, the end of the era of freebooting in the railroads was signaled. Cornelius Vanderbilt's son had to come for help to Junius Morgan's son. New generations, new ways.

While the old Commodore was alive, his blustering and bribery kept his critics at bay; but with his death, reformers in the New York legislature began to ask how his son William had inherited $60 million and 87 percent of the stock of the New York Central Railroad. It was simply too much for a tugboat captain to have amassed for his heir in one lifetime. The legislature now proposed to control railroad management, prevent stock-watering, and tax profits. Jay Gould's hidden hand was behind the reformers because he wanted access to the Atlantic for his ailing Missouri tracks. And Pierpont Morgan himself had an interest in the Wabash, St. Louis & Pacific, which would do better by combining with the New York Central than by cutting freight rates and bleeding both to death.

William H. Vanderbilt was a petty, stingy man with a gift for annoying the public even if he did not actually tell them to be damned. He had none of the style or physical presence of the huge Morgan with his flaming nose and piercing eyes. He made a secret agreement to sell through the Morgan syndicate 250,000 shares of his New York Central stock to English investors. He also agreed to combine the Central with the Wabash. This would stop a freight war, hamstring the legislature's attack on monopoly and personal ownership, and connect the Atlantic coast with the Midwest in one system.

With his usual secrecy, Pierpont Morgan disposed of the stock through his father to English investors, clearing $3 million in the transaction. When the news broke, Vanderbilt announced that he had put his cash into United States bonds — also through the Morgan syndicate. Thus profit stood with patriotism, combination with diffusion of ownership. The age of Morganization had begun. Pierpont himself insisted on joining the board of the New York Central to protect the interests of his investors, while Drexel, Morgan and Company remained the financial agents of the Pennsylvania Railroad and also helped to raise

$50 million to keep the Northern Pacific afloat on its sea of watered shares.

Morgan was even to lease the Wabash line to his old enemy Jay Gould's Missouri & Pacific Railroad in return for certain undertakings from that system. His aim was to increase profits by eliminating price-cutting and alternative routes. He wanted to prove George Stephenson's famous dictum: where combination is possible, competition is impossible. And he insisted on indirect control through ownership rather than direct control through administration. He wanted the profits and was content to leave the presidents of the railroads with the headaches and the blame. When one of them finally exploded and asked him why he should turn over his road to Morgan's nominees, the banker replied: "Your roads! Your roads belong to my clients."[1]

As Morgan was starting to make some sense out of the scramble for an American railroad network, the wives of the plutocrats were also trying to establish a fresh pecking order in New York. If the railroads needed to be Morganized, society needed to be Astorized. The old American–Dutch aristocracy was not rich enough to compete with the new mercantile princes, whose women were demanding marble palaces on Fifth Avenue. Not since the days of the Venetian Empire would successful trading families display so much wealth on their facades and balconies.

The first mansion was commissioned by Alexander T. Stewart, a department-store owner who built a four-storied, ornamental stone packing case on Fifth Avenue. Not to be outdone, William H. Vanderbilt ordered twin, connected Greek Renaissance blockhouses, while his sons and relatives constructed four huge edifices nearby, all modeled on châteaux from the Touraine, some awkward with spires and some as solid as wedding cakes topped by green-icing roofs. Pierpont Morgan himself did not join in the early rush for self-advertisement, preferring to move to a larger and more luxurious home at 219 Madison Avenue, which was fronted by the traditional brownstone. His father was still head of the family. He would not flaunt himself too soon.

Mrs. William B. Astor, who was to become the arbiter of New York society for the rest of the century, was living in a huge brownstone house in the Murray Hill area. She asserted herself with the help of the extraordinary Ward McAllister, who understood perfectly that a new social aristocracy was like a new art collection — it needed a catalogue to establish an order of merit and of price. Half Yankee and half southerner, he loved the combination of brashness and birth. Although he did not exclude the old Knickerbocker families from the smart set he was forming, he declared that they wished to sit upon Mount Olympus up the Hudson while a fresh society took their place in the city. He carefully chose himself and twenty-four "Patriarchs," including two male Astors, to pick who should be invited to exclusive subscription balls. These lists of the elect were to determine the Four Hundred invited to Mrs. Astor's ball, which was to open her own brand-new marble palace on Fifth Avenue.

The number was arbitrary. Mrs. Astor's new ballroom could only hold that many, although McAllister was to expand the list to six hundred. But he had grasped with his exact snobbery the principle that Pierpont Morgan had also grasped. The chaos of postwar society needed regulation and organization. The Patriarchs' lists, which would become the Four Hundred, were, in his words, "organized social power, capable of giving a passport to society to all worthy of it."[2] If he selected himself to be the judge and front for Mrs. Astor's financial power, he was doing what Pierpont Morgan was doing in choosing to act as the arbiter of the railroad wars and the front for the international Morgan syndicates. In his autobiography, McAllister quoted with approval the anonymous lines sent to him after a party he had arranged for some English aristocrats at Delmonico's:

They sat in order, as if "Burke"
Had sent a message by his clerk.
And by whose magic wand is this
All conjured up? The height of bliss.
'Tis he who now before you looms,—
The Autocrat of Drawing Rooms.[3]

McAllister's social power existed because he was known to have Mrs. Astor's backing, just as Pierpont Morgan's power existed because of Junius's strength in Europe. But it also existed because he was seen to use it. On his own, Ward McAllister made Newport fashionable by holding picnics there, just as Pierpont Morgan would create a railroad system he wanted by choosing where to put the financial resources behind him. Power is held to be in the hand of its dispenser, not its possessor. And Ward McAllister and Pierpont Morgan were visibly two of the prime movers in the national urge toward the consolidation of society and wealth.

McAllister tried to combine birth and riches in his social list. "We wanted the money power," he confessed, "but not in any way to be controlled by it."[4] Of course, he failed. His standard that it took four generations of gentlemen to make an American aristocrat had to be lowered to one, if he were rich enough. For the fortune needed to keep up a place in society was growing. To be a mere millionaire was to be poor, and McAllister had to admit that a man now had to possess between ten and a hundred million dollars to pass as wealthy.

Even the proud Mrs. Astor had to yield to the governing principle of consolidation. Her chief rival was Mrs. William K. Vanderbilt, who was one generation less of an instant aristocrat than she was. Yet when Mrs. Astor was faced in 1883 with Mrs. Vanderbilt's preparations for the largest fancy-dress ball ever to be held in New York, she could not allow herself to be excluded. She had to call on her rival at last and form a combine in the spirit of the times. She was invited with her close friends, and from that day on, the two great ladies shared the social world of New York and Newport between them. Sometimes Mrs. Vanderbilt so blazed with diamonds that she was called the Electric Light, and sometimes Mrs. Astor wore so many jewels on her bodice that she glittered like a cuirass. They might compete, but in tandem. Better a common and exclusive list of guests than a competitive and diluted division of the acceptable few.

Ward McAllister, indeed, became unnecessary. Once he had defined the Four Hundred, he was rejected by them as too poor and too undistinguished. A committee formed by a Fish and a Gerry and a Jay eliminated him from the Patriarchs, stating that he was "a discharged servant. That is all."[5]

Short of total ruin, a Pierpont Morgan could not share McAllister's fate. He had the resources, the pedigree and the power, and he was adding to his influence all the time. In the early 1880s he did not join in the extravagances of the Astors and the Vanderbilts. He had his own quieter set of Drexels and Tracys and Osborns, old family friends and business partners.

Elizabeth Drexel, who was to become the unhappy wife of the society prankster Harry "King" Lehr, left an interesting portrait of Morgan's life in his new home on Madison Avenue. He ruled his household, she wrote, like the autocrat he was, and noboly dared to disobey him except for his youngest daughter, Anne. She was a thin elf of a child with his disconcerting, brilliant eyes. On one occasion, her father asked her what she would like to be when she grew up. "Something better," she said, "than a rich fool, anyway."

Pierpont Morgan's domestic life and sober financial friends and attachment to Episcopalian bishops gave him a stability that many of the other plutocrats lacked. He was still curbed by the family tradition of saving, and he could not spend like a Vanderbilt. It was to his advantage, as he gathered in the reins of power, not to waste his energy and resources on the extravagances of the Gilded Age. Elizabeth Drexel Lehr wrote:

> It merited its name. There was gold everywhere. It adorned the houses of men who had become millionaires overnight, and who were trying to forget with all possible speed the days when they had been poor and unknown. It glittered on their dining-tables when they sat down to unfamiliar awe-inspiring banquets of rare dishes whose high-sounding names conveyed nothing to them; it enriched the doors of their carriages in which their wives and daughters drove round Central Park behind the high-stepping thoroughbreds imported from England. Gold was the most desirable thing to have because it cost money, and money was the outward and visible sign of success. They cultivated the Midas touch to such good purpose that truth to tell they were often bewildered by their own magnificence.[6]

Among these wonderers at their own orgy, Pierpont Morgan watched and waited. He would not imitate William H. Vanderbilt and build a new palace to house a second-rate collection of contemporary French painters such as Detaille and Meissonier and Bouguereau. He would not rush in to spend where experts feared to tread. And he certainly would not copy Vanderbilt's ostentation in being the first and last of the billionaires to give a press showing of his private art gallery.

If Morgan wanted novelty, it did not lie in art but in technology. The Drexel building in Wall Street and the Morgan house on Madison Avenue were two of the first places in the city to install Thomas A. Edison's invention of electric lighting. At the house, the system was run from a generator in the stables, a change of horsepower that smoked worse than dung and neighed loudly from its dynamo. Never too busy to check the household accounts, Morgan picked a quarrel with Edison himself, claiming that the meter was wrong and that he was being overcharged. The fault proved to be a janitor who kept the lights blazing while he cleaned downstairs through the night. Morgan ended as one of Edison's financial backers. He knew how to put his money where the future was. When Edison's next extraordinary invention, the phonograph, was produced, Morgan backed it and bought one personally, loving to hear the needle scratching out shrill hymns and songs from the round wax cylinders.

He found it almost impossible to change his mind, once he had faith in someone or something. The result was that he could show a surprising tenacity and mercy in calamity. These traits were evident during the frequent rewiring jobs in the Madison Avenue house. He never seemed to mind living under conditions of permanent earthquake and declared that he hoped the Edison Company appreciated using his house as its experimental laboratory. Once a faulty connection caused a fire in his library, which destroyed the desk and the oriental rug. Instead of giving up the invention or dismissing the electrical engineer, he brusquely told the man to fix it right away. Nothing else. Like Nero, he would rather Rome burned than admit he was wrong.

He was already perfecting the later legend of his infallibility and his taciturnity. He knew that those men who talked little were held to think more, and that silence implied wisdom. He still liked to do most of his exchange business personally at Drexel, Morgan and Company. He was open to all comers and any proposition, and built up his reputation and the business enormously. In the recollection of one veteran broker, who often dealt with him in the Drexel building:

> He sat there in the front of his private office, his head down at his desk, and a big cigar cocked up in the corner of his mouth. When you offered him exchange, if he thought it was too high he'd say, "No"; nothing more. Never an offer of what he'd give. You'd never know what he thought. Then you'd go out. If you could, you'd come back and offer it again, lower. If he thought the price right, he'd say, "I'll take it"; nothing more. It was always "Yes" or "No"; no other talk at all.[7]

So the fame of a man grew who knew his own mind and what to do with his money. He convinced others by his certainty. Soon he would have the authority to use other people's minds and tell them what to do with their money.

6

Blackmail, Water and Order

That is not what I asked you. I asked you to tell me how it *could* be done legally. Come back tomorrow or the next day and tell me how it can be done.

— J. Pierpont Morgan to ex-Judge Ashbel Green (1885)

In the scramble for wealth, the railroad wars not only beggared investors but also made workers into paupers. Excessive competition cut dividends and wages. In 1877, there had been a great railroad strike on the four major eastern lines after wages had been cut for the fourth time in seven years. For one week the strikers had prevented all traffic and had persuaded the soft-coal miners to come out in support. The outbreak of something approaching a general strike had scared President Rutherford Hayes enough to send out federal troops to back up the state militias, already in open war against the strikers. Poor families had starved, dozens had died before a settlement was reached. Anarchy on Wall Street was provoking anarchy in the shacks and the slums.

This lesson was lost on the rival railroad companies, which could not pay a living wage while they were cutting each other's throats. The recovery of the American economy after 1879 had led to another mania for building new railroads. Within two years, the total number of miles of track had been increased by a third. Within five years, there were five independent lines running between the Atlantic coast and Chicago with another two under construction. Yet there was only enough business for three of them. And there were no standards. The rival roads had four different gauges, and a passenger traveling from New York to Buffalo sometimes had to change trains ten times. Neither the worker, the investor nor the traveler mattered to the promoter. He bought a charter and issued worthless railroad bonds as if he had found a new philosopher's stone that could turn water into gold.

Such counterfeiting could not last forever. By the end of 1883, the influential investors' guide, *Poor's Manual,* stated that nearly the entire capital stock of the American railroads, about $4 billion worth, was muddy water. Half of this had been formed during the past three years and did not represent tracks laid on the ground. Fortunes had been collected to construct nothing but blackmail lines.

These phantom railroads were a speculator's dream. Given the current madness for investing in the future of communications to the West, any plausible group of partners could gather in tens of millions of dollars by issuing railroad bonds for a line that would duplicate another already in existence. They could double their money by owning the construction company that began to build the tracks and could treble their money by selling their own stock to their rival, once a freight war had proved that acquisition was wiser than mutual ruin. These partners were paid three times over: by a gullible public, by a false front, and by an angry competitor. The only brief beneficiaries were those western farmers and travelers who could take advantage of the railroad wars that sometimes reduced the cost of a fare from New York to Chicago to one dollar.

Yet no railroad could long survive by cutting its rates until it bled to death. The fact that its watered stock demanded swollen dividends made its position even more desperate. Some spirit had to be conjured up from the vasty deep to mediate between the rapacious and suspicious railroad owners and presidents, who seemed hell-bent on ruining themselves and the nation as long as they could ruin their rivals as well. That spirit was J. Pierpont Morgan. His two successes against Jay Gould and on behalf of William H. Vanderbilt had given him a small reputation, which his size and silence only enhanced. In particular, the floating of the $50 million loan to the Northern Pacific on the London market had confirmed his strength in Europe through his father. The Morgan family seemed able to allay the doubts of foreign investors about the quicksands of American railroad companies.

Yet there was a catch in it. Soothing fear and inflaming greed may be the chief talents of a financier. But a promise implies performance. Although the American railroads dealt in hope and the hereafter, the Morgans were staking their reputation on steady dividends. They had persuaded their investors against the evidence that the American railroads had reformed and would not engage in a further orgy of irresponsibility. Already foreign investors had been bitten twice by widespread defaults during financial panics, and they were thrice shy. The situation was serious and asked for intervention. The benign neglect of the past simply would not do.

In December, 1881, Pierpont Morgan set off for his second consultation with his father that year in London. Junius was now aided by his son-in-law Walter H. Burns in order to keep the business in the family. After the three conferred, he proposed to take Pierpont with him on a luxurious pilgrimage to the Holy Land. The conferences about the railroad situation could continue aboard a British steam yacht chartered for the winter cruise. It was aptly named *Pandora.* For the task of Junius and Pierpont Morgan was to keep the lid on the box of evils which the American railroad promoters were loosing on European investors along with enough hope in the future to prevent mass suicide.

Pierpont's wife as usual did not go on the trip. Her place was in the home, and she stayed there. In one of his rare surviving letters, Pierpont wrote back to her about the effect of visiting Jerusalem with his father. Like another Son, he felt a sensation beyond imagination as he entered the Holy City through the Jaffa Gate. In the Church of the Holy Sepulcher, he was awed at the deathlike stillness, broken only by the sound of a distant organ. He could only say to himself, "It is good to be here." And at the slab on which Christ had been laid out, an irresistible impulse made Pierpont fall onto his knees.[1]

With his absolute belief in Father, Son and Holy Ghost, Pierpont continued to obey his father and follow his own inspiration in business. Enthused by the convenience and grandeur of the hired steam yacht, he cabled his friend George Bowdoin in New York to buy for him one of the two best-equipped steam yachts in America, a 165-foot craft he wanted to call *Corsair.* She was a seaworthy slow boat, comfortable on deck and stuffy below. But she could provide a place for secret conferences and a communications system between his New York office and Cragston up the Hudson, supplanting his little launch *Louisa.* He could even fly his personal pennant to show his love of the Middle East — a white crescent and star on a red background.

Even upriver at his country house, Morgan could not escape the turmoil of the railroad wars. His old opponent Jay Gould was still intriguing for an Atlantic connection for his prairie tracks, and he also wanted to put pressure on William H. Vanderbilt and the New York Central. With the energetic and ruthless General Horace Porter to front the operation, he arranged for the floating of the West Shore Railroad to compete with the Central from New York to Buffalo and on to Chicago. With the help of Pierpont Morgan's debonair friend Charles Lanier — one of the six founding members of the exclusive Corsair Club — Gould and Porter raised $40 million of mortgage bonds to begin the construction of the line, which was planned to run past Highland Falls along the banks of the Hudson River.

So the peaceful retreat at Cragston sounded as if it were under artillery attack. Blasts of explosives rattled the windows and made Pierpont's headaches worse. Gangs of Irish and Italian laborers invaded the village and brought their families, breaking down his careful segregation from the immigrant poor. The Morgan children were forbidden to ride out on the main road for fear of the tramps and jobless hoboes passing through the construction camps. The brutal facts of railroad competition were being banged into the financier's skull by rock-crushing hammers and spikes driven home. Beset by clamor and fear for his family, he learned to hate the West Shore line and what it represented. He did not want a railroad so close to his house. He wanted it under his control or out of business.

William H. Vanderbilt agreed with Pierpont Morgan. To him, the West Shore was a blackmail line, "a miserable common thief caught with its hands in my pocket."[2] He had already been blackmailed by the Nickel Plate Railroad running between New York, Chicago and St. Louis. This had been built, in the words of Vanderbilt's lawyer, solely to be unloaded on Vanderbilt or Gould. Furious at its price-cutting, Vanderbilt had first half-ruined himself in a freight war and then had acquired it in an explosion of rage, paying too much a few weeks before it would have been forced into bankruptcy.

He resolved not to repeat his mistake on the West Shore Railroad. He knew that one of its directors, George M. Pullman, had a vendetta against him because he had refused to use Pullman's luxury cars on the New York Central. In retaliation, he decided to drive the rival line out of business at any cost. As he told the board of directors of the Central: "Our old road will not be behind any of its rivals, whether they are young or old. . . . The fact is that there has got to be a further liquidation."[3] That was the best way to pick up competitors cheap.

Suspicious that the Pennsylvania Railroad, led by the pugnacious and difficult George Brooke Roberts, was buying out Jay Gould as the chief backer of the West Shore, Vanderbilt decided to strike back at the heartland of the enemy. He instigated a new railroad, the South Pennsylvania, to link up with the prosperous Philadelphia & Reading line and break the Pennsylvania Railroad's monopoly on freight to Henry C. Frick's anthracite mines and the steelworks of Andrew Carnegie. Both Vanderbilt and Carnegie combined with the new oil dynasty of the Rockefellers to shatter the autocracy of the Pennsylvania Railroad. Gradients were leveled, forests were cleared, cuttings were made, and some two thousand men reputedly died to make way for tracks that were never laid — and, without knowing it, for the Pennsylvania Turnpike.

So folly fought folly, and parallel lines were drawn that by design were not to converge even in infinity. This chaos and cutthroat competition was compounded by another financial collapse in 1884, when the broking house of Ward and Grant failed, wiping out hundreds of investors. The ex-President of the United States was ruined by his own son. At this moment of panic, Cyrus Field used the transatlantic cable he had pioneered to advise Junius Morgan of the catastrophe. His words were:

> Many of our business men seem to have lost their heads. What we want is some cool-headed strong man to lead. If you should form a syndicate in London to buy through Drexel, Morgan and Co. good securities in this market, I believe you would make a great deal of money and at the same time entirely change the feeling here.[4]

After watching his son mature during his interminable junior role after the Civil War, Junius Morgan felt that Pierpont might now be that cool-headed strong man. However much he plunged, he could not ruin his father as Ulysses S. Grant had been ruined. Pierpont now had two new excellent partners to back him up: George S. Bowdoin and Charles Henry Coster. Bowdoin was a sensible and cautious financier like the Drexel brothers, a brake on Pierpont's arrogant search for authority, while Coster was a human calculating machine, a genius at gutting balance sheets and suggesting suitable reorganizations. Until his death in 1900, Coster was to be the secret agent and adviser behind Morgan's more lasting schemes of combination, chiefly the railroad mergers, which were to begin to shape sense out of waste.

Junius Morgan once more called his son across the Atlantic in the spring of 1885. He had two purposes. The first was to arrange for his son to take his place in the London office as the copartner of his son-in-law Walter H. Burns, in case he might die or retire. The second was to plot out ways of ordering railroad finance in America after the numerous defaults of the previous year. Even Vanderbilt's New York Central, the steadiest of all the lines to the West, had halved its guaranteed dividend.

The father decided to send out his son to bang the heads of the speculators together and booked Pierpont on the same steamship back to America that William H. Vanderbilt was taking. He could now afford to stay behind the scenes and leave it all to his son, who had lusted for so long for a limelight of his own.

Called later to the witness stand to explain his actions in 1885, Pierpont took full responsibility, never mentioning his father's name, not even talking of the conversations held with Vanderbilt on the voyage home. Out of loyalty, discretion or vanity, he put everything upon himself. His evidence was this:

> When I came from Europe in June of this year, I became satisfied that it was necessary that something should be done with a view to securing harmony among the trunk lines, and after conversations with various parties here, and also with friends in London, I made up my mind that the principal thing was to secure a harmony between the Pennsylvania and the New York Central.[5]

So he began the legend of the master who could impose his will on the economic anarchists of his time. It was only a legend. There had been months of diplomacy between the two interests, during which either could have denied him. At first he had to persuade Vanderbilt, who had needed his services before and knew he had to keep the Morgans' financial backing in case his freight wars went too far and had to be funded. If Vanderbilt was not wholly convinced during the voyage, he would be through Chauncey M. Depew, the president of the New York Central and one of Pierpont Morgan's friends from the Union Club. It was evident to any rational man that exchange was the better part of valor.

George Roberts of the Pennsylvania Railroad was far tougher to crack, another Welsh-American whose ancestry was nearly as old as the Morgans'. He would not admit to his backing of the West Shore against Vanderbilt, whose backing of the South Pennsylvania he considered piracy. He instructed his railroad vice-president, Frank Thomson, to tell Pierpont Morgan, "Mr. Vanderbilt has seen fit to go into Pennsylvania. No one wanted him to come here and build a railroad, and why should the Pennsylvania, the road he would injure most, give him back the money?" To Morgan's Drexel partner Roberts was more explicit, saying that "he would not buy a hole in the ground." If Vanderbilt was stuck in that hole, he himself would not make it a rat-hole for his money.[6]

Meanwhile, the West Shore line was already in the hands of the receiver. Its capitalization of $40 million, supplemented by a further $10 million, had already been swallowed up by the promoters' construction company, which claimed that it had spent more than $70 million in building less than four hundred miles of track. Pierpont Morgan pointed out to the fuming Vanderbilt that the rival route from New York to Buffalo would actually help the New York Central's expanding traffic commitments and stop Vanderbilt himself from having to build more track. Having made him reconsider, Pierpont pushed him further until he agreed to come for a conference with Roberts on the *Corsair*, where nobody could overhear them.

So the secret railroad conference was held afloat. The *Corsair* sailed from New York harbor to Sandy Hook and back again, then up to West Point and back to Sandy Hook. Pierpont Morgan glowered above the smoke of his endless series of black cigars, saying little. Chauncey Depew complained about the blackmail of the West Shore line, while George Roberts complained about the blackmail of the South Pennsylvania. Morgan's proposal that each major railroad should swallow up its sore spot to eliminate competition did not suck out the sting.

"Can't you see it?" he burst out. "In the end you would have to come to it. In the end you would have to buy out or control this other road only to make your connections. You must come into this thing now."

The rivals would not see it throughout a long lunch and a longer afternoon of cruising. They wanted to teach each other a lesson at the price of their own ruin and that of their shareholders and workers. Above all, they did not like Morgan's reorganization plan, in which the watered stock of both minor railroads would be written down to half or less of its nominal value, losing many millions for those who had speculated in it, Carnegie and the Rockefellers among them. Morgan himself was pleased with that prospect. "They'll not get out whole," he said.[7]

At seven o'clock in the evening, Roberts was the last to concede. Effective control of the South Pennsylvania Railroad was given over to the owners of its rival for a mere $3.5 million, while the Morgan interests and Depew bought in the West Shore Railroad for $22 million at a foreclosure sale. For their services, the Morgans would make a profit approaching $3 million. The fact that the laws of Pennsylvania forbade railroad mergers was simply solved by Pierpont himself in his lordly way. At the later inquiry, he stated that he had evaded something as petty as a state law without involving Drexel, Morgan and Company or his father: "As a firm we could not do it, but as an individual feeling the importance of what was at stake, I was prepared to do what I could and to give the use of my name and signature to act as purchaser of one for the other, and the papers bear that out."

In fact, Pierpont Morgan was acting as high-handedly as he had when a young man in the Hall Carbine and Gold Room affairs. He was risking himself by skirting the edge of the law, but he was not risking his firm's name or his father's. When one adviser told him that his actions would be illegal, he replied that he only wanted to hear how the thing could be done. Not finding a way, he simply did it himself, taking advantage of the fact that American law is even kinder to the individual than to the corporation pretending to be be an individual. Later, when Elbert Gary warned him on another occasion that he was breaking the law, Pierpont Morgan would reply that he did not want a lawyer to tell him what he should not do. "I hire him," Morgan explained, "to tell me how to do what I want to do."

Overmastering as he was, Pierpont Morgan could still be held to ransom by the law. A certain Syracuse lawyer called Belden bought ten shares in the West Shore line and obtained an injunction to block its sale to the New York Central. A few other discontented shareholders joined him, and he demanded a million dollars to drop his injunction on their behalf. Pierpont Morgan was ill with influenza and had to concede, although he insisted that the payoff be entered in the accounts as "a payment of blackmail authorized by Mr. Vanderbilt." So personally did he take this squeezing that he dreamed he was tied to a bell cord and pulled through little brass holes the entire length of a New York Central train.[8]

The laws of Pennsylvania also did not allow Pierpont Morgan to escape scot-free. An inquiry was held into the whole affair, and Morgan was put on the witness stand. He gave his evidence openly and almost contemptuously, hiding what had to be hidden by his apparent frankness. When asked by the state attorney, Cassidy, why the decision about the railroad mergers had to be taken so speedily, the following dialogue took place:

MORGAN: I do not remember anything in particular nor in general. When I have business on hand I think it is better to have it done quickly. That is my experience.

CASSIDY: Why did you go on the yacht?

MORGAN: Because it was a convenient place.

CASSIDY: Then it was not for the purpose of having nobody know what business you were engaged in?

MORGAN: I do not know that that was a part of the consideration. It might have been. I fixed upon that place, but I do not know of any special purpose or view in that connection.[9]

Although there was no question of indicting Morgan for conspiracy or for any other crime in the silence of the laws of the time, further investigations by burned stockholders like Andrew Carnegie were to upset the reorganization plan for the South Pennsylvania seven years after the event. In 1892, the state supreme court ruled that the Pennsylvania Railroad could not acquire control of its rival line through the fiction and the deception of an intermediary sale to Pierpont Morgan. But by then it was too late. William H. Vanderbilt was dead and his heirs were in Morgan's pocket, trying to keep the New York Central afloat without adventuring again into Pennsylvania. Illegal or not, the reorganization had worked for the competing railroad financiers, although not for most of the old stockholders nor for the travelers, who now had to pay all the fares that a monopoly could gouge from them.

Pierpont Morgan's victory had been a personal triumph. He had risked his reputation and had won. The new combinations, indeed, had done so much to drive up the value of the New York Central and Pennsylvania railroad stocks that Jay Gould could unload his holdings on the open market and be eliminated from his forays toward the Atlantic. Morgan had also proved how essential he was to the Vanderbilt heirs, who now trusted him with most major decisions, and even to the independent Roberts of the Pennsylvania, whose bonds were so dependent on financing through the Morgan houses.

One of the two moral censors of Pierpont's life, his mother, had died the year before. With her passed an evangelical conscience that had never praised him much. Nor had his father Junius ever complimented him on anything. But now Pierpont's success elicited from Junius a few words of praise, not directly, but through Pierpont's wife. "Pierpont handled the West Shore affair," he was said to say, "better than I could have done it myself." In fact, Pierpont was doing so much that Junius feared for his health, writing at the end of 1887, "I do hope now, my dear son, that you will 'rest upon your oars.' You have done your work well, and I would not now take up any new reorganization. . . . *Hold off* and let the 'small fry' go to some other Doctor."[10]

Pierpont was very pleased. At the age of forty-eight, he had been allowed to come of age. He was magnanimous even to his friends in victory, forgiving Charles Lanier for helping to finance the West Shore line. But there was always a sermon in his mercy. "My time or anything else I have is at your disposal," he wrote to Lanier. "I say this because I feel that you are surrounded by men in those companies without the least particle of honor."[11] He was quite sure of his own.

If the construction of the West Shore line had brought poor workingmen too close to Cragston for the comfort of segregation, the new pastor of St. George's Church also jolted Morgan from his autocratic complacency about the vestry and the congregation. The church was in a bad way. Smart society had moved uptown, leaving the church in an unfashionable area. Unlike the Morgans, leading men did not go there anymore, preferring the unctuous comforts of Bishop Potter, famous for saying grace at rich men's tables with the words, "Bountiful Lord, we thank Thee for all these Thy blessings . . ." while the poor dinner table heard, "Dear Lord, we give thanks for even the least of these Thy mercies . . ."[12]

The new rector of St. George's, W. S. Rainsford, found that the pews were difficult to rent now and that the church was nearly empty on Sundays. Allegience had been transferred with residence. He was not prepared to accept the decline. A man of exceptional physique and manic-depressive temperament, he looked like an Anglo-Saxon St. George himself and behaved as it he were personally slaying the dragon of sin. He was certainly a match for Pierpont Morgan.

Morgan called the first vestry meeting in his study in Madison Avenue instead of in the church. The rest of the vestrymen were dutifully in attendance. The Reverend Rainsford decided to grab the bull by the horns and assert his authority at once. In his memoirs, he declared that he said the church had gone too far to be pulled up, but that he would undertake the task on three conditions.

> "Name your conditions," said Mr. Morgan; and I did.
>
> "First, you must make the church absolutely free — buy out all those who will not surrender their pews; next, abolish all committees in the church except the vestry; and, third, I must have $10,000 for three years, apart from my salary, to spent as I see fit; my salary I leave to you."
>
> "Done," said Mr. Morgan.[13]

Morgan liked a man who knew his own mind and did not waste his time. He did not, however, expect the challenge Rainsford would provide. The new rector went out into the neighborhood to find a new congregation, and he found it by "altering the machinery to the needs of the people." He realized that he would attract "a lot of bums" by breaking down the barriers of the exclusive church, and he even started street missions to bring in more of the poor. He would stand no nonsense. If his silver tongue could not persuade a drunk to behave, he would knock him down with his fist. His success with the homeless and with workingmen led to a full church and the respect of some of the rich, including Pierpont Morgan, who sometimes found it hard to find a seat at divine service since he could no longer reserve a pew.

If Morgan ever had a confessor, it was Rainsford. The financier felt himself judged by the rector; for Rainsford had set out his beliefs in these words:

> The dangerous men are not the masses; but often men we know and dine with; the men prominent in religious and philanthropic enterprises who are all the time trying to buy something that the law does not allow to be bought and that enlightened public opinion knows to be wrong: these are the men who do not trust the people — the great lawyers, great corporations, great insurance people — men who are always trying to do something that the law does not quite allow.[14]

Morgan was one of these, as was clear in the West Shore affair. And Rainsford knew his man well, describing accurately how a rich man puts his religion into one compartment and the rest of his life into another, comfortably apart. And yet he learned to admire his powerful vestryman. He battled with him over having a mixed choir that wore surplices, and Morgan conceded. When Andrew Carnegie refused to endow a church community center unless he was given control of the choir, Morgan listened to Rainsford's defiance of the other financier and, twelve months later, handed him a sealed envelope just before sailing off to Europe. In it was a piece of paper guaranteeing the full cost of the center, some quarter of a million dollars. And when Rainsford fell ill of nervous depression, Morgan paid for his long convalescence and set up a trust fund for him and his wife so that they need have no worry about their future. He did this in spite of or because of the fact that Rainsford would stand up to him.

On one occasion, Morgan decided to control the vestry completely. He proposed a vote that would reduce the vestry to a few of his business friends and ensure that they met only in his study. Rainsford opposed the motion, saying that the vestry had to meet in the church under his supervision and should be enlarged to include a workingman. Morgan expected to browbeat the other vestrymen into supporting him, but all took Rainsford's side. He rose, saying, "Rector, I will never sit in this vestry again." He submitted his resignation in writing, but Rainsford sat on it. In a month of sullen weekly breakfasts, he and Morgan did not refer to the matter; but just before Morgan sailed off to Europe, he agreed to serve again with good grace and in good faith.

Rainsford's estimate of Morgan is shrewd and unexpected. He testified to the financier's extraordinary and winning charm and to his gift for inspiring loyalty. The eyes that pierced other people and cowed them into obedience seemed to Rainsford to be compounded of both penetration and extraordinary kindliness. They certainly had the power to make others believe in Morgan. "When he said a thing, and looked full at you as he said it, to doubt him was impossible."

Rainsford was even more interesting on the subject of Morgan's faith. If it was in a separate compartment like the faith of other rich men, it was real.

> His faith was threefold: Faith in himself and his business judgment (when I first knew him I should say that outside of his office, where he was king, he was singularly self-distrustful and diffident. This diffidence passed as years brought him power and flattery); faith in the religion of Jesus, as formulated by the Puritan Calvinistic divines; and faith in the stability and greatness of the United States. He was intensely and unselfishly patriotic.
>
> In religious matters, and he was deeply religious, he had no vision of reforms, and generally little sympathy with reformers. On the religious side of his nature, he was intensely conservative. His beliefs were to him precious heirlooms. He bowed before them as the Russian bows to the "ikon" before he salutes the master of the house. . . . So Mr. Morgan had the peace and power of religious assurance, while the very nature of his assurance precluded in him the possibility of spiritual development. His religion was a talent to be wrapped in its own napkin and venerated in the secret place of his soul; laid aside in safe disuse, rather than passed from man to man.[15]

So Pierpont Morgan moved out of his father's shadow in 1885 into the responsibility of his own actions and faith. He was not, as he confessed to Rainsford, a good judge of men; but he could inspire their loyalty and awe them into obedience. He was an intensely private man, turned even more on himself by the spreading deformity of his nose. He felt himself called to support his threefold faith: in the rationalization of American business under his guidance; in a personal Calvinistic creed expressed through the hierarchy of the Episcopal Church; and in the future greatness of the United States. He rarely doubted that he was the right man in the right place at the right time.

7

Trust, or a Gentlemen's Agreement

> You say we have a gentlemen's agreement. The trouble is this — I only see one gentleman in the room.
>
> — Alexander Korda

Pierpont Morgan had arrived at the crossroads of his life. He was hugely ambitious. There were four ways he could go; each route taken would seem a different direction to his friends and his enemies. He could continue to amass money like a Frick or a Rockefeller and hope that future museums and foundations would obscure the grubby origins of his fortune. He could become the center of a loose alliance of international bankers, which might attempt to control the worst excesses of the swings and roundabouts of the American economy. He could interfere in the chaotic competition of American business to rationalize it in the way he thought it ought to be run, but many did not. Or he could try to concentrate the communications, the industry and the money power of the United States for the good or ill of his country.

Pierpont Morgan took all four roads. Like Stephen Leacock's hero, he galloped off in several directions simultaneously. He continued to pile up a fortune and began to collect manuscripts and works of art to embellish it. He called meetings of bankers to develop his father's syndicates into more coherent financial groups that might halt panics before they became disasters. He went on with his policy of trying to combine railroads and other industries into associations that would provide better public service at greater expense to the public. And he worked for the concentration of financial power in the hands of a few New Yorkers, as a part of a gigantic international web. To some, this would seem stability; to many, conspiracy.

His first job was a hangover from his previous success. Squeezed by the monopoly of the Pennsylvania Railroad and inefficiently managed, the lucrative Philadelphia & Reading Railroad was in difficulties. By 1886, its deficit was $6 million a year. Pierpont Morgan was called in with his shears and pruning hooks to slash the value of the watered stock, reduce interest rates on the bonds, and assess the shareholders for more money. After another year of wrangling, his scheme, drawn up by his partner Coster, was accepted. The railroad was put into profit again. Unfortunately, its new manager, Archibald McLeod, aspired to become the Napoleon of the railroads even more than Morgan aspired to be the Alexander of his age. He fought the attempts of the financiers to dominate him, saying that he "would rather run a peanut-stand than be dictated to by J. P. Morgan." Yet for all his brave words, he was to resign after eight years. The road would be left in Morgan's hands, who would learn in this long struggle to insist on controlling what he had agreed to reorganize and finance.

His work, indeed, provoked congressional action against the anarchy of the railroads. What one man had elected to do to serve himself might be better done by those elected by the people to serve them. In 1887, Congress passed a bill setting up the Interstate Commerce Commission. It was in response to popular agitation after the conservative United States Supreme Court had struck down in *Wabash* vs. *Illinois* the right of the states to regulate interstate commerce or even to interfere with any traffic crossing their borders.

Farmers, western manufacturers, shippers and workers were up in arms against a ruling that threw them on the untender mercies of the railroad owners. They pestered their congressmen and senators, who were forced against their will and the lucrative lobbies to debate a regulatory bill for a year. Finally they passed a cosmetic measure, which gave the protestors some official paragraphs and left the magnates in control of the railroads. "A bill that no one wants," one congressman called it, "and everybody will vote for."[1] Its importance for the future lay in the fact that it did forbid price-fixing and special rebates and conspiracies to drive up fares and rates on goods. Fair competition was the shibboleth of the act. But the Interstate Commerce Commission, set up to enforce the act, was a toothless, feeble creature without even the power to fix freight charges, and was further emasculated by the Supreme Court in favor of the owners, until the watchdog of the people could hardly bark and never bite.

Still, Pierpont Morgan would rush in where governments feared to tread. In December, 1888, and in the following January, he summoned to his home on Madison Avenue all available railroad magnates along with the leading railroad bankers. He wanted to form an effective, self-regulating mechanism in the hands of the owners, not of the government

— an Interstate Commerce Railroad Association, which would police the communications industry and have teeth.

The meeting provoked intense speculation. Its open secrecy meant national publicity for Morgan. One of the western railroad presidents warned, "The public are sure to think we are conspiring to do something that we ought not to do." But Morgan kept the meetings closed and sworn to silence. Reporters besieged the house ceaselessly. Spies with opera glasses hung out of balconies across the street. Nothing was known except that Morgan was trying to increase his power as a mediator. He wanted a general principle established, an informal "gentlemen's agreement." He looked for mutual trust between competitors and financiers, which would develop into the later railroad trusts, the great combinations so essential for orders and profits, so demoniacal for farmers and governments.

When the meeting opened, Morgan immediately made it clear that the money power would not permit the unnecessary competition of the railroads to destroy reasonable profits. During the previous three years, he had already pushed the coal-carrying railroads into an agreement to fix tariffs and charge the same rates, even when their lines ran parallel. To Morgan, civilization was founded on dividends, while savagery was the result of anarchy in business.

"The purpose of this meeting," he declared, "is to cause the members of this association to no longer take the law into their own hands when they suspect they have been wronged. . . . This is not elsewhere customary in civilized communities, and no good reason exists why such a practice should continue among railroads."

George Roberts of the Pennsylvania had been disciplined by Morgan once before on the *Corsair*. He found such patronage intolerable. He objected to "this very strong language, which indicates that we, the railroad people, are a set of anarchists, and this is an attempt to substitute law and arbitration for anarchy and might."

Roberts was correct. The association and "gentlemen's agreements" proposed by Morgan were ways of avoiding the new act, which forbade price-fixing by formal documents or cartels. Unrestricted competition was actually the requirement of the law. Roberts also pointed out that the bankers themselves were responsible for financing the blackmail lines which were ruining the old railroads. If there was no money available, there would be no undue competition. As trade followed the flag, so tracks followed the finance. Yet, respectful of Morgan's powers of persuasion, Roberts left the door open for an agreement. "It is a little harsh language for us to hold here," he said, "but I can stand it, I suppose, if the others can."

Morgan moved in for the kill. Now he listened less and ordered more. He said what the other bankers had authorized him to say: if an organization with an executive committee were formed of railroad men and financiers, then its members would do everything in their power to prevent any speculator from building parallel tracks. He would pledge their financial power to deter any backing of blackmail lines. Two years before, he had already done so, when he and his associates had put out of business the freebooter Henry S. Ives and his Vandalia line by ganging up on him and calling in his loans. His group had also chosen to rescue the Baltimore & Ohio Railroad, and then the Chesapeake & Ohio. If the financiers would agree to eliminate unfair competition, why not the railroads, who most suffered from it?

Morgan's proposal would have given the railroad men a solution, but the trouble lay in themselves. Charles Francis Adams, now the president of the Union Pacific, already knew this. Before the Morgan meeting, he and the western railroad tycoons, Gould and Strong and Huntington, had tried to form a clearinghouse to standardize rates; it had not lasted a week, given the storm of public opposition. The small railroads that had not joined cut their rates immedately to pick up more business. With his Brahmin righteousness, Adams denounced his own kind, blaming railroad managers for their "covetousness, want of good faith, and low moral tone." He asked any one of them in the room to stand up and positively declare he preferred to disobey the law and refused to submit to arbitration. The representative of the Chicago & Northwestern line did so at once.

In the words of Morgan's contemporary biographer, the meeting was like that of the chiefs of the fighting clans of Scotland. Each man was passionately certain, convinced in his own mind, that his neighbor was at fault.[2] Cosmetic but futile resolutions were passed. In the end, nothing of substance was agreed on. Morgan had showed that he wanted harmony and fair dealing among the railroads so that he could guarantee dividends to his weary investors. But the western railroad men were not impressed, and they continued to do what they wanted on the far side of the Mississippi, where Morgan and his friends had no influence.

The failure of his "gentlemen's agreements" because there were not enough gentlemen in the room led Morgan inexorably into exerting personal control. It was being forced upon him in the Philadelphia & Reading

Railroad affair, and it would be forced upon him by the contumacy of the railroad barons. In the absence of mutual trust, there had to be an economic trust. If new government regulations forbade price-fixing between rivals, and if the railroad managers could only agree to disagree, then one single holding company had to bind them and fix rates before they all ate each other alive.

Morgan tried again the following year to reach a western agreement that would prove binding. A board was appointed to arbitrate and levy small fines on those who broke the rules of the association. For the credit of the railroads was in jeopardy once more. A single one of those quoted on the London Stock Exchange was still paying dividends, although the Morgan houses had encouraged European investors to buy great amounts of their stock. In order to create confidence, Morgan even called in the press and exaggerated the strength of the association. "Think of it," he declared, "all the competitive traffic of the roads west of Chicago and St. Louis placed in the control of about thirty men! It is the most important agreement made by the railroads in a long time, and it is as strong as could be desired."[3]

His optimism was far from the truth. Even at the conciliation meeting, one of the thirty had said that he would not trust the other railroad presidents with his watch out of sight. He was then ungently reminded that he also was a railroad president. The western lines may have been controlled by only thirty men; but fierce egos and short-term interests, regional and private animosities, destroyed all attempts at cooperation. One western vice-president denounced Morgan's association as "a colossal fancy of some eastern bankers whose sole excuse for foisting it upon the practical managers of the West was the supposed necessity of doing something to satisfy demands of Wall Street."[4] So the public fear of financial conspiracy was used to sabotage attempts to organize capital investment at least as efficiently as the railroad unions were trying to organize the workers.

It was no accident that Morgan's syndicates were matched by the rise of the syndicalists, and that his drive for a national association of employers was met by a push for one big union. Overweight creates its own counterpoise; might conjures up a common resistance. While Morgan or his nominees were joining the boards of most major eastern railroads to keep them in line and coordinate their policies, the growing railroad unions were also in communication, trying to end the wage-cutting caused by the railroad wars. Actually they stood to gain from rationalization as much as Morgan and the nation did. It was far easier for one big union to deal with one big employer in control of one big continental system. But many wasted decades of strikes and cutthroat competition were to pass before necessity would cut the railroads down to size.

Morgan's methods of railroad reorganization followed a standard pattern with small variations. They were created by himself and his partners, chiefly Coster; they were soon known as Pierpontifex Maximus and his Apostles, or "Jupiter" Morgan and his Ganymedes. First, an insolvent railroad would be put on a paying basis by squeezing the water out of its stock, issuing new bonds at a lower interest rate, assessing its stockholders for more capital, and eliminating all waste. Second, when possible, its lines could be consolidated with other lines. When not, a common interest was sought to avoid ruinous competition, whether by association or by agreement or by collusion to fix rates outside the knowledge of the law. Third, a large fee would be charged by Morgan and his associates, not less than half a million dollars. As Morgan often used to say, "I am not in Wall Street for my health."

Various devices were invented or developed to assure control by Morgan and his Apostles: the voting trust, by which the shareholders voted to give their rights to Morgan's nominees on the board; the majority shareholding, by which Drexel, Morgan and Company actually held most of the stock; the interlocking directorate, whereby Morgan found himself sitting on the boards of a dozen railroad companies and his Apostles on the boards of fifty more. The final device was the great holding company, which would make real Morgan's dream of total domination. This structure was the apex of a vast pyramid which exchanged its nonvoting shares for other railroad company shares until it held power over all at the top.

Yet in the end, whatever stratagem Morgan used to establish order in business, his authority was personal. Where he was neither feared nor respected, he could still lose. He lost, indeed, to a young upstart, the new railroad financier E. H. Harriman, who began representing the Illinois Central in 1886. Harriman had retired early as a stockbroker after learning all the tricks of Drew and Fisk and Gould in the New York market. He was as secretive as Morgan, but far more deceptive. While Morgan liked to bully other business leaders into recognizing the art of the possible, Harriman liked outmaneuvering them until they were forced to accept his art of the implausible. A raider rather than an organizer, Harriman knew the niceties of a legal situation even better than the Morgan partners did and exploited his local knowledge to defeat them.

The battleground was the control of a minor line in Iowa, the Dubuque

& Sioux City. Although Drexel, Morgan and Company held the majority of the stock as trustees for the reorganization of the road, Harriman had all the Morgan proxy votes rejected at the next stockholders' meeting because of a technicality. The members of the firm personally had signed the vote approving the new Morgan-dominated board, but not as trustees. This action invalidated their vote under Iowa law, and Harriman had his board of nominees elected even though Drexel, Morgan and Company were the majority stockholders.[5] Morgan never forgave Harriman for the trickery, but he had to recognize the astuteness of his new rival. On his father's advice, he tended to avoid lawsuits. "I hope you will not be tempted into litigation," Junius had advised him in a fight over the Baltimore & Ohio Railroad. "Life is too short for that."[6]

Yet in spite of minor reverses, steadily and surely Morgan and his partners were gaining control over many of the eastern and midwestern railroads. Whenever a line was in trouble — and all were, at one time or another — it usually went to Morgan for reorganization. Given the cycle of boom and slump in American business, there would have to be another panic, another crash. The railroads with their dried-up dividends and sloppy capitalization would be the first to go into liquidation. Then Morgan could collect them as he had already begun to collect manuscripts, tapestries, and works of art, *en masse*, as if his appetite were never satisfied, as if he wanted to possess them all.

Once more, Pierpont Morgan's family pointed out the way to the dutiful son. For a decade, Junius Morgan had been collecting English masters to furnish 13 Prince's Gate and Dover House with family portraits, which might make him seem an aristocrat by association, if not by birth. Using Agnew and Company, which dominated the international market until the Duveen family moved into picture dealing, Junius concentrated on buying portraits by Reynolds and Romney and Gainsborough. It was a conservative and moderate collection in a known style, impressive without being remarkable.

Pierpont was still too much in awe of his father to compete with him. His own house at 219 Madison Avenue was crammed with Victorian objects of somber taste. In art, his standards were not yet different from those of his rich contemporaries, who liked the English school of painters for its nobility and story pictures, and the French school for its landscapes, nudes and sugary images. Until the rise of the Morgan of the international art world, Joseph Duveen, the American plutocracy bought Bouguereau and Rosa Bonheur, Landseer and Millais. Morgan himself admired them, but did not think they were too suitable in the home. With the advice of Joseph Duveen's "Uncle Henry," the founder of the house's fortunes in America, Morgan filled 219 Madison Avenue with grandiose junk and a little good porcelain and delftware, the two things Uncle Henry know well at that time. In fact, after Morgan's death, his librarian, Belle da Costa Greene, asked Uncle Henry what he thought of his decoration job on Madison Avenue. He replied: "It iss orful!" — and began redecorating the house from top to bottom for Morgan's son.[7]

Yet from his association with the Metropolitan Museum, Morgan was already learning to be more independent in his judgment of art. He was fundamentally a romantic collector with a developing taste in royal and religious history. The first painting he had ever acquired had been an idealistic portrait of a young woman by George A. Baker, which used to hang in the place of honor in his library; it bore a remarkable resemblance to his first wife; and Morgan also treasured another portrait by Baker of his daughter Louisa at the age of two. Even after he had acquired a host of great works of art, he loved mixing the homely with the grand. One actress, who was staying in the London home he had inherited from his father, was astonished to see a reproduction of *Cherry Ripe* hanging in her bedroom beside some Renaissance altarpieces.

But before his father's death, Pierpont owned little of value beyond a few Egyptian antiquities. Then a nephew sent along a friend with a manuscript by Thackeray. Pierpont picked it up, turned over the leaves, and said: "Are you sure that this is in Thackeray's own handwriting?"

"Quite certain."

"You are too young to be quite certain."

"I think not, sir, because I have been dealing in manuscripts since I was seventeen."

"Very well. What's the price?"

"One hundred pounds."

"Is that cash?"

"No, sir. Ninety pounds cash."

"Very well. My secretary will give you a check. Let me know if you get any more really good authors' manuscripts."[8]

That was the end of the conversation. Pierpont Morgan was as laconic in buying works of art as in dealing in foreign exchange or with railroad presidents. He wanted a good bargain without wasting words about it. The Thackeray manuscript, however, although put in the cellar of 219 Madison Avenue, was the acorn that planted the oak forest. Soon Morgan was to acquire manuscripts by Dickens and the original draft of Keats's

Endymion. It was safe stuff from the English school of major nineteenth-century writers, bound to appreciate in value, but it was also the foundation of the great Morgan Library to come. And it was an independent choice: his father did not collect manuscripts.

Suddenly and accidentally, Junius Morgan died and liberated his son. He had been living on and off for four years on the French Riviera near the outrageous Frank Harris, who had found Pierpont's father very anglicized, with all the reticences of the English and none of his son's tendency to extravagance. He lived, Harris wrote, as an English gentleman would live who was making only forty or fifty thousand a year. Pierpont was sailing from the United States to make his annual report to his father when the tragedy occurred in the south of France, where Amelia Sturges had died and where young Pierpont had broken down. Now, in 1890, Junius Morgan was thrown from a victoria when the horses bolted, frightened by a train. He was flung onto a pile of stones by the roadside, never regained consciousness, and died a few days later. A series of telegrams was sent to his son. They were meant to be read in sequence to prepare him for the shock of his father's death, but they all arrived at the same time. In his impatience Pierpont ripped open and read the last one first.

Again he had a brief collapse. He was traveling with his daughter Louisa, who comforted him enough to have her travel with him to Monte Carlo. There his sister Mary Burns was waiting with the embalmed body of Junius. Pierpont sailed with it back to New York, organized a funeral service in Hartford, and had his father buried in the new Morgan plot at the Cedar Hill Cemetery under a massive block of red Nova Scotia granite. So powerful was Junius in the memory of his hometown that the flag on the state capitol and those on all other government buildings were flown at half-mast.

Yet if Pierpont Morgan was briefly broken in spirit, he surged up soon in the knowledge that he was finally master of the house of Morgan. He had to return to London to reorganize his father's firm. His son Jack would play his old role of commercial spy and agent there, reporting back regularly to him across the Atlantic as he had had to do for so long himself. But before he left for New York, he began the acts of personal extravagance and advertisement that would signal his emancipation from his father's caution and censorship. He ordered a new *Corsair* to be built; it had to be as large as possible, yet able to turn round in the Hudson River opposite Cragston. He gave its designer a book of signed blank checks drawn on his firm. "When the builders need money," he said grandly, "you draw the checks until you are stopped." Then he sailed to London. His partners did not stop the checks or the building.

Corsair II was more than two hundred feet long and had three engines, a strong and speedy boat painted glossy black like its predecessor. Named again in memory of Pierpont's supposed pirate ancestor, Henry Morgan, it was to fight against the Spanish Empire as he had done. But for the time being, it was a lavish present to himself from a man who had waited until the age of fifty-three to inherit the confidence to indulge himself.

Junius Morgan left nearly ten million dollars. Most of his money went to his daughters, but Pierpont was left with a million dollars and the two houses in London. His real legacy was his liberty. He had been the son. Now he was the father of the family, the head of the house of Morgan. And in case his future role might not be understood, he even purchased George Washington's sword.[9]

8

The Enemy of the West

I have done nothing except stop men fighting. I don't like to see men fighting. There is too much waste.

— J. Pierpont Morgan (1893)

Pierpont Morgan inherited his power from his father in the year that the American frontier was officially said to be ended because the subcontinent had all been marked out into states and territories. The limits had been reached in the land, although not in the making of fortunes. The seized ground had to be developed, the barriers had to be broken down. Mass communications were needed to erode the mutual suspicions of East and West and South. Only then could the farmer by the stove become the brother to the men of the cities, losing his ignorance and his innocence along with his isolation.

In the twenty years after 1870, the population of the West had grown from seven million to seventeen million, too quickly for its own comfort. The farmers' hope in cheap land and easy money had often been killed by the sufferings inflicted by nature, and they put the blame on the urban melting pot from which they had been refugees. They had fled, after all, to an agricultural myth, which told them that their exclusion was a successful repudiation of wealth and aristocracy and luxury. Farmers were the only true democrats, the representatives of the best in the American tradition. The cities held the idle rich and the owners of farm mortgages and the dregs of Europe. When the new western champion William Jennings Bryan denounced the East as "the enemy's country," he voiced a rural prejudice older than the Declaration of Independence.

Suffering breeds radicalism. The discontent born of poverty and unending labor forged the rural organizations of protest: the Grange and the Farmers' Alliance and the Populist movement. The ideology of these movements was a peculiar mixture of reaction, xenophobia and progressiveness. But, above all, it was set in terms of black and white. At the time of Pierpont Morgan's birth in the days of Andrew Jackson, the Second Bank of the United States had been held responsible for the slump in the West. Later, the Roman Catholics, Wall Street, gold, the immigrants, the railroads and the trusts all became the scapegoats for western ills. The country radicals rarely admitted the guilty truth, that their own plundering of the land and heavy borrowing from the banks of the East had caused many of the sufferings they blamed on others.

There is a traditional theory of conspiracy at the grass roots of American politics. It was at first the product of geography and hardship and religion. Later, when farming on the prairies became dependent on urban and international markets, the money power of the East grew into a real enemy, capable of ruining farmers surely and inexorably. Commercialization, specialization, business methods, new machinery and communications, the mail-order catalogues called "wishing-books," all destroyed the self-sufficiency of farm and village and made them dependent on the wicked city. Bryan's campaigns for free silver were less an economic matter than an expression of the rural hatred of eastern financiers, who waxed fat under the mysterious protection of the devilish gold standard.

Yet if the gold standard was the distant Satan, the railroad was the present Lucifer. The tracks were, after all, not merely lines on the map. The small market towns depended on them utterly. In 1890, the United States was still a skein of localities that hardly knew each other. Although the new migrants from Europe were filling the city slums, three fifths of all Americans still lived on farms or in villages. Dirt roads and covered wagons still made local travel possible; but the railroads were the iron nerves of the continent, transmitting the hogs and grain to the cities and the goods from the factories. Where the railroad was routed, a town prospered and hoped to become a small city; otherwise it died. Two thousand settlements in Illinois became ghost towns within fifty years because the railroad passed them by. One Ohio writer noted that his small town used to be a crossroads and was now a water tank. The engines and the cars and the tracks were the condition of survival for rural America.

This dependence was the source of the growing hatred of Pierpont Morgan's arrogance. Of the old villains of railroad manipulation, Jay Gould was the last survivor. He had ousted the righteous Charles Francis Adams from control of the Union Pacific and was approaching his dream of being the first man to manage a transcontinental railroad. But, unable to float his new bonds, he was forced into the hands of his opponent, Pierpont Morgan. Morgan agreed to accept notes endorsed by Gould because his ambition was the same — to control a comprehensive railroad system linking North and South and West. Once again he proved his mastery over Gould, forcing him to subscribe to new notes on the Union Pacific and accusing him of "juggling with the property." Gould was summoned to Morgan's office like a naughty schoolboy and was told that, if he did not act frankly, he would be thrown out of control of the line.

Yet the old speculator had a last rebellion in him. He went back to rate-cutting on his railroads, destroying Morgan's attempt at an association of the western owners to fix prices. But death soon did Morgan's business for him. In December, 1892, Gould died after a pathetic attempt to become accepted by the smart people who had always accepted Morgan. On the day after his last Christmas on earth, Gould had attempted to launch his daughter Helen in New York society. He had cast his net wide and had invited three thousand people to come rather than the Four Hundred beloved by Mrs. Astor and the twelve hundred on the list of Mrs. Vanderbilt — neither of whom came to visit the Goulds. But a few hundred guests did arrive, and among them were Mr. and Mrs. J. Pierpont Morgan. It was an unusual courtesy on the part of Gould's most formidable opponent.

Gould had done the other railroad tycoons one strange service during his life. He was so notorious for the trickery of his dealings and the poor quality of his railroads that he had attracted most of the hatred of the farmers and the reformers. He was the scapegoat of his time and of the economic system that permitted him to exist at all. When he complained to an editor about a venomous attack on him in the press, the editor replied that Gould was one of only three or four men in the country worth abusing. Just before his death, he admitted that he knew he was the most hated man in America. Now his role as the whipping boy of the plutocrats was open.

Morgan elected to fill Gould's shoes and his sacrificial place. His motives were different. The age of the raiders was ending; the investment bankers were taking over. Although Morgan wanted to enrich himself as much as Gould did, he could claim that his wish to consolidate was in the national interest. But by choosing to act as the symbol for the new financial power structure, he would finally attract most of the popular odium looking for an outlet. He who would master be must also be a mark.

Having asserted his power over a group of northern railroads, Morgan first moved toward the agrarian South. There, thirty-five separate railroad corporations were competing in a tangle of tracks, rates, low wages and insolvency. The key firm was the Richmond & West Point Terminal line. Its stock had fallen into the hands of a few speculators, who played bulls and bears with it as Daniel Drew had done with the Erie Railroad in the bad days. Morgan refused to reorganize the company unless he and his associates controlled the stock. At first, the speculators did not accept and tried to adjust matters on their own; but when they failed, they had to go back and surrender to Morgan on his terms.

So he acquired control over the hub of the southern railroad system. And as the economic situation worsened before the panic of 1893, he watched the other thirty-four southern lines plunge toward receivership. He then produced a mammoth reorganization plan, developed by the indispensable Coster and another friend, Samuel Spencer of the Baltimore & Ohio road. Using his trusted methods, he had the total debt of the new Southern Railway System written down by a third, while the shareholders were assessed for fresh capital and new stock was issued at a lower rate of interest, enough for the traffic to bear. His fee was $850,000, and a voting trust left the whole Southern System in the hands of his men. Samuel Spencer became its president, responsible to Morgan himself, to Charles Lanier and to George F. Baker, the president of the First National Bank of New York, a man so silent he made Morgan appear to be a babbling brook. During the rest of Morgan's life, Baker was to serve as his financial counselor and restraint; Wall Street would call him Morgan's Secretary of the Treasury.

As always, the whole reorganization was rushed through to forestall blocking by Congress, the courts or dissident shareholders. Morgan had to consolidate quickly and secretively, or not at all. The western radicals had worsened the political climate for him. The Interstate Commerce Commission had been followed by the Sherman Antitrust Act of 1890, which was intended to break up the growing number of trusts and cartels, in particular the railroad mergers and Rockefeller's ruthless Standard Oil. Actually, the Sherman Act was as much a sham and a delusion as its predecessor; both were designed to placate the West and leave the Morgans in power. "What looks like a stone wall to a layman," Mr. Dooley commented, "is a triumphal arch to a corporation lawyer."[1]

But all the same, the Republicans no longer controlled the presidency of the United States, which had seemed theirs by right since the Civil War. The Democrats under the forceful Grover Cleveland twice broke the fifty-year Republican monopoly on the White House. They were responsible to the southern and western votes that had put them in power. Placebos might not be enough against the unrest now bursting through, even through the complacency of the rich.

The plutocrats had gone too far in cutting wages to survive in their suicidal price wars against each other. Two major strikes — at the Carnegie steelworks at Homestead, Pennsylvania, in 1892 and the Pullman strike two years later — pulled the nation to the brink of a social war of the classes. Faced with a prolonged strike at his plants if he forced the steel unions to stick to a twelve-hour day and a lower piece rate, Carnegie decided on a lockout and went overseas, leaving his partner and deputy Frick to stand in the breach. When the strikers blockaded the Homestead plant, Frick sent for three hundred Pinkerton strong-arm men, miscalled detectives. They came upriver in armored scows, were fired on, and shot back. Three of them died, and so did five of the strikers before the "detectives" surrendered and were beaten out of town. The governor of Pennsylvania sent in eight thousand militiamen to restore order, and Frick himself only just survived after being shot and stabbed by the anarchist Alexander Berkman. Although Carnegie was absent when the strike was broken, his reputation never recovered. Frick was admired for his toughness, but Carnegie seemed a politic coward, the new villain of American capitalism. "No pangs remain of any wound received in my business career save that of Homestead," he wrote later. "That was sufficient to make my name a by-word for years."[2]

In 1894, Morgan's old rival George Pullman played the villain of the piece. His Palace Car Company tried to cut wages and was faced by Eugene V. Debs's growing American Railway Union. Debs ordered his 150,000 members not to handle Pullman cars on the roads. The strike spread across two thirds of the United States. Grover Cleveland called in federal troops to keep the railroads running, while the Sherman Antitrust Act was misused to indict Debs for conspiracy in restraint of trade. So the law passed to curb the trusts was used against their chief challengers. And the strike was broken after something near a social war.

The Pullman strike concentrated the wrath of the western reformers on the railroads and on those, like Morgan, who were the new powers behind them. There were calls from the Populists for nationalization of the roads and government operation. "We must run the railroads," one reform paper declared, "or permit them to decree and collect tribute of us all and carry on war against their employees."[3] That same year, the march on Washington of Coxey's Army of unemployed men increased social unrest and hatred against the financial power of the East, in which Morgan's name was becoming preeminent. The four years of the depression in the mid-nineties would be the time that he replaced Gould and Carnegie and Pullman as the Golden Calf of western paranoia.

Such confrontations appalled Morgan. The loss during the Pullman strike was estimated at $80 million. The railroads were already rocky and could not afford that. If Morgan could be accused of instigating the labor wars by forcing lower wages in the first stages of his reorganizations and neglecting the living conditions of his workers altogether, he would not have understood such charges. To him, his job was to provide financial stability for the prosperity and communications of the United States. Outside that, twelve-hour working days or starvation wages were none of his concern.

He had, indeed, helped to alleviate the panics of 1890 and 1893. The first had begun with the insolvency of the Baring Brothers, who had overspeculated in the gold markets of Argentina. The Bank of England had raised its bank rate to an unprecedented 6 percent; loans had been called in; and the Argentine government had defaulted on its bond payments because of two years of bad harvests. In his first international financial crisis, Pierpont Morgan had behaved with his new decisiveness. He had contributed to a pool of £7 million to bale out the Baring Brothers. And through J. S. Morgan and Company, he had guaranteed the sale of $75 million worth of Argentine government bonds to refund the whole national debt of the country. He was using the same techniques that he had used in the railroad reorganizations: the elimination of old bonds and the issuing of new ones at a debt level which could be serviced. Only now he was treating a foreign nation as if it were just another American railroad line.

The panic of 1893 was a more serious matter, although the failure of the many was the opportunity of the few. The Sherman Compromise Silver Act of 1890 had directed the Secretary of the Treasury to buy 4½ million ounces of silver a month to satisfy the westerners who thought they were being starved of cheap credit because of the cross of the gold standard. Within the next three years, until the repeal of the act, the Treasury lost nearly $150 million from its gold reserve. This outflow went into private banks and abroad. A speculative gold situation was created as it had been in the Civil War, but for another reason — the growing popular hatred of the Gold Bugs of the East.

Fear for the stability of the currency, industrial troubles, and the perennial problems of railroad finance combined to cause a panic on Wall Street, which began four years of depression under the Democratic regime. By December, more than fifteen thousand firms, over five hundred and fifty banks, six mortgage companies, and thirteen trust companies had collapsed. Nearly one quarter of the railroads also went into bankruptcy. The rich went down with the poor. Even the cautious Henry Adams, who kept himself outside every possible financial risk, was "caught in the cogs, and held for months over the gulf of bankruptcy, saved only by the chance that the whole class of millionaires were more or less bankrupt too, and the banks were forced to let the mice escape with the rats."[4]

Morgan met the crisis with his partial boldness and selective generosity. He lent money to men of reputation and let those without it go to the wall. One of those who went to him, Colgate Hoyt, remembered the great man's directness. In fear he entered Morgan's office and asked for a loan. He had to have a million dollars. Morgan checked that the loan was absolutely necessary, rang a bell, and had a check drawn up immediately for the sum at the legal rate of interest. Hoyt then offered to bring in his portfolio of securities for Morgan to select the collateral. "You may need your collateral with the banks," Morgan replied. "I am lending you the money on your business record in Wall Street and upon what I know your character to be."[5]

Morgan was less involved in the crisis than usual, but it was the last time a brake could be put upon him — by his senior partner, Anthony J. Drexel, who was still alive. The Wall Street Pepys, Clarence W. Barron, was told that year that Drexel was a man of great reserve power, and that nobody had ever come to the end of Drexel's money. "He always had money to lend and he made his millions out of other people's necessities. He saved Morgan two or three times, for Morgan is a plunger."[6] But it was to be the last time, for Drexel died at Carlsbad a month after the worst of the panic, leaving a fortune of thirty million dollars and taking away the safety net and halter from his partner. Within two years Morgan would drop the name of Drexel from the firm and go back to trading under his own name, something he had not done since the days of the Civil War, when he had been young and reckless and uncurbed.

The endless work of international financing and railroad reorganizations at Drexel, Morgan and Company put great strain on Morgan and his partners. There was a changing of the old guard with the death of Drexel, a coming of the new to the firm of Morgan on his own. Although the essential Coster still carried on until his premature death in 1900, as pale-faced and scurrying as the White Rabbit in *Alice in Wonderland*, two of the old partners retired, broken by the overwork: Egisto P. Fabbri and J. Hood Wright. Rising to take their places in the continuing railroad mergers were Morgan's astute personal counsel, Francis Lynde Stetson, and the Harvard football hero Robert Bacon, who was warned not to "overwork like Coster just because you can and like to do it. He is wonderful — and unwise — to do so."[7]

Bacon looked like an Adonis and was the forerunner of the young Angels who would replace the older Apostles as Morgan's new lieutenants. According to one of the older Morgan partners, Morgan had "fallen in love" with Bacon and wanted him always near at hand, admiring the young man's industry and charm and skill at negotiation as well as his strength and good looks. He never cared for physical weaklings nor for men who had not accomplished anything. In fact, he seemed to take pleasure in surrounding his disfigured strength with the vigor and beauty of the young. His new associates, indeed, would cause the saying on Wall Street that, when the angels of God took unto themselves wives among the daughters of men, the result was the Morgan partners.

There was something in the man too large even for his time. In the opinion of his quiet competitor James Stillman, now become president of the National City Bank, Morgan was a powerful man, heavy and virile, curt and decided, charged with vitality, physical and mental. His tastes had a Renaissance gorgeousness and his desires a naive directness that savored of simpler days. His manner, too, was not without a certain masterful quality, which heightened the Renaissance effect. Genial and accessible, he had a natural heartiness and warmth that never affected in the faintest degree the purpose he had set himself.[8] It was Morgan, after all, who said that there were always two reasons for doing anything: the apparent one, which showed, and the real one.

There was also a hidden Morgan, subject to depressions, headaches and melancholies. Three times he broke down in front of his confessor Rainsford, calling aloud for help, although Rainsford still found him in general the most reserved person of them all. He would sit in church at night with only an organist to play him hymns, which he would boom out to keep back the terrors of the next day. And he was still prey to sudden nervous collapses which were known on Wall Street to happen at the times when he had plunged too deeply. In fact, Barron was told in 1894 that Morgan would live only two years more because he had fits and would die suddenly.[9]

Yet few knew of the secret self-doubt in Pierpont Morgan. Outwardly, he was flamboyant and dominant, a "tremendous adventurer in the world of reality."[10] He had been the chief subscriber to the syndicate behind the new arena at Madison Square Garden, over which Saint-Gaudens's gilded nude Diana shot her golden bow toward the pleasure-seeking city below. He had commissioned from the outrageous Stanford White the building of the palatial Metropolitan Club, which he helped to found just because a friend of his had been blackballed from the Union. He was presenting "Morgan cups" to the New York Yacht Club, so that he could feel master of its races from his high seat in *Corsair II*. He was buying a thousand acres of wilderness upstate and a house in Newport. He intended not to be matched by anyone or anything.

His physical size was now paralleled by an external magnificence. He knew the secret of a good show. He would attract more power by displaying more patronage. He would achieve domination by proclaiming it. Without seeming to advertise himself, he would make his presence known behind the scenes through the actions played in front of them. He would act the omnipotent legend that, once printed, would become the fact.

Yet as he hid his nervous instability behind an overwhelming physique and piercing stare, so he made himself seem indispensable in the railroad reorganizations by pretending that he was. His previous successes had led to an excessive myth of his invincibility. As a commentator in the *Wall Street Journal* noted in 1894, "Mr. Morgan reminded him of three men stranded in Missouri, too proud to beg and too honest to steal. One of them told the other two to go and contract a certain annoying but not dangerous complaint, mingle with the community, thereby circulating the complaint, when he would come along, cure it and receive fees for so doing. Within three or four months this amateur physician had all the money there was in that part of the country." The commentator then added that, if he were young enough, he would set up shop as a reorganizer.[11]

Morgan did achieve another success. He gained a practical monopoly of the anthracite shipping industry by taking over the Lehigh Valley Railroad, which could combine with the tracks owned by his Vanderbilt and First National Bank associates. Then his gadfly Harriman challenged the myth of his necessity and caused him to make two bad mistakes in a row. The first was in the ancient swamp of the Erie Railroad, the second in the promising quicksands of the Union Pacific.

When the Erie went bankrupt in 1893, Morgan was summoned in his savior's role. As the owner of a few second-mortgage bonds, Harriman objected to Morgan's reorganization plan as financially unsound and an infringement of the creditors' rights. His resistance was backed by the important investment firm of Kuhn, Loeb and Company, August Belmont representing the Rothschilds, and the Astor family. Although Harriman's lawsuit, which was heard by the Supreme Court, was unsuccessful, his predictions were correct. The Erie defaulted on the newly issued Morgan bonds twice, and Morgan had to come up with another plan to satisfy the creditors.

This prescience of Harriman's was turned into an outright victory over the Union Pacific line. That railroad also went into the hands of the receivers, and a committee headed by Senator Brice and including Morgan was appointed to rescue it. After two years of discussion, the committee failed to agree on a plan. Jacob H. Schiff of Kuhn, Loeb and Company was approached. "That is J. P. Morgan's affair," Schiff said. "I don't want to interfere with anything he is trying to do."[12] But when Congress persisted in blocking any attempt to reorganize the railroad and settle its debts with the government, Morgan became disgusted. He washed his hands of the line, not believing in its future.

It was a great tactical mistake. Kuhn, Loeb did not get any further with the reorganization until they had co-opted Harriman onto the committee. He had been putting up obstacles in Congress because he wanted the line to join the Illinois Central. Soon, mysteriously, Congress approved the reorganization plans and the settlement of the government's loans. Harriman, now backed by Kuhn, Loeb, had become a force in railroads whom even Morgan could not ignore.

This loss of interest by Morgan, which resulted in his rival's victory, showed that he was neither as omniscient nor as invincible as his image suggested. His grandiose style of life, his three months' holiday a year on his yacht or in Europe, his liking for large social occasions — these meant that he could not give his full attention to all things at all times. So he let the Union Pacific go. It was too much of a nuisance, and he hated endless political wheeling and dealing to gain his point. He despised congressmen almost as much as he despised the robber barons of the railroads.

He was, after all, as even Henry Adams pointed out, not like most of the other plutocrats of the period. "Scarcely one of the very rich men held any position in society by virtue of his wealth," Adams claimed, "or could have been elected to an office, or even into a good club. Setting aside the few, like Pierpont Morgan, whose social position had little to do with greater or less wealth, riches were in New York no object of envy on account of the joys they brought in their train."[13]

Yet outside New York, Pierpont Morgan's riches were becoming objects of envy. Very obviously, they brought joys in their train. Along with the big black yacht and fine houses and estates up the Hudson, there were the friendships with the famous, ranging from bishops to actresses, and a social position that was second only perhaps to the Dutch–American founding families of the state. He seemed to have the best of all possible worlds in the East and to be invulnerable there. The criticism of him was in the West and the South, in the Democratic and Populist areas that were meaningless to him. He was becoming the new emperor of the Atlantic coast, which did not see that he had no clothes on. He would be even more naked to the wind of blame after the Gold Crisis.

9

The Gold Bugs and the Government

> The man who is a bear on the future of the United States will always go broke.
>
> — J. Pierpont Morgan (1895)

> If a man needs beef, he goes to a butcher; if he needs gold, he goes to a banker; if he needs a great deal of beef, he goes to a big butcher; if he requires a great deal of gold, he must go to a big banker and pay his price for it.
>
> — Grover Cleveland (1895)

THE only time Pierpont Morgan switched his allegiance from the Republican party to the Democratic party was during the election of 1884. He voted for Glover Cleveland, partly because Cleveland's opponent, Blaine, was tainted with financial scandal, but mostly because Cleveland was known as a sound money man who shared Morgan's own qualities of directness and "ugly honesty." He was as heavy and bull-necked and imposing as Morgan, and he knew the financier through counseling the law firm of Bangs, Stetson, Tracy and McVeagh, which sometimes acted for Morgan. Charles Tracy was the father of Morgan's second wife and a political figure in the city; upon his death, Francis Lynde Stetson rose to head the firm and became the chief legal adviser of the Morgan interests.

During the two Cleveland administrations, Morgan used Stetson to influence Cleveland, who supported the repeal of the Sherman Compromise Silver Act in 1893, despite the protests of the westerners and farmers in his own party. They were finding in the depression that it took twice as many bushels of wheat to pay off their mortgages as it had taken a few years before. They thought that their President was selling out to the Gold Bugs and foreign bankers represented by the house of Morgan; if they wanted cheaper credit, they were right.

Cleveland himself was in great difficulties. The drain on the government's gold reserves was not stopped by the repeal of the Silver Act. The price of minted silver had dropped to nearly half its face value because of excessive mining, and the Treasury, forced to redeem silver certificates and greenbacks for gold, watched its reserves melt away below the legal level of $100 million. Two issues of government gold bonds in 1894 did not help matters. With one hand, the speculators bought the bonds for gold; with the other, they took the gold back by insisting on Treasury redemption of its paper.

The leading bankers of New York tried to behave responsibly and discourage a wild market like the one in the Gold Room during the Civil War — an excess which Morgan knew only too well. The industrial and western unrest and the power of the silver movement made European investors want to cash in their United States Treasury bonds. The loss of the yellow metal could not be halted. Even Morgan was deeply worried. Although his syndicate picked up the second government bond issue because the Secretary of the Treasury appealed to him, he hardly knew where to find the gold to cover it.

His quiet rival, James Stillman of the National City Bank, gave an unusual picture of Morgan at this time of financial crisis. He claimed that Morgan had refused to pick up the second government bond issue of $50 million until Stillman himself went around to see him in his office:

> He was greatly upset and overcharged, nearly wept, put his head in his hands and cried: "They expect the impossible!" So I calmed him down and told him to give me an hour and by that time I cabled for ten millions from Europe for the Standard Oil and ten more from other resources and came back. I told him:
>
> "I have twenty millions."
>
> "Where did you get them?" And when he heard — he leapt from the pit of despair to the height of happiness — and became perfectly bombastic and triumphant, as the Savior of his Country. . . . But then you see, he is a poet; Morgan is a poet.[1]

Morgan did not often show his fallibility. In Washington and elsewhere in the country, he seemed to be more solid than the Treasury and to possess more gold. Politics were going his way. In November, the Republicans demolished the Democrats, seizing control of both houses of Congress. The only bad omen for the Gold Bugs of the East was the rise in the Populist vote to almost one and a half million; the party returned four senators along with two sympathizers. These were pledged in their party platform to press for an income tax on the rich because "the fruits of the toil of millions are boldly stolen to build up colossal fortunes for a few, unprecedented in the history of mankind."

Grover Cleveland was correct when he said that the electoral debacle had much to do with the split in the party between the Gold Democrats like himself and the majority of western and southern Democrats, convincingly led by the quicksilver tongue of William Jennings Bryan. Although Cleveland was conscious of the feeling against eastern bankers in the grass roots, he had already failed to sell the second government issue of gold bonds by public subscription and had been forced to turn to the Morgan syndicate. Yet within two months, there was a greater run on gold than before. By the end of January, Cleveland had received disquieting news from Europe that American securities were being sold as fast as possible there in return for gold shipments across the Atlantic. In January alone, the Treasury was depleted by $45 million in bullion, and the rate of withdrawal would make the United States technically insolvent within weeks.

The situation was clear. Either the administration gave way to the silver lobby and left the gold standard, destroying its credit abroad, or it had to sell more gold bonds to the eastern bankers like Morgan. In the future world depression of the 1930s, many nations would leave the gold standard; but in Cleveland's time, it was hardly thinkable for America to go it alone. In a message to Congress on January 28, 1895, Cleveland showed his annoyance. In his view the most dangerous and irritating feature of the crisis was that the Treasury had to give back, in exchange for legal-tender notes, all the gold it brought in "without canceling a single Government obligation and solely for the benefit of those who find profit in shipping it abroad or whose fears induce them to hoard it at home."[2]

Measures to issue more gold bonds and retire the legal-tender notes were blocked by an unsympathetic Congress. "Outside the hotbeds of goldbuggery and Shylockism," one southern newspaper declared, "the people of this country do not care how soon gold payments are suspended."[3] So the government found itself within a shaving of insolvency as the federal gold reserves fell to $45 million, less than was needed even to meet the gold certificates redeemable during the next month.

Aware of this crisis from his Rothschild connections, August Belmont took a train to Washington to warn the Secretary of the Treasury, John G. Carlisle, of the necessity of a new bond issue, through which European sources could return to America the bullion they had just taken from it. Belmont then went back to New York to consult Morgan, already alerted by his London office. The Europeans, so often burned by their American investments, were demanding a high interest rate, so that the Morgan–Belmont combination was asking for 3¾ percent to provide $100 million in gold for the Treasury. "It was not really a question of price," Morgan said later. "It was a question of success."[4] The thing had to be done and interest rates were irrelevant.

Rumors of a new bond issue helped to staunch the outflow from the government, but they also inflamed the Populists, who feared profiteering by the Gold Bugs. Faced with this outcry and Cleveland's own dislike of going cap in hand to the financial magnates, Secretary Carlisle refused the Morgan–Belmont offer, implying that he would once again offer the American public Treasury bonds in spite of the previous failures. He was backed by the New York *World*, which fed Joseph Pulitzer's fortune and its own circulation through politic demagoguery in gutter language. If the banks would not take a 3 percent loan, the *World* declared, the people would.

Belmont and Morgan now traveled to Washington to persuade the government from its path of folly. Morgan took along Stetson to draw up papers and young Bacon for general support. The following morning, they called on the President, who showed none of his usual cigar-puffing amiability to Morgan. The meeting was inconclusive. Cleveland was unwilling to surrender to the bankers and risk a popular explosion. "Thank you for calling, Mr. Morgan," he said, "but I have decided to rely upon Congress. The Government does not desire a private loan."

Two days later, the House of Representatives voted down a bill allowing the administration to issue gold bonds. Before Morgan heard the news in New York, he cabled his London office:

> CONSIDER SITUATION CRITICAL. POLITICIANS SEEM TO HAVE ABSOLUTE CONTROL. SHALL MAKE STRONGEST FIGHT POSSIBLE FOR SOUND CURRENCY. IF FAIL AND EUROPEAN NEGOTIATIONS ABANDONED IT IS IMPOSSIBLE OVERESTIMATE WHAT WILL BE RESULT UNITED STATES.[5]

He called for Stetson and Bacon and left with them in a private car for Washington on the icy February afternoon of the House debate. His arrival was reported, and Secretary of War Lamont met him at the station, bringing a message from the President that he would not consider a private bond sale nor see Morgan at the White House. According to some accounts, Morgan declared that he would stay in Washington until the President did see him. According to other accounts, his pride was hurt, and he talked of returning to New York and letting the government go bankrupt. He was, however, eventually persuaded to spend the night at the Arlington Hotel, where he received a stream of worried visitors and then played "Miss Milliken," a kind of solitaire, alone in his room until four in the morning.

A blizzard was raging outside. During the next twenty-four hours, nineteen hundred people would file through the soup kitchen of the central Union Mission. Out on the prairies, the price of wheat was down to six cents a bushel. Poverty and unemployment stalked the land. But Morgan was thinking back to his gold speculations in the Civil War and the measure taken by Lincoln's administration, which allowed the Secretary of the Treasury to buy gold when the government required it. The law had probably not been repealed, but was lying forgotten on the statute books. If so, Cleveland would not have to go to Congress for authority to make a gold deal with Morgan.

Next morning, on February 8, Cleveland agreed to meet Morgan. The Secretary of the Treasury, Attorney General Olney and Bacon were also present. Morgan began by complaining that his previous offer with Belmont had been agreed with the Treasury, and then refused. Cleveland replied that he would still prefer to sell gold bonds by public subscription, as long as a bridging loan could be made to keep the gold reserves respectable until the receipts from the bond sale arrived. According to Cleveland, Morgan then mentioned the law of 1862 (Section 3700 of the Revised Statutes) — a proposition wholly new to the President.[6] Jay Cooke had financed the Civil War by private contracts with the government. Why not now?

Morgan then made an incredible claim to Cleveland. He declared that he and his syndicate "were absolutely able not only to find the gold we needed, but to protect us . . . against its immediate loss." In fact, Morgan was proposing to control the whole international gold market in the interest of his syndicate and the United States. It was a bold, almost reckless, assertion; but in the hours that followed, Morgan worked on convincing the President. He was, he said later, never so excited in his life. "Everything depended on my changing Mr. Cleveland's mind. When I went into the room, I had an unlighted cigar in my hand; as I arose from the chair to go, I had no cigar, but saw on the floor a little pile of snuff."[7]

Outwardly, Morgan seemed composed and certain, even if inwardly he was fuming as he waited like a messenger for an answer. The President took time to believe Morgan's claim that he could manage the gold trade.

"I had a feeling," Cleveland later said, "not of suspicion, but of watchfulness. . . . I had not gone far, however, before my doubts disappeared. I found I was in negotiation with a man of large business comprehension and of remarkable knowledge and prescience . . . of clear-sighted, far-seeing patriotism." When Cleveland later asked Morgan how he had actually *known* that the great financial interests of Europe were with him, Morgan replied with total arrogance, "I told them that this was necessary for the maintenance of the public credit and the promotion of industrial peace, and they did it."[8]

Morgan's presence had convinced the unwilling President. His clinching remark was that a check for more than $10 million was outstanding in New York, and if it were to be presented for payment to the sub-Treasury, there would not be enough gold to cover it. The President was finally certain that something had to be decided there and then. Morgan again proposed to provide $100 million in gold, this time at 4 percent; but Cleveland only wanted 3.5 million ounces, worth some $65 million, of which half should be shipped in from abroad. As a sop to their critics, Cleveland and Morgan agreed that if the bonds were all redeemable in gold rather than coin, the interest rate should drop to 3 percent. Neither of the men expected the balky Congress to agree to this, but a contract was drawn up and signed.

Morgan returned to New York to try and control the gold trade. The news of the contract immediately caused $18 million of gold to be taken off the liners, which were still in harbor and had not sailed for Europe. Morgan made it known to the bankers that he would offer more for their gold than they could get overseas. Moreover, he cabled his financial sources in Europe to send over their gold to America.

The lever was the high rate of interest. Morgan and his syndicate were successful. The Treasury reserve once again rose to over $100 million. Unfortunately for Morgan's reputation, the gold bonds offered at 104½ by the government and sold at 112½ to the subscribers rose more than seven points in the open market, netting an additional $5 million for the syndicate, although Morgan's own share seems to have been less than $300,000. Altogether, the Morgan group probably cleared more than $7 million from their patriotism at a price.

At a later Senate inquiry, Morgan absolutely refused to reveal how much he had made from the business. "What I did with my own property subsequent to that purchase," he declared, "I decline to state."[9] Even when a friend asked him about the terms of the deal, he replied, "Can't give you any particulars. If you want to make some money and have got the gold, subscribe. If not, *au revoir*."[10] He was fortunate that the offer of bonds coincided with a boom on the London stock market from speculation in South African diamonds and gold mines, which also increased the flow of the metal. The offer was oversubscribed six times in New York and more than ten times in London. "No Americans need apply" was the bitter comment of some of the disappointed.

Yet Morgan, like Clive of India before him, could stand astonished at his own moderation. At modern interest rates, he had taken little from his country's necessity. He had also risked a disastrous loss if his pledge to corner the gold market had not coincided with the London boom. He could have made as much money spending his time doing other things. His patriotism and his belief that he was indispensable had been his only motives. When he was later examined by two senators, he was explicit about that:

SENATOR PLATT: And so your real purpose, as I understand you, in this transaction was not the idea that you could take this bond issue and make money out of it, but that you could prevent a panic and distress in the country.

MR. MORGAN: I will answer that question, though I do not think it necessary, in view of all that I have done. I will say that I had no object except to save the disaster that would result in case that foreign gold was not obtained.

SENATOR VEST: If that was your sole object, why did you specify in your telegraphic communication to Mr. Carlisle that your house, or you and Mr. Belmont, were to have exclusive control of the matter?

MR. MORGAN: Because it was absolutely impossible for more than one party to negotiate — to make the same negotiation for the same lot of gold. It would only have made competition.

SENATOR VEST: If the gold was abroad I take it for granted that anybody could get hold of it who had the means to do so. If you were actuated by the desire to prevent a panic, why were you not willing that other people should do it, if they wanted to?

MR. MORGAN: They could not do it.[11]

Morgan's arrogance and exposure were increased in the eyes of the Populists when the Supreme Court struck down the income tax law. There was evidently one law for the rich and another for the poor, and no redress. The ugly side of the radical movement was revealed when William Jennings Bryan asked for the terms of the "Shylock's bond" (the gold-syndicate loan) to be read in the House of Representatives, adding that the gratitude felt by the Democrats to Cleveland was the same that a passenger felt toward the trainman who pulled a switch and caused a wreck. Cleveland had attempted to inoculate the Democrats with the Republican virus, and blood poisoning had set in. "We cannot afford to put ourselves in the hands of the Rothschilds," Bryan concluded, "who hold mortgages on most of the thrones of Europe."[12]

Bryan's attack on the foreign influences behind the gold loan were mild compared with the assaults of Pulitzer's *World*, which declared that the whole of the gold syndicate was composed of bloodsucking Jews and aliens. Morgan was hardly that. He was an American of Puritan stock without prejudice over matters of money. He associated himself with Belmont and the Rothschilds as he did with a Peabody or a Baker or a Stillman. Neither country of origin nor religion had anything to do with it. In the international circles of the rich, bigotry was bad business.

So was the threat of war. Morgan bitterly opposed Cleveland's foreign policy, which was now directed against the British Empire. Seeing the popular hatred of foreign bankers and the increasing intervention of European capital in the Americas, Cleveland decided to provoke a confrontation with Britain over the frontier dispute in Venezuela. In Henry Adams's opinion from Washington, the quarrel was bound to come sooner or later. "We are at the mercy of England as far as our finances go," one Oregon newspaper declared, "and this is our only way out."[13] For his party's sake Cleveland had to assert American independence of foreign capital — exactly what Morgan was aiming to increase. The financier was appalled. He had been trying, he said, "to build up such relations of confidence between the United States and the money markets of Europe, that capital from there could be secured in large sums for our needs, and here is a threatened disaster that will put an end to our borrowing."[14]

Yet what was a disaster for Morgan was politically successful for Cleveland. The American people could be counted upon to rally round the flag. The President had never been more popular, or Morgan and the foreign bankers more unpopular. Before Christmas, 1895, there was another run on gold. Again Morgan went to Washington to offer $200 million of gold coin to the Treasury. This time he declared the members of his syndicate, all good American names like Adams and Fisk and Stewart and Stillman, but he excluded Jewish and foreign names along with English banking sources. Populist prejudice had made him wary.

All expected Cleveland to accept Morgan's new offer. That summer, the President had even had a secret conference with Morgan on the gold question, mooring his yacht beside *Corsair II* in a secluded cove. But he had not been convinced. He could make political capital by refusing the unpopular Wall Street syndicate. He had already been looking for direct arrangements with the Bank of France and other national banks to buy gold for the Treasury in time of emergency without having to go to Wall Street. He saw the storm rise again in Congress after the new Morgan bid was known. At home as abroad, he decided to show his independence. He refused to meet Morgan at all or to negotiate with him. Henry Adams exulted in a letter to his brother on December 27, 1895:

> We were all deeply depressed, and assumed that the President would surrender. That was a week ago. . . . When the dethroned monarch, J. P. Morgan, came on a few days ago, the President did not send for him or see him. . . . We all see here that political independence implies financial independence, which means either silver or paper. . . . The quarrel with Wall Street is even more bitter at the White House [which is] exasperated with the money-lenders, and indifferent to their doings.[15]

Yet, as before, Morgan would not take no for an answer from a mere President who had been his legal adviser. The run on gold was draining the Treasury. Again something had to be done. Once more Pulitzer inveighed against Morgan with an inflammatory editorial on January 3, 1896. Pulitzer instructed his editor to make a public pledge that the *World* would buy a million dollars' worth of gold bonds at the highest market price. "It will compel a public loan," Pulitzer said, especially as a blizzard of telegrams had brought in offers of support from financiers throughout the country for $235 million. The editorial was headed: GROVER CLEVELAND'S OPPORTUNITY: SMASH THE RING. It bade the President trust the people. The most damaging thing that could happen was for the Democratic administration to be regarded as "a Government by Syndicates for Syndicates."[16]

Although the editorial gave Pulitzer national publicity, it angered Morgan and Cleveland. A cartoon was also run showing Morgan in a pirate's costume demanding a ransom of $12 million from Uncle Sam for him and his mates. (For once, Morgan's nose was not exaggerated — he had protested about this to his clubmate Pulitzer on previous occasions.) The next day, Morgan sent a personal letter to the President making the excuse that the serious financial situation forced him to write and offer 11.5 million ounces of gold coin to the Treasury through a syndicate. Morgan did, however, say that he would accept a public advertisement for the loan if the President would convince him in a personal conference that this had to be done.

Cleveland ignored Morgan's offer and used him as a scapegoat, not a savior. On January 5, he wrote to a senator that he would not deal with Morgan or any syndicate. Morgan had been relying entirely on his own judgment when he had formed his group. The *World*'s assertions and acccusations were unfounded, sensational and maliciously mendacious:

> No banker or financier, nor any other human being, has been invited to Washington for the purpose of arranging in any way or manner for the disposition of bonds to meet the present or future needs of the gold reserve. No arrangement of any kind has been made for the disposition of such bonds to any syndicate or through the agency of any syndicate. No assurance of such a disposal of bonds has been directly or indirectly given to any person. In point of fact, a decided leaning toward a popular loan and advertising for bids has been plainly exhibited on the part of the administration at all times.[17]

The very next day, the Secretary of the Treasury announced the fourth issue of gold bonds for $100 million, open to the highest bidder. Rebuffed, Morgan dissolved his syndicate, but declared his support for the public offer. There was no corner in gold, he declared to the press, and the notion that he had one was absurd.[18] In fact, he made one of the high bids for the gold bonds through his own firm, now called J. Pierpont Morgan and Company. He took up $33 million worth of the bonds, making Pulitzer look stupid, and another $5 million of the issue went to him by default. This final service to the government solved the gold crisis that had bedeviled Cleveland's administration. Another would not occur for many decades owing to the increase in the world supply of gold from the discoveries near Johannesburg and in the Klondike.

Morgan had, after all, proved his point, that it was difficult to do without him. Since the American public had not subscribed willingly, he had taken up the second issue and one third of the fourth issue, as well as the whole of the third. Henry Adams, who had gloated over the "dethroned monarch" at the end of the year, was forced to eat his words at the news of the Morgan bid on the open market. As he wrote to his brother on February 7, 1896, about the next election and the probable Republican candidate, McKinley:

> The monied-interest can't help winning and running the country. There is no other interest competent to run a hand-cart. Silver is lost. Gold will need five or ten years to fill the void, but it will come. . . . Mr. J. P. Morgan gets practically the whole loan, and the small thieves are furious. My view of the case is always to encourage the big thieves and to force the

pace. Let's get there quick! I'm for Morgan, McKinley and the Trusts. They will bring us to ruin quicker than we could do it ourselves.[19]

Certainly the Democratic candidate, William Jennings Bryan, thought that the campaign issues were Morgan, the gold bonds and the trusts. Although the Senate investigating committee failed to uncover a conspiracy between the Treasury and the Morgan syndicate, Bryan believed there was one. He shared both the paranoia and the business instincts of his backers. He won the nomination with his famous speech that conjured up the image of a crucifixion on a Cross of Gold. The man who had driven in the nails was unnamed, but was evidently Morgan. So conspiratorial was Bryan that he told one of McKinley's campaign financiers, Charles G. Dawes of the City National Bank in Chicago, that Pierpont Morgan had given the Republican campaign a check for $5,000,000 to defeat the Democrats and free silver. When Dawes replied that McKinley's whole campaign had only cost $3,560,000, Bryan would not believe him.[20] The wicked power of the money trust must have brought about his defeat.

What Bryan did not know was Morgan's true contribution to McKinley's nomination, effected through a secret conference on *Corsair II* with two of his campaign managers. When he returned from a European trip in the previous June, Morgan met the press and curtly stated his position on the election:

> The dominating question of course is the currency problem. If that is settled satisfactorily Europe will buy our securities. If it is not she won't. That is all there is to be said. By a satisfactory settlement of the currency I mean a decision that this country will maintain the single gold standard.[21]

Morgan's leadership of what the Democrats called the Aristocracy of Gold brought to him another banker, Myron T. Herrick, who was working with the Ohio iron-ore magnate Mark Hanna on behalf of McKinley. He first encountered Herrick at his Wall Street office and thundered that McKinley had a "backbone of jelly." Herrick then pointed out that a candidate was needed who would conciliate and straddle the divisive questions threatening to split the country. Unconvinced, Morgan pulled down the cover of his rolltop desk with a bang.

"There is not going to be any more business in this office," he said, "until the election is over."

He then asked to meet Hanna, and invited Herrick to bring his candidate to dinner on *Corsair II*. By Herrick's account, "Hanna that night got a good deal of education from Mr. Morgan in what the gold standard meant to our country's business. Mr. Morgan also learned a few things about how Presidents are nominated. He had never attended a national political convention."[22] Both sides got what they wanted: Morgan his gold policy; Hanna his available man. As William Allen White noted at the Republican convention, the New York bankers wrote the gold plank and forced it down Hanna's throat, even though McKinley chose to remain wisely silent on the currency issue during the campaign.

> McKinley was trustworthy, as the phrase goes in politics. He was not given to illusions of leadership. The advocates of sound money had confidence in McKinley after he became their candidate, and his former record did not worry them any more than it worried him. They apparently construed his silver utterances as the Pickwickian deliverances of a gentleman indulging in the harmless pastime of soft-soaping the electorate. McKinley grew into their respect and confidence later, but when the gold standard champions in the Republican party took him they did not think particularly well of their bargain, though it was the best they could make.[23]

If Bryan's defeat was not brought about directly by Morgan and the gold trust, they did contribute to the result. On the Saturday before Election Day, there was a parade of eighty thousand people through New York City. Their song was:

We'll hang Bill Bryan on a sour apple tree,
As we go marching on!

The whole of the Morgan banking house was decked with Republican banners six stories high, and its employees were given a holiday to join in the parade. Morgan himself was too discreet to be present, although the crowd shouted for him. He knew that after the Cross of Gold speech, he was the scapegoat of the Bryan Democrats. Cartoons pictured him as a big-bellied, swollen-nosed plutocrat, arm in arm with Andrew Carnegie, whose hands were dripping with the blood of the Homestead strikers. Morgan was anathema, and he kept his head down.

The western assault on him was hysterical and unjust. The injustice lay in the fact that Bryan did not want to destroy the free-for-all competition that had allowed Morgan to flourish, but merely to alter the system for the benefit of the small businessman. He made it clear that the American wage earner, clerk, farmer and miner were "as much businessmen as the few financial magnates who corner the money of the world." The problem was to curb the Morgans and force them to give more opportunity to their small rivals — who only wanted to become rich enough to be Morgans. Bryan never saw the futility of the dream of opportunity, that true competition eliminated competition and that there was room only for the few at the top of the golden heap.

Yet Morgan, in a way, deserved the role of the symbolic scapegoat. He had deliberately chosen to represent himself as the savior of the currency through the gold standard. He believed he was. He had persuaded the Treasury in Washington that he was, although actually the gold crisis was not to be solved by his personal intervention, but by the toil of thousands of miners in the Rand and the Klondike. Yet by proclaiming himself, he was damned by the westerners as if he were really responsible for the few at the top of the golden heap.

He had begun to affect the West directly only after 1895, when he had begun his alliance with James J. Hill of the Great Northern Railroad in order to swallow up the Northern Pacific. If Morgan had lost the Union Pacific to Harriman and Kuhn, Loeb and Company, he was striking back through Hill and the northwestern lines in order to secure his own rival group on the Pacific coast. A preliminary merger plan had been made at 13 Prince's Gate and had been called the London Agreement. In it, the three dominant parties in the Northern Pacific reorganization, Morgan and Hill and the Deutsche Bank, had agreed that the Great Northern should swallow up its competitor and control freight rates to everybody's profit.

For once, the merger was struck down by the state courts and the Supreme Court, which thus put the first tooth into the Sherman Antitrust Act. As a result, Morgan reverted to the device he had used in the West Shore affair. He arranged for the new stock of the reorganized Northern Pacific to be held by individuals like himself rather than directly by the Great Northern. Naturally, the house of Morgan and the Deutsche Bank would form a syndicate to monopolize the selling of the stock for ten years, while a voting trust dominated by Morgan would control the railroad. Nothing was said about fixing rates between the two competing northwestern routes, but that was understood. As the *Economist* commented, the stockholders were powerless; it was one more lesson in a long and dismal series of lessons about American rails.[24]

McKinley's defeat of Bryan confirmed the lessons of Morgan's railroad reorganizations. At the last resort, the majority of the American people still had enough faith in the free enterprise system, however much misused by the organizers of the trusts, to choose the opportunity of getting rich personally over cutting the magnates down to size. Competition was more important than regulation, liberty than equality. Like Henry Adams, they wanted to encourage the big thieves and force the pace. Although Morgan was widely hated and envied, he had vaunted his strength so often that he was almost thought to be as necessary as he thought himself. Even Bryan, by making him a sort of golden Satan, had confirmed his status for ill or good, depending on the point of view from either side of the street.

If the Bryan Democrats saw the plutocrats as devils, the plutocrats saw themselves as archangels, if not saviors. A Rockefeller could speak of making money as a sacred duty, because he made work for others and spent money more wisely than they did. A Carnegie would take the word "trust" to mean, not his steel business, but the fortune put in his hand to use on behalf of public education. Philanthropy began to mask plunder; selfishness was described as self-sacrifice.

For finally, even the big bankers were human. They desired public approval and were vulnerable to criticism. "It is most painful," James Stillman wrote to President Cleveland during the Gold Crisis, "to hear of leaders in finance spoken of in Congress as robbers and must be very discouraging to them in their efforts to cooperate with you in maintaining the country's financial honor."[25] Throughout the decade, the financiers kept their influence in the White House. But if ever the President were to turn on the plutocrats or the western clamor were to reach the streets of the eastern cities, even Morgan's vast confidence in his necessity and patriotism would not be immune.

10

The Grand Style

> Morgan was born a gentleman, and did everything he could to fortify that fact and impose it upon an admiring world. He had a childish aversion to "mixing" with such people as Carnegie and other less finely bred rulers of the financial robber barons and promoters of his time. Apart from that idiosyncrasy, the great man was indifferent even to the point of callousness to the opinions of the world. What he did was right; what he wanted he got.
>
> — James Henry Duveen, *Collections and Recollections* (1935)

The McKinley years at the end of the nineteenth century were the age of gold and the swansong of Morgan and the trusts. The long depression ended; prosperity seemed to fall like cakes from the rich man's table. Administrations had come and administrations had gone, but Morgan was still reorganizing railroads. He had even dared to plunge into the Erie, squeeze its watered stock moderately dry, and add it to his networks. By 1898:

> He had largely reorganized the railroad system of America. He was in complete voting control of the great network of lines radiating throughout the South Atlantic seaboard; he entirely dominated the Erie Railroad; he was the chief factor in the policy of the Reading; he controlled the vast Northern Pacific; he had a powerful voice in the administration of the Baltimore and Ohio and also an important interest in the affairs of the Atchison, Topeka and Santa Fé; he had the entire capital stock of the rejuvenated Central of Georgia locked up in his safe; he controlled the Hocking Valley, the Chesapeake and Ohio; and he was the real financial power behind the vast system of the Vanderbilt lines.[1]

Two years later, he and his allies Hill and Vanderbilt controlled some forty-nine thousand miles of track with only two major competitive systems standing out against them: Harriman's and the remnants of Gould's last empire, with some thirty-six thousand miles of track between them.

Morgan also had an indirect influence through partners and associates over another fifty thousand miles of track. Effectively, he dominated the communications of the United States in the age before the automobile. Only the Southwest was not his territory. His thrust and Coster's plans had given him a transcontinental power that had escaped the robber barons. Stealthy finance had proved mightier than stock frauds. What, indeed, was robbing an investor compared with owning a bank.

Yet Morgan's dominance provoked the beginnings of his downfall. Protest was in the wind. In Pennsylvania, for instance, the stranglehold on freight rates angered rival magnates like Frick and Carnegie, who did not want high carying costs for their steel and coke. "If you would call public meetings," Frick wrote to Carnegie, "and denounce the railroads, you would create such an outburst as has never been seen . . . peacefully if we can, forcibly if we must; but competitive rates we shall have."[2]

With industrial money available to back popular feeling against the railroad trusts, Morgan and his associates misused the language to make it appear that their combinations encouraged fair competition, their mergers were in the name of independence, and their control was a public service. These declarations were less hyprocrisy than a belief in efficiency as practiced by themselves. James Hill put it most clearly in a letter to J. P. Morgan and Company in 1898 after their mutual takeover of the Northern Pacific through the Great Northern. The sole object of Hill and his friends in bringing together the two rival railroads was "that both companies could be operated on such lines of general policy as would preserve their mutual independence and allow each one to discharge all its duties to itself and to the public in such a manner as to avoid unnecessary expenditure of money either in building new lines or in the operation of existing lines. We believed this could only be done by the holding of a large and practically a controlling interest in both companies by the same parties."[3]

Morgan took the misuse of language even further when he had to testify during a stockholders' suit against his railroad mergers. He claimed that such combinations would be a "community of interests." He did not mean that he and Hill would run the railroads in the interests of the community, but as if the companies were their own personal property.

"The community of interests," Morgan said, "is the principle that a certain number of men who own property can do what they like with it."

"But they shan't fight one another?" he was asked.

"There is no fighting about it," he answered. "If they choose to fight their own property — but people don't generally do that."

"Is not this community of interest one of working harmony?"

"Working in harmony," Morgan replied, "yes."

"Even though they own competing and parallel lines?"

"No," Morgan said. "They own them all."[4]

Morgan simply did not want to see the point. What he and his associates controlled was theirs. They should be free to do what they wished with it. Through competition they had acquired it on the market. So they used the language of independence for the few to deny the independence of the many. If Morgan was doing a public service by amalgamating many wasteful and inefficient parallel lines, he did so for profits before the public good. He had chosen to act in the absence of government; but if the government chose to intervene, he could not claim that the people had chosen him as their organizing genius. In point of fact, Morgan's concentration on railroads was to prove his greatest lack of foresight, his refusal to recognize that the infant automobile would replace them in a few decades. He did not see the future of Henry Ford as he had seen Thomas Edison's.

Yet as he rose to the zenith of his power, Morgan found the United States too small for his ambition. His father had backed Cecil Rhodes, who had once declared that he would colonize the planets if he could. Rhodes had enriched himself and the house of Morgan through the De Beers diamond syndicate, but Pierpont Morgan wanted more. He would reorganize the globe if he could.

He was not particularly patriotic in his foreign transactions. Money knows no frontiers. In spite of the Monroe Doctrine, he aided the Seligman brothers to buy the Panama Railroad, once built and owned by Americans, on behalf of the corrupt French Panama Canal Company. With the Deutsche Bank, he helped to refund the Mexican national debt, allowing the Germans to develop their penetration of the border country. And he came to the rescue of the British Empire during the Boer War, eventually funding a fifth of its war costs through American loans underwritten by his firm.

It was a great reversal of fortune. Junius Morgan had used British capital to develop the American interior; now it was time for Pierpont Morgan to come to the assistance of America's imperial rival. He was so well considered in England that his name was suggested for the post of ambassador at the Court of St. James's in 1898 by the retiring ambassador, John Hay, who wrote to Whitelaw Reid: "Quite a number of the best people want Pierpont Morgan."[5] His fame was spreading internationally as the symbol of the rise of American financial power. "No telling where he'll stop," Senator Mark Hanna said. "I wouldn't be surprised to hear he was getting up a syndicate to buy the British Empire. It isn't safe as long as he's over there."[6]

His transatlantic ties did not make him an enthusiast for McKinley's new policy of American expansion abroad in competition with the European empires. While he did not oppose the acquisition of new territories or markets, he did not want conflict with the other imperial nations. This did not apply, however, to the Spanish Empire. There, it was a question of picking up the pieces before somebody else did.

Yet when the *Maine* exploded in Havana and war was declared against Spain, Morgan was not amused. The American navy was too small to blockade the Spanish fleet. Three rear admirals were appointed to select and buy any suitable craft to support the fleet. They chose *Corsair II* for its speed and strength. If Morgan was patriotic about America's future and its finances, he did not think that his patriotism should extend as far as his personal property. He tried, as his family biographer admitted, to put off the rear admirals in every way, even offering to build another ship for the government if he was allowed to keep his yacht.[7] But *Corsair II* was needed now. Bought for $225,000, she was stripped down and converted into the gunboat *Gloucester*. Furious at this appropriation of his property even though it was a time of national emergency, Morgan hired the steam brigantine *Sagamore* to keep the pennant of the New York Yacht Club commodore flying on the Hudson while the *Gloucester* flew the Stars and Stripes off Cuba.

Incredibly, the *Gloucester* performed as well against the Spanish fleet as Henry Morgan's pirate ship had two hundred and fifty years before. "These pleasure toys of the very rich in times of peace," the New York *Journal* had to admit on December 11, 1898, "called to a service for which they were never intended by the exigencies of national emergency, responded readily, splendidly, and with admirable efficiency." In the decisive naval battle off Santiago, the *Gloucester* was stationed with her four six-pounders inshore on the east of the two American battle squadrons blockading the port. When the four main Spanish armored cruisers broke out of the harbor, they turned west and assaulted the main American fleet, ignoring Morgan's converted yacht. But they were followed out by two torpedo boats, the *Furor* and the *Plutòn*, equipped with fourteen-pounders, six-pounders and torpedoes.

As the battle moved west, only one American ship was left behind to intercept the torpedo boats, the little *Gloucester.* Its lieutenant commander, Richard Wainwright, had survived the sinking of the *Maine* and wanted revenge. He cut across the course of the two enemy boats, concentrating his fire on the *Plutòn*, blowing up its forward boilers and driving it onto a coral reef. He then chased the *Furor* in front of the American battleships, which rained shells on the Spanish craft, its steering already out of control because of the *Gloucester*'s gunfire. A shell from the *Oregon* landed in the *Furor*'s engine room and blew her to fragments. The *Gloucester* was hardly hit in the engagement and capped its day of glory by rescuing the Spanish admiral Cervera from the wreckage of his sunken flagship. It would remain in service in the United States Navy for another twenty years, ending by escorting convoys to France and chasing U-boats during World War I.

This naval action by the armed *Corsair II* was the nearest that Pierpont Morgan ever came to emulating the exploits of his pirate namesake. At a celebratory dinner after the victory, he found himself on his feet delivering a speech off the cuff, something he never did. He had been given by the Navy Department a piece of the ship's mast, which had been struck by a Spanish shell. He spoke of his pride in his yacht until his voice broke and he had to sit down abruptly in midsentence. He had betrayed his emotions in public about a patriotic gesture he had not wanted to make.

Morgan's yachts did mean a great deal to him. On losing *Corsair II*, he had immediately commissioned a third *Corsair* to be built identical to the second except that twin screws would replace the single one. He was fiercely loyal to things he loved. The furniture and the fittings had to be duplicated even down to the pattern in the carpeting, which was now out of stock. As commodore of the New York Yacht Club, he wanted a flagship for show as well as for secret business conferences.

And a good show he made of it. He sailed out on *Corsair III* at the head of ninety-four steam yachts to greet Admiral Dewey's *Olympia* on its triumphant return from the Philippines. He intended to be an even more legendary commodore than Cornelius Vanderbilt. He had won his title because of his interest in the Yacht Club, presenting Morgan Cups for the races and then serving on the committee for the America Cup, which had to be preserved from all foreign challengers. He had also served on the special committee of inquiry which had heard the Irish peer Lord Dunraven's charges against the American yacht *Defender* after its defeat of *Valkyrie III* in 1895. Dunraven's charges were frivolous and were dismissed; he was that rare Englishman, a bad loser. "No one takes him seriously," a friend said. "He even applied for admission to a maternity hospital."

Commodore Morgan and his friends never took an English challenge for the America Cup too seriously. When war with England threatened over the Venezuelan question, the New York Stock Exchange cabled its counterpart in London that it hoped the British warships were better than their yachts. Morgan himself organized the syndicate that financed the building of *Columbia*, which successfully defended the America Cup against the first of Sir Thomas Lipton's *Shamrocks*. When *Shamrock I* originally appeared with its beautiful great mainsail, Morgan and his friends were relieved. The sail was all white and did not sport in huge printed leters: USE LIPTON'S TEA.[8] In fact, *Shamrock*'s topmast broke during the races, and with *Columbia*'s victory, Morgan was seen literally dancing with joy on board in the arms of another member of the syndicate.

Morgan's yacht was an important part of his transport system. Its chief job was to ferry him and his guests from New York up the Hudson to Cragston for the weekend. It would leave on Saturday morning and arrive in time for lunch. Morgan and the guests would spend the weekend ashore and embark again on Sunday night to get a good sleep. The following dawn, *Corsair III* would steam for New York, where it would arrive at nine o'clock in the morning. Morgan would sit down to a gigantic breakfast in the English country-house style — seven or eight courses, including porridge, fruit, fried fish, eggs, bacon, tomato salad, rolls, butter and veal-tongue hash. He ate vastly, keeping his weight at 210 pounds, and took no exercise at all.

Morgan followed Henry Ford's dictum: A man who is well needs no exercise, and if he is ill, it will kill him. On one occasion, however, he climbed a rope ladder up the side of the liner *Oceanic*, hauling his bulk upward sixty feet by the strength of his arms, his usual cigar stuck in his teeth, and the passengers at the rail betting against his chances of arrival and survival. His arms were always strong, and three times he pulled up bolting horses on the brink of destruction — although his friends thought he handled his carriage so roughly that he made the horses bolt in the first place.

Morgan's yacht was also used for his business and pleasure in New York. Many evenings he and his guests would steam out to Great Neck and anchor off Execution Light. Dinner would be served below in the luxurious saloon, and then entertainments would follow, given by actresses and singers. The yacht would steam back in the morning. Nobody ever reported what happened aboard, although Broadway legends made such a cruise appear to be a merger of the Arabian Nights, Bluebeard's Castle and a Global Gold Corner.

Each year, Morgan would also use the yacht to run from the millionaires' winter resort of Jekyll Island off Georgia up to Newport for the races. Ward McAllister had made Newport fashionable, and both Mrs. Vanderbilt and Mrs. Astor had built marble mansions there, huge in size, small in taste. Morgan did not like the Newport social life too well and preferred to rule the seas, the arbiter of the offshore. But even the occasions he had to attend as commodore of the New York Yacht Club soon proved too much for him, and he retired from the post in 1899 to spend more time at his favorite recreation, business.

Three remarks made him famous in yachting lore. The first was his wise advice that, unless a man had at least two male friends prepared always to join him on his yacht at the drop of an anchor, it would be too lonely to have one. He himself could always choose his company from the young Angels in his firm, the members of his private and select Corsair Club, and Dr. James Markoe of the Manhattan General Hospital. Morgan had endowed the Lying-In Ward there and treated the athletic young doctor as a friend and as a personal physician.

Morgan's second remark on yachting was to a rich man who was worried about the cost of owning a boat. "If it is of any consequence to you," Morgan advised," keep out of it." There was also the question of keeping yachts exclusive. Morgan dealt with that in his third dictum. "You can do business with anyone," he said, "but you can only sail a boat with a gentleman."

"Oddly enough," the art dealer James Henry Duveen wrote of Morgan, "his art collections and his open intrigues with women accelerated at the same rate as the improvement in his business morals. . . . Morgan almost invariably 'saved his country,' always with the result that, whoever may have been ruined, he emerged with more power and more millions."[9]

Morgan was now beginning to use his millions and his power to try and dominate the art world as he did American business. But this time he was meeting dealers with less discretion and sharper pens than his financial rivals. More knowledgeable about their specialties, they resented his checkbook collecting and rifling of European treasures — and profited from it. "He was a big man in every respect," Duveen's memoirs continued, "had an inordinate pride of birth, and considered very few things and even fewer people good enough for him. That explains his bearlike manners, as well as his smashing of all competition by offers of hundreds of thousands of pounds in acquiring works of art."[10]

Even though Morgan used the same methods as he did in his Wall Street office, art collecting could not finally be Morganized in the same way as American railroads. There were too many treasures in the world to amass, and too many princely and ducal collections whose owners might think Morgan's pedigree and manners beneath their notice. Only with dealers could Morgan impress by his breeding and curtness. In Uncle Henry Duveen's galleries in New York, he did not swear like the other American plutocrats and spit on the carpets from the Royal Savonnerie. He neither needed a cuspidor nor wasted time. "How much?" "I'll have it" or "Too much" was all he said. "That was usually the end of any particular deal; just as it was when he treated with the greatest financiers in connection with his enormous exchange deals."[11]

After buying a few forgeries from suspect dealers, Morgan learned quickly to trust only a few and to pay over the odds for things with an authenticated pedigree. He liked testing the assurance and veracity of his contacts. On one occasion, he invited Uncle Henry to bring along his brother, who was also said to be an authority on Chinese porcelain. As a test, Morgan had set out on the chimneypiece of his house in Prince's Gate three genuine ancient Chinese beakers and two reproductions. "Now, if you're such an authority," Morgan declared, "which are which?" The Duveen brother looked carefully, raised his walking stick, and smashed the two false ones.[12] Morgan was gratified that his guest proved right in his choice.

Morgan also discovered that works of art came cheaper by the dozen. Through his agents, chiefly in the Duveen family, he began acquiring whole collections in the last years of the nineteenth century. At first he was chiefly interested in ancient Anglican religious missals, the Sarum liturgies, and prayer books from the time of Henry VIII and Charles II. He then began to acquire whole libraries: the Toovey collection of books from the Aldine Press of Venice, and the Earl of Gosford's library, which included the first tome ever printed on hunting and hawking, *The Book of St. Alban's*. He bought the Ford collection of early American documents to donate to the New York Public Library and the de Forest collection of early French literature, which he stored in his own cellar on Madison Avenue. The storeroom was so crammed with his books that he had to rent a warehouse on East Forty-second Street and transfer his treasures there.

The next logical step was to build a library for his books and manuscripts. He set out to do this in a typically convenient and grandiose way. He secretly bought the two neighboring family houses on his block on Madison Avenue, razed them, and commissioned Charles McKim to design a Renaissance marble palace in which to house his collection. McKim and his library plans became as common a fixture at breakfast as Rector Rainsford and his church plans. Morgan continued to try and serve Mammon and God together by collecting priceless religious texts, including an eighth-century illustrated gospel and a Gutenberg Bible. But he still had a taste for the romantic and the profane. He sent off an agent to Greece to negotiate with the heir of Byron's mistress Countess Teresa Guiccioli for the poet's manuscripts that had been in her possession. Bishop Lawrence gave the details:

> The persistency with which he could follow up what really interested him was remarkable. I remember his telling me how he obtained the Byron manuscripts. "I was told," he said, "in London, that the Byron manuscripts were in the possession of a lady, a relative of Byron, in Greece. Libraries in England were after them. I wanted them. I therefore, through the advice of an expert, engaged a man, gave him a letter of credit and told him to go to Greece and live until he had gotten those manuscripts. Every once in a while, during several years, a volume would come which the relative had been willing to sell, until the whole was compete.[13]

He did not only buy for himself but for favored institutions. He bought Benjamin West's *The Raising of Lazarus* for the Wadsworth Atheneum in Hartford, the Badia and Vives and Baron textile collections for the Cooper Union, and Sebastiano del Piombo's *Christopher Columbus* for the Metropolitan Museum of Art, among other lavish gifts to that place. His donations in England were more practical. Unable to see the impressive interior of the dome of St. Paul's Cathedral, he contributed five thousand pounds to a lighting system, so that electricity could illuminate what only God could see.

When Henry Adams went to the Paris Exhibition of 1900, he wrote back: "Apparently Pierpont Morgan owns the British building. At least, he is credited with most of the pictures."[14] In fact, they were mainly the British eighteenth-century portraits collected by Junius Morgan in his later years and hung at 13 Prince's Gate. One of them was missing, a Gainsborough portrait of the Duchess of Devonshire, which Junius had intended as a present for his son, but which had been stolen from Agnew's in Bond Street before delivery. When it turned up on the market again in 1901, Pierpont raced across the Atlantic in a liner and demanded that an Agnew's man visit him at Prince's Gate.

"What my father wanted," he said, "I want, and I must have the *Duchess*. . . . What is the price?"

"That is for you to say, Mr. Morgan."

"No," Morgan answered, "whatever price your firm thinks is fair, I pay."

Reported to have paid the absurd sum of $150,000, Morgan followed his usual policy and would not speak of it. "Nobody will ever know," he asserted. "If the truth came out, I might be considered a candidate for the lunatic asylum."[15]

His reputation of paying huge sums without bargaining and of acquiring whole collections made him the mark of every dealer in Europe. While he could get some peace in his homes in London, his usual apartments in the Hotel Bristol in Paris or in Rome were besieged with people carrying dubious treasures to sell. Morgan soon discovered the trick of taking a work of art on approval and having its authenticity checked by other dealers and experts before paying for it. He was never a man to be deceived twice.

The lavishness of his spending and that of other American multimillionaires like Huntington and Widener began to alarm many of the major families of Europe, who thought that the American collectors were parvenus and pirates. They chose to forget that all great collections in any country had once been acquired by plundering other countries, chiefly Italy. To them, the growing competition of Morgan and his peers on the international art market seemed intolerable. The hallowed spoils of old wars were being lost to the unhallowed spoilsmen from the New World. Although laws hardly existed to prevent the export of works of art and "national" treasures, Morgan's huge acquisitions began to raise the same sort of protest that his railroad mergers were raising in the American West.

But this time the privileged were offended, not the poor. In one of her letters to her mother, Queen Victoria, the Crown Princess of Prussia had already foretold the eventual European reaction to the transatlantic invasion. "If our *great* English families are obliged to sell their unique collections," she wrote to the Queen, "at least I think if possible the nation *ought* to *secure* them. The day will come when these things *can* no longer be had — and all is readily snapped up by the *new* collections of America."[16]

Yet for the moment, Morgan was allowed to snap up art works and railroads, scarcely challenged by laws or deterred by protests. His international image was now both of a Maecenas and a Midas, a patron and a tycoon. His art purchases increased his legend because of his secret dealing and in spite of it. The very scale of his life condemned him to publicity, although he spoke little, especially to the press. His avid pursuit after the best could not go unnoticed. The more he hid and the more he did, the more everybody wanted to know his secret and feel his golden touch. As his son-in-law Herbert Satterlee, who married his favorite daughter, Louisa, in 1900, wrote:

> As long as he was in active life, and in whatever field he entered, he bought the highest-priced corner lot; he added championship horses to his stable; built the best steam yacht, and purchased the most notable pictures, books, and objects of art for his collections, yet no one ever accused him of doing these things for self-advertisement. His natural shyness, his avoidance of interviews, and his hatred of publicity, all precluded such an idea. Nevertheless, everything he did seemed to increase public interest in him and in everything connected with him. At this time it is probable that more columns of newspapers in more different countries were filled with stories about Mr. Morgan than about any other man in public or private life. What he did seemed to catch people's imagination. He always showed perfect disregard of the element of investment or "getting his money's worth," and yet almost everything that he bought increased in value.[17]

It was the size of Morgan's wants that created his legend. His silence only increased the tall tales about him. His thirst for acquisition, after all, was beginning to make Gargantua look like Tom Thumb. His appetites seemed to feed upon themselves, until he would be ready to devour everything to quench his dissatisfaction. He did not know the meaning of enough. His next plan was to gobble up all of the American steel industry.

Morgan used his presence and his silence to overawe his partners as much as his rivals, and to make them overwork. He had found that a refusal to explain implied a great certainty, and that a refusal to speak was taken as wisdom. When the young financial reporter Lincoln Steffens visited the Drexel building in Wall Street, he found that Morgan was in sight all the time. He sat alone in a back room with glass sides and the door open. It looked as if anyone could walk in at any time. But nobody did. Even his partners did not enter unless they were summoned, "and then they looked alarmed and darted in like office-boys."

Young and brash, Steffens decided to try it. He walked into Morgan's office and stood in front of the flat, clean, clear desk. Morgan was examining a sheet of figures. "He was absorbed, he was sunk, in those figures. He was so alone with himself and his mind that when he did glance up he did not see me; his eyes were looking inward." By ignoring Steffens, Morgan persuaded the reporter that he was a mathematical genius — and Steffens slunk out. If he had spoken, there would have been an explosion. "It was generally believed on the Street that J. P. Morgan was a dangerous man to talk to, and no doubt that made it unnecessary for him to be guarded by doormen, secretaries, and stenographers. He could protect himself. I know that I came to feel, myself, what others on Wall Street felt, a vague awe of the man."[18]

So Morgan created awe and respect and overwork. Although he sat in his glass booth and proved that he concentrated more than anybody else, he did take long periods of rest away from the firm, which piled even more of a load on his partners. Even his favorite, Robert Bacon, was forced to admit to his wife that he had no time for her or the family during one of Morgan's absences. He had been left with such responsibility and was so engrossed in the maelstrom that, as he said, "My head fairly buzzes night and day with business and its worries. Like Louis XIII, I never sleep now — '*je ne dors plus, Monsieur, je rève quelquefois, voilà tout.*' "[19] The indispensable Coster, working toward what would seem Morgan's greatest triumph, the amalgamation of the United States steel industry, finally exerted himself too much and expired in 1900. Being a Morgan partner may have meant becoming a millionaire, but it was also a shorter route to the hereafter.

Morgan's power and notoriety gave him a commanding position in the age of McKinley, which seemed to Henry Adams to be a time when the government encouraged the financiers to pool interests in a Great Trust. Combination was in fashion and legal in New Jersey. Since 1896, the syndicate operations pioneered by the house of Morgan had become so profitable that many of the banking houses would engage their money in nothing else. The boom in America coincided with poor harvests in Europe, and gold flowed back across the Atlantic in return for grain. A New Jersey law written by the shrewd "Hammurabi of holding companies," James B. Dill, allowed mergers and conglomerates "not only indulgences but absolution."[20]

The result was a huge increase in the sale of new securities on Wall Street, and a time when the investment banker became the undertaker of old companies and the promoter of new ones that swallowed up the remnants of the old. As the New York *Times* declared, looking back on New Year's Day of the new century: "Money was easy; profit-making easier; the speculative disposition developed with rushes; the industrial fever was high. Promoters crowded into Wall Street and madly rolled out gigantic capitalizations. The era of consolidation was on all sides proclaimed as present and as full of blessings." Even a sharp fall in share prices was called a "prosperity panic."[21]

Morgan and his partners had cleverly arranged huge pools of American capital by cross-linking banks, trust and insurance companies. Morgan obtained direct control of the National Bank of Commerce, and part control of the First National Bank through his friend George F. Baker. He also had connections through his partners with the Chase, Hanover and Liberty banks. His insurance sources were the enormous Equitable Life, the Mutual, and the New York Life, whose vice-president, George W. Perkins, was to become a partner in the house of Morgan without giving up his insurance post or seeing a conflict of interest in holding both jobs. Backed by the savings and insurance funds, Morgan created holding companies and industrial trusts with new stock that attracted even more funds. As Mr. Justice Brandeis was to point out, he was controlling the people through the people's own money.[22]

As well as creating something near a money trust, Morgan and Coster and the other partners were trying to reorganize competing American industries. Their efforts resulted in such giant combinations as the General Electric Company. But the steel industry particularly engaged their interests, at first partially, then obsessively. After testing the climate, Morgan found himself more and more drawn into rationalizing a cut-throat situation just as bad as the railroads.

It began with a suicidal war between the wire manufacturers in the Midwest. As one of them testified: "Every man's hand was against his neighbor; we were all Ishmaelites, every one of us." Eventually, a small merger was arranged by the swashbuckling gambler John Warne Gates and the canny "Judge" Elbert Gary, who was the nearest thing to a Methodist bishop that any lawyer could look. It was called the Consolidated Steel and Wire Company, but it was not strong enough to fence in its own preserves and make profits in depression years. In 1897, Gary went to Morgan to seek help in financing a larger corporation. Morgan turned him over to Coster, who put together a scheme for a trust to be capitalized at $80 million. After many months of negotiation at the Waldorf-Astoria, where "Bet-a-Million" Gates spent more time at poker tables than at conference tables, Morgan withdrew his offer to finance. Market conditions had become bad because of the war with Spain. "The jig's up," Gates said. "There's nothing to do but go home."

Yet on the way home, Gary worked out with Gates a smaller scheme to combine the western manufacturers in the American Steel and Wire Company of Illinois. Both men were also interested in the Illinois Steel Company, which was being badly hurt by Carnegie's and Frick's harsh domination of the iron-ore and coke markets. Gary advised Illinois Steel to buy its own coke and ore supplies in Minnesota and then went to Morgan to finance the merger. Gary worked on it with Robert Bacon and came up with the Federal Steel Company, which Morgan capitalized at $200 million, although there was only one twentieth of that sum in liquid assets in all the companies involved in the merger. As usual, Morgan valued the far future in his present prices.

When the question of the presidency of the new corporation came up, Morgan showed his characteristic decisiveness and quick judgment. He demanded that Gary become president, even though he was a lawyer who knew nothing much about the steel business.

"But I must think it over," Gary protested.

"No," Morgan insisted, "we want to know right now."

"But who are the directors to be?"

"You can select the directors," Morgan said, "name the executive committee, choose your officers and fix your salary."[23]

Thus he gave Gary the dictatorial powers he always took himself. As long as Gary ran an efficient dictatorship, and as long as he kept the profits coming in, Morgan would be satisfied. He liked to deal with a single man, whose head would roll if he did not perform well. He did not believe in the modern tricks of management, which set up systems of spies in high places to inform on each other's defects to a distant owner.

So Morgan became involved in the problems of the steel industry. There was not yet a question of a national steel trust. Although Gary and Carnegie did come together for price-fixing agreements, Carnegie himself was officially against pooling forces and resources. "Surely my views about going into Trusts are pretty well known," he wrote from Scotland to his trusted deputy Charles M. Schwab at the end of 1898. "The Carnegie Steel Co. should never in my opinion enter any Trust. It will do better attending to its own business in its own way. . . . We hope our competitors will combine, for an independent concern always has the 'Trust' at its mercy."

Yet Carnegie was a slippery man, whose righteousness concealed his ruthlessness and duplicity. He let it be known that he wanted to retire to his Scots castle at Skibo, where personal bagpipers and footmen could persuade him that he really was the laird of his dreams. He also wanted to devote himself to philanthropy, so that his public giving should disguise his bad treatment of his steelworkers: his untaxed income was $15 million a year; the average wage for a worker in his anthracite mines was $500 a year; that was the God-given differential between the rich steward and the poor man. He wanted to end in a kilt of illusion and a smell of sanctimony.

Yet Carnegie would sell out, at the right price. Schwab knew that, and so did Carnegie's partner Frick. And so did the house of Morgan, and so did the Moore brothers, who had put together Diamond Match and National Biscuit, and whose combinations of tin plate, sheet steel, steel hoop and straight steel companies had given them a power second only to Carnegie's own.

Combination was the name of the game, but Carnegie's game was a waiting one. Profits had never been higher. The price of his holdings was rising. "This seems to me," he wrote again on January 23, 1899, "a time for us to keep very quiet, pursue our business steadily, close five-year contracts as you are doing, and let the tumult in iron circles go on until it boils over."[24]

Carnegie did not have to wait for long. His ambitious, ruthless and variable partner Frick was ready to oust him. Backed by the Moore brothers, he said that there was an offer for the Carnegie and Frick companies of $320 million, but that he could not disclose the names of the bidders. Carnegie was both tempted and angered by the offer. He insisted on a forfeitable deposit of $2 million, of which his personal share would come to $1,170,000. Once the option was secured, the Moores went up and down Wall Street trying to raise the balance; but they were blocked everywhere by Morgan and his friends, who despised these rival steel operators as mere Chicago adventurers. When Carnegie was told that the Moores and Frick himself were behind the bid to buy him out, he refused to extend the option date and pocketed the deposit.

He now felt that Frick had betrayed him and decided to get rid of him. The official reasons were the high price of Frick's coke and an inflated sale of Frick land to the Carnegie company. At one moment Frick became so enraged that he chased Carnegie out of his office, but he was removed from the boards of Carnegie's companies. The rest of his life was poisoned by his hatred of Carnegie, and even the commissioning of a marble hall in New York and the buying of a supreme art collection could not solace his bitterness.

The knowledge that Carnegie had actually accepted a bid for his company encouraged his rivals to underrate him. In his usual fashion, he struck back at his enemies, undercutting them and trying to ruin them. He declared that he would build hoop, rod, wire and nail mills to process his own steel and compete with the Moore brothers and the house of Morgan, which had just helped to consolidate nineteen steel-goods companies in National Tube. He even threatened to revert to the bad old days of railroad buccaneering and to build a track running parallel to the Pennsylvania monopoly, which had put up its freight rates under direction from its Morgan-dominated board. Morgan himself confided his fears to James Hill, and later to Gates and Schwab: "Carnegie would demoralize the entire railroad situation as he had demoralized the steel situation."

Morgan stood for organization, not for demoralization. Yet until the election of 1900 was finished and McKinley's second term assured, he did not feel ready to make an approach to Carnegie, a man he was learning to treat warily. The unpleasant truth was out. Those who were organizing the trusts, which Carnegie called swindles, did not have what he had. As one witness told the chairman of a later investigating committee, "These gentlemen who organized the Steel Corporation were about to make a very fine plum pudding, and they ascertained that Mr. Carnegie had all the plums."[25]

Morgan's methods of installing his hand-picked directors in ailing businesses were not always successful. His admirable rescue of the insolvent publisher Harper and Brothers was a case in point. Founded in 1812, the firm had become an American institution with its textbooks and magazines. Yet during the late nineties, it walked the brink of bankruptcy. Morgan lent the company $2.5 million, declaring, "The fall of Harper and Brothers would be a national calamity."

Unfortunately, he knew no more about the book business than about the steel business. So he decided to replace the comfortable family editors with a group of dynamic young men like the Angels in his office. He knew that the small independent publishers S. S. McClure and Frank N. Doubleday were aggressive and efficient; *McClure's Magazine* competed with the four Harper's magazines and made more money. He proposed that they should run Harper and Brothers. They accepted the challenge for a trial period with an option to buy the Harper stock in ten installments.

It was as though, one later commentator noted, a small independent steel-maker should suddenly be invited to take over the whole industry.[26]

McClure and Doubleday called on another helper, Walter Hines Page, the editor of the *Atlantic*, and moved in to Harper and Brothers. The knowledge that Morgan had personally installed them deterred even the entrenched resistance of the old editors in the building. For six months, the young men investigated the situation. They found that the publisher owed more than $5 million, that all the profits of *McClure's Magazine* were going to pay off the Morgan loans, and that the debts of Harpers were not worth the prestige of the name. They would be the bondslaves of Morgan finance for decades. So they disappeared as curiously as they had arrived, McClure to develop his magazine, Doubleday and Page to set up their own successful publishing house.

The Harper staff came to work soon afterwards to find a notice pinned to the door that the firm was in the hands of the receivers. It did survive under its own name, slowly paying off its debt to Morgan, but only because the financier found an efficient reorganizer the second time around. He was the saturnine George Harvey, who would use *Harper's Weekly* to help many of Morgan's policies and would even become Henry Frick's most partial biographer.

This remained Morgan's greatest problem, the choosing of his partners, his lieutenants, and the sentries in his outposts. He was concerned with far too much. Nearly every promoter of the McKinley period came to Morgan first of all, when it was a question of a reorganization, a syndicate or a New Jersey corporation. He was spreading himself too thin and was making decisions too quickly on people and possibilities of action. Despite the myth of his omniscience, he was often deceived, once confiding to Rainsford that he was a bad judge of people and trusted them too easily.

Yet by 1900 he was the dominant power on Wall Street and in the popular imagination. His chief competitor remained James Stillman of the National City Bank, who had Rockefeller backing and supported Morgan's railroad rival Harriman through his successful reorganization of the Union Pacific; but Stillman believed in a low profile while Morgan bestrode the Street. In the words of the chief financial commentator of the period:

> Physically and intellectually, Morgan reproduced the traditional old-time London banker. . . . Morgan's personality was one of great dignity; his presence was impressive, and everyone who came in contact with him

> recalled particularly his eyes, which seemed to penetrate the mind of his interlocutor. But, except with his intimates, he was reticent rather than communicative. Those who met him personally found him gruff and often stern in manner. . . . By pure force of personality, Morgan broke down resistance or opposition of other important financiers to any plan which he had adopted. His individual driving force in organizing and putting such a plan into operation was immense. It was even then a familiar tradition of Wall Street that, under the strain imposed upon them, his active junior partners, to whom was committed the aggressive work on details of the programme, one after another broke down physically.[27]

Stepping on the bodies of others, of partners and rivals and promoters and politicians and dealers and workers, Morgan had forced himself inexorably toward financial preeminence. Only two areas lay outside his control — mass politics and the White House. Yet when McKinley won an easy second victory over Bryan in 1900, his unorthodox Vice-President, Theodore Roosevelt, took pains to come to terms with the most powerful man in New York. "I hope you can come to my dinner to J. Pierpont Morgan," he wrote to the Secretary of War. "You see, it represents an effort on my part to become a conservative man in touch with the influential classes and I think I deserve encouragement. Hitherto I have given dinners only to professional politicians or more or less wild-eyed radicals. Now I am at work endeavoring to assume the Vice-presidential pose."[28]

Roosevelt knew why he should court Morgan, for the financier had once again helped McKinley in the election. There had been a prolonged and dangerous strike among the anthracite miners, caused by the foul conditions and low wages forced on them by the mine owners, who in turn were compelled to accept low prices for their coal by the steel and railroad magnates. Mark Hanna had been worried about Byran's exploiting the situation for the Democrats and had called in Morgan to settle the strike. Because of his power in railroads and steel, Morgan had given his orders to the mine owners and had made them accept the miners' compromise demands.

This was financial power used directly for a political purpose. That was why Roosevelt invited Morgan to dinner, and why Morgan listened carefully to a speech by Schwab at another dinner, also given that December in his honor. Possibly prompted by Carnegie's throwing out a trout fly all the way from Scotland, Schwab gave a eulogy on the need to consolidate the steel industry in the name of efficiency. Morgan was worried by Carnegie's campaign of demoralization and was reassured by the political situation. So he took Schwab to one side after diner and fired a hundred questions at him. When he had heard the answers, he left for home, satisfied. After the election, the trusts now seemed to be trusted. Greater combinations were possible under McKinley's second term. Who could imagine that an assassin's bullet would affect the great mergers to come?

11

Steel, Rails, Raids and Murder

> Morgan was a bull. "He gets it coming and going," the Street used to say, "but he always says that for the long pull the bull side is the winning side in America. The U.S.A. is a bull country."
>
> —LINCOLN STEFFENS (1931)

AFTER Schwab's golden-tongued speech at the December dinner, the negotiations for forming a huge steel corporation continued through the January snows of 1901. Robert Bacon wrote that a new light had come into Morgan's mind, which had also noted the booming profits in the steel industry. Morgan called in the steelman Gates, whom he thought a good dealer at everything but cards. Gates acted as his agent with Schwab, who was afraid of repeating Frick's error and going behind Carnegie's back. He had not forgotten Carnegie's warning to him: "You can make as many mistakes as you like, but don't make the same one twice."[1] So he arranged to meet Morgan "accidentally" in Philadelphia; but when he reached there, he received a call from New York summoning him onward. Morgan had a cold, a blizzard was raging, and Schwab was the younger of the two men.

So Schwab left for Morgan's home. There in the library in front of the medieval missals, the London-style merchant prince and his aging Adonis of an assistant, Robert Bacon, met the slick Pittsburgh administrator who was also a midwestern speculator. The meeting lasted all night, while Schwab talked in detail about the past of the Carnegie companies and their likely future. "To listen to him," one commentator wrote, "was to be converted to his views: he could talk the legs off the proverbial brass pot."[2] He confirmed that Carnegie meant to go into manufacturing steel goods and owning rival railroads and integrating all his operations, unless a group was formed consolidating his companies with the elements they lacked. He would either expand into a trust or sell to one. When the question of a total steel monopoly came up, Schwab advised that certain firms like Bethlehem Steel and Jones and Laughlin should be left out of the proposed combination. This would provide the illusion of competition to a merger of Federal Steel, Carnegie, Frick, National Tube, and the various wire companies under Gates's management. The merger would realize Gates's unlikely dream of a billion-dollar corporation.

It is hard to imagine what a billion dollars meant at the time. It represented a twenty-fifth of the whole national wealth, more than the combined dividends from the railroads for eight years, and more than the value of all the wheat and barley and cheese and gold and silver and coal produced in 1900 in America. It would have built twenty Krupp steel plants, the largest in Europe and the pride of Germany.[3] No merger on this gigantic scale had yet been attempted. The question was not would it work, but would Carnegie sell out. Schwab was doubtful because he knew the changeable moods of the old Scotsman of sixty-six. "Well," Morgan said in the dawn light, closing the conference, "if Andy wants to sell, I'll buy. Go and find his price."

If Morgan was best at doing business at midnight on his yacht and in his library, Carnegie was most at home on a golf course. At the St. Andrew's Club north of Yonkers, Schwab told him of the Morgan interest. At first, Carnegie blew cold. He was reluctant to sell. He had decided to fight any steel trust. He did not want a repetition of the humiliating Frick and Moore offer. Yet he did respect the house of Morgan. Junius had given him his first great help in the matter of the Allegheny Valley Railroad bonds, and Pierpont was the only financier of sufficient stature to arrange a sale of that size. After a night's thought, Carnegie penciled his terms on a piece of paper. They were the same as for Frick and the Moores plus $100 million for the two previous successful years of trading. "All that I asked Morgan," Carnegie testified later, as if astounded by his own modesty, "was $420 million; and it was taken at that; and I owned just about half, and I got $213 million."[4]

Faced with the penciled figures on the single sheet, Morgan looked at them and said to Schwab, "I accept." There was no meeting between the principals at the time, although some weeks later Morgan invited Carnegie to come down to his Wall Street office and see him. As Carnegie was two years senior and the seller, he invited Morgan to come up to Fifty-first Street and see him. For once, Morgan accepted. He drove uptown, and settled the whole thing with Carnegie in precisely fifteen minutes. He conceded that the Scotsman would receive his money in first-mortgage,

5 percent gold bonds. When he left, he shook the other man's hand. "Mr. Carnegie," he said "I want to congratulate you on becoming the richest man in the world."

In terms of convertible assets, it was an astounding amount. For Carnegie had already creamed off his companies a personal fortune of another $100 million. Even Lord Rothschild was driven to comment that Carnegie in one generation had amassed more than all of the Rothschilds in a century of accumulation. Yet such was Morgan's confidence in his ability to sell the stock of his new corporation that he would have offered even more. Shortly afterwards, Morgan found himself on a transatlantic liner with James Stillman and Carnegie. At first, he and Stillman played cat and mouse with the little Scot, who seemed to have something on his mind. Eventually, Carnegie cornered Morgan alone and said:

"Do you know, Mr. Morgan, I have been thinking it over, and I find I made a mistake. I should have asked you another hundred million for those Carnegie properties."

"If you had, I should have paid it," responded Morgan with frank, unfeeling truthfulness. In its report on the conversation, the *Wall Street Journal* asserted that Carnegie "was so soured in his soul that he could take no more toast and marmalade."[5]

Stillman, who was always quietly malicious, said that Morgan spoke more bluntly, telling Carnegie, "I'd have given it, if only to be rid of you."[6] For Morgan had to have the Carnegie holdings to make an integrated structure for his United States Steel Corporation, and he could always issue more stock to pay a surplus to Carnegie. The next problem was not to pay too much to the owners of the other elements in the proposed trust, the group led by the piratical Gates. Although Gates had first brought Schwab to Morgan, he was expendable because of his reputation as a gambler who would risk a thousand dollars a time on racing raindrops down a windowpane.

The negotiations for buying Gates out of the American Steel and Wire Company were protracted. Morgan bullied and threatened, then left the room and stayed away while Elbert Gary cajoled. Yet Gates still stood out for a ridiculous price. Morgan fumed in another room, breaking down Gates's resistance by the threat of his absence and his refusal to negotiate. Then he made a studied and furious reappearance, "big and fierce, his eyes like coals of fire," in Gary's words.

> "Gentlemen," he said, pounding the desk, "I am going to leave this build-in ten minutes. If by that time you have not accepted our offer, the matter

will be closed. We will build our own wire plant." And he turned and left the room.

John W. Gates scratched the top of his head and . . . said, "I don't know whether the old man means that or not."

"You can depend upon it he does," I said.

"Then," said Gates, "I guess we will have to give up."

I sent for Mr. Morgan. "The gentlemen have accepted your proposition," I told him when he came in.

"Is that right?" Mr. Morgan snapped.

"Yes," they all said.

Never have I seen Mr. Morgan more elated. "Now," he said, "let's go home." We went up on the Elevated to Fiftieth Street, where his old electric car met him. He was like a boy going home from a football game.[7]

That was only one spectacular episode in what proved to be interminable negotiations during the first three months of 1901. Gary and Bacon and Francis Stetson on one side, and the attorneys of all the various steel interests on the other, argued and redefined terms day by day. Once Morgan exploded with a celebrated phrase, "Oh you lawyers!" He preferred Carnegie's single piece of penciled paper as the whole basis of the deal, but as other contracts were signed with the other parties, even he had to send Stetson down to ask Carnegie to sign a more formal letter.

Another problem arose. Because of the laws, the trust could not seem to be a trust. The language used during the railroad mergers had to be resurrected to allay public fears about a mighty conspiracy. Gary announced to the press that J. P. Morgan and Company was considering the acquisition of large iron and steel companies in order to "*secure perfect and permanent harmony* in the larger lines of this industry." It was not intended, however, "to obtain control of any line of business or to create any monopoly or trust, or in any way *antagonize* any principle or *policy of the law*."[8]

Technically, this might have been true. There were other steel companies and other minor competitors of the corporation, perhaps comprising one third of the American steel industry. And one element was still lacking: guaranteed supplies of iron ore. Although Carnegie's holdings near Lake Superior were immensely valuable, their full extent was not yet known. The Rockefellers also held large ore deposits at Mesabi. If these could be secured, the United States Steel Corporation's future would be assured. The trouble was that Morgan personally did not like the Rockefellers, whom he considered unscrupulous upstarts. He said as much to Gary, who told him not to let a prejudice interfere with the success of his great undertaking.

Morgan again took his hat in his hand and called the next day on the old John D. Rockefeller. Because he had been ignored by Morgan for so long and had backed Harriman in the railroad wars, Rockefeller would not talk business at all, but indicated that his son would do that later. After a few days, the young John D. Rockefeller came down to Morgan's office. This time he was rebuffed while Morgan talked to one of his partners for some time. Then the young man was given the usual blunt treatment.

"Well, what's your price?" Morgan asked at once.

"Mr. Morgan," the young Rockefeller replied, "I think there must be some mistake. I did not come here to sell. I understood you wished to buy."[9]

The confrontation between the old financier and the young one was total. Rockefeller picked up his hat and left. His father thought he had done what he had to do, but was not surprised to receive an emissary. Frick, now promised a place on the board of Morgan's new corporation, arrived to continue the negotiations. Rockefeller told him that he did not like Morgan's tactics, but that he would not stand in the way of a worthy enterprise. How could the founder of Standard Oil block the founder of United States Steel?

This was the preliminary for settling on a price $5 million higher than the outside price suggested by Morgan and Gary. Morgan was forced to accept the inflated figure in order to complete his integrated corporation. It was a punishment from a rival who was already richer than he was and who used to say of him that he was never able to see "why any man should have such a high and mighty feeling about himself."[10]

With the terms agreed, the last problem was to incorporate the company under the easy laws of New Jersey and to float the stock of the new United States Steel Corporation. There were many millions to be made for everybody concerned with the transaction. First, a syndicate was formed to provide $200 million of working capital. Those invited to participate in the syndicate were Morgan's favored friends in finance and politics, bound to him by his largesse. He knew they would not refuse him. On one of the rare occasions when a client had turned him down, Morgan had replied, "You can stay out, but do not think you will share with us again."

This time, no member of Morgan's syndicate dared to stay out. One of them, a former mayor of New York City, received a letter stating that he had been allocated $100,000 worth of United States Steel Corporation stock. He was not consulted, he was told. He knew that if he did not take up the offer Morgan would write him off forever. Fortunately, he only had to put up $8,000 in cash for immediate capital. He accepted the "invitation" out of faith that Morgan would always look after his own. He was not called upon for more money. After some months he was paid his profits for joining the first underwriting syndicate: 100 percent in cash and 200 percent in dividends. "I never made money as easy as that," he said.[11]

Morgan capitalized the Steel Corporation at $1.4 billion, of which nearly half was watered stock discounting the future. The underwriting syndicates made a profit of $57.5 million, of which $11.5 million went to the house of Morgan. In order to make that profit, the syndicates had fully guaranteed the sale of all the stock and bonds during the spring of 1901. The name of Morgan had ensured the success of the sale. Yet one month later, after the panic of Blue Thursday in May, the stock might have been unsalable and an irreparable disaster might have overtaken Morgan and his associates.

But for the time being, Morgan's reputation as a financial wizard had never been higher. The steel stock, offered at 38, rapidly rose to 55. A flood tide of speculation flowed into the stock exchange. Of course, hired brokers were manipulating the price to create an illusion of success, and the house of Morgan was beginning to use the sharp practices it had denounced during previous deluges of watered stock and public greed. Half a million shares changed hands in the first two days of the stock's appearance; one million during the next week.

This speculation was deliberately provoked by Morgan. His "high and mighty feeling" about himself had become an article of faith to the many. His belief that the bull side was the winning side in America enabled him to sell optimism to the investing public rather than real assets. The flaws in his logic were that the boom would only last as long as confidence in him lasted, and as long as the market did not get out of control. For as sure as night followed day, a panic followed a stock market bubble.

In the opinion of the leading financial commentator of the time, Alexander Dana Noyes:

> The outburst of speculation during April, 1901, was something rarely paralleled in the history of speculative manias. Not only did the younger men who had sold out to the Steel Corporation, now made into many times millionaires almost overnight and bewildered by their extraordinary for-

tune, toss into stock market ventures the money which they saw no other way of using, but old and experienced capitalists lost their heads, asserted publicly that the old traditions of finance no longer held and that a new order of things must now be reckoned with, and joined the dance. The "outside public," meantime, seemed to lose all restraint. A stream of excited customers, of every description, brought their money down to Wall Street, and spent their days in offices near the Stock Exchange. . . . The daily record rose to a million shares, to two million, and finally, on April 30th, to three million and a quarter. . . . The mere posting of this enormous business compelled commission houses to keep their office forces working into the small hours of the night. Execution of the orders on the floor of the Stock Exchange, under the prevalent conditions of excitement, manifestly threatened physical break-down of the brokers. . . . The newspapers were full of stories of hotel waiters, clerks in business offices, even door-keepers and dressmakers, who had won considerable fortunes in their speculations. The effect on the public mind must be imagined.[12]

Not all were convinced. Those who knew the real value of the Carnegie company within the U.S. Steel Corporation were selling out. Both Frick and Phipps, the other major partner, liquidated their holdings in secret and became even richer. Carnegie himself held onto his mortgage gold bonds, jesting in earnest that he would soon repossess his company by foreclosure when it went bankrupt. Everything depended on the public faith in Morgan remaining unshaken. Exuding confidence, he sailed for Europe in April. Unfortunately, he was preparing to return to his old battlefield, the railroads, where he had sometimes suffered a defeat. "We had better go to work and secure . . . a road to Chicago," he had told his associate James Hill, "and if you will share with us, we will do it together."[13]

Finally convinced by Hill that the best road for their purposes would be the Chicago, Burlington & Quincy, Morgan committed his people to buy up its stock. If secured, it would compete with Harriman's empire and complete the Morgan–Hill lines. As one authority said, the Burlington was like the point and moldboard of a plow to the rich Midwest, while the Great Northern and Northern Pacific were the beam and handles to the ocean.[14] Furthermore, the combined lines would join at Chicago with the New York Central, which Morgan dominated, and complete a transcontinental link. Nothing could be more desirable than the acquisition of this last eight thousand miles of track.

With his usual arrogance, Morgan refused to deal with Harriman and ordered the stock to be acquired from the Burlington owners in secret.

He forgot the sensible compromises he had forced on rival operators in the early days of his railroad associations. He would have all, and he provoked his crisis. As he sailed away, the music halls were singing that every place on earth and in hell was already taken over by one man:

It's Morgan's, it's Morgan's,
The great financial gorgon!
Get off that spot,
We're keeping it hot,
That seat is reserved for Morgan!

His trouble was that he now believed in his demonology. He thought he could outface anyone and do anything.

Before sailing to Europe, Morgan had tried to replace the irreplaceable Coster, who had died in harness the year before. His leading partner now, Charles Steele, was reliable but conservative. Robert Bacon was the best of lieutenants at conducting the steel-trust negotiations, but he lacked initiative and flair. Morgan had heard of an astute young man with a nose for business, George W. Perkins. Perkins had brought off coups for his company, New York Life Insurance, in Germany and Russia, even securing a government loan to float from the Czar's chief minister. If insurance companies were beginning to compete directly for foreign loans, the house of Morgan might have to look to its international position. Morgan wanted Perkins out of the New York Life office and in his own.

James Stillman moved first and made Perkins a director of the National City Bank. Morgan then asked Perkins to call on him without giving a reason. Perkins used the opportunity to plead for money for the preservation of the Palisades on the Hudson River. Morgan offered him all he wanted if Perkins would do something for Morgan.

"Do something for you," Perkins said. "What?"

"Take that desk over there," Morgan said, pointing to an empty one in his office.

"I have a pretty good desk up at the New York Life," Perkins said, choosing to misunderstand.

"No," Morgan said. "I mean come into the firm." He would not wait for an answer. "Let me know tomorrow if you can."[15]

At first, Perkins refused and arranged for a raise in his salary at New York Life. But within two months he was invited to breakfast and inveigled by Morgan into a partnership in order to complete and manage the new steel trust. Perkins would now be dealing only with "the larger things instead of the detailed things," no longer a glorified bookkeeper, but a reorganizer and grand schemer second only to his chief.

Perkins, however, would not leave his post at New York Life. Morgan saw the advantage of having a man in his firm with access to the huge pool of insurance funds available to Perkins. He could leave behind him in New York a man of proved resourcefulness and financial resources. That would be his stroke of good fortune in the time of trial to come.

When Harriman discovered that the Morgan and Hill railroad interests were buying up the Burlington on behalf of their Great Northern and Northern Pacific lines, he came immediately from California to New York for a conference. Morgan was then at the Grand Hotel in Aix-les-Bains, where he was diverting himself with a tall and dark French countess. But Hill met Harriman in the library of his chief banker, Morgan's friend George F. Baker, the man who attributed his success to keeping absolutely silent. Harriman brought along his banker, Jacob H. Schiff of Kuhn, Loeb and Company, who was annoyed that Hill had deceived him about buying up the Burlington stock, particularly as he had failed to buy up enough of the stock himself for Harriman and had sold what he had unknowingly to Morgan. Both Harriman and Schiff strongly urged Hill to give their rival Union Pacific line a share in the Burlington. They would rather split than fight. But Hill knew of Morgan's antipathy to "that little man" Harriman. He refused to deal.

"Very well," Harriman said, "this is a hostile act and you must take the consequences."

Harriman was distrusted in many circles, but he was probably the only financier as determined as Morgan in getting what he wanted. "He was a human dynamo and had wonderful confidence in himself," his associate Robert Scott Lovett said of him. "When he started upon a course nobody could swerve him from it. He would go right through despite all opposition and carry the situation alone. He would not understand public sentiment or why he had public opposition in many cases."[16] James Stillman estimated his qualities even higher than Morgan's. "I have been acquainted with all of the prominent men of this country," he once said, "and I can truly say that Harriman, in his conception of vast achievements, and his skill, energy and daring in bringing them to realization, far surpassed any other man I have ever known. His brain was a thing to marvel at; and yet if you could take it apart as you would a clock, you would find its mechanism extremely simple."[17]

Harriman was stronger now than on the occasion when he had

previously defeated Morgan. He had built up the bankrupt Union Pacific into profitability and power, and he had added Huntington's Southern Pacific to his holdings. Consequently he dominated the Southwest and confined the Morgan–Hill group to the Northwest. The secret of Harriman's success lay in his funding by Rockefeller and Standard Oil through Schiff and Stillman. If the Burlington road, however, were to fall into the hands of his rivals, he would lose the best feeder line into the Midwest. He would also face direct competition on the Union Pacific's tracks from Cheyenne to Kansas City. The Burlington might well complete the Morgan–Hill transcontinental empire at Chicago, but it threatened the Harriman one.

So Harriman decided to raid the enemy camp at its one weak point. If the Northern Pacific had acquired the Burlington, then he would acquire the Northern Pacific. He had noticed that the Morgan group had neglected to buy up a majority of the stock. Although their holding was large, it was not invulnerable. Harriman determined to beat the enemy at their own game and gain control of the Northern Pacific by buying its shares secretly. He would need at least $80 million to do so, but with Standard Oil and the Union Pacific behind him, he thought he could manage that.

He instructed Schiff to begin buying up all the Northern Pacific stock on the market, both preferred and common. By April 15, 250,000 shares had been bought for the Union Pacific. The share prices moved up by one third for the common stock, but the brokers thought that the rise was because of the Burlington purchase, not because of a raid. Taking advantage of the situation, Hill's friends sold off their shareholdings, and as late as May 2, 23,000 shares were sold by direction of J. P. Morgan and Company and the Northern Pacific board itself.

In charge in New York, Robert Bacon was concentrating on the new steel corporation and was glad to raise cash by selling off shares in companies which he felt were safely in hand. Morgan was overseas, and only Hill in Seattle now smelled a ruse. He discovered that his and Morgan's holdings of Northern Pacific had fallen by a third — to danger levels if they still wanted to keep control. Somebody was raiding, and Schiff would know who it was.

Hill ordered a special train across his own tracks. "The road is yours to St. Paul," the superintendent of the western division told him. "Everything else on the line will be held up to let you pass."[18] The special broke all records to the Mississippi River, and then Hill hurried on to New York. He reached Schiff's office to meet the banker on May 3,

Friday afternoon. Revenge was sweet for Schiff. It was tit for tat, trick for track. Hill was told that Schiff and Harriman already had secured the greater part of the Northern Pacific and so controlled the Burlington, from which they had been excluded. According to Hill, he was told he could stay on as chief executive of the Northern Pacific if he deserted Morgan. He would not accept, but went to confer with Bacon and Baker and Perkins. A cable was sent to Morgan, asking his authority to buy up all available stock to protect their position.

Morgan may have been on holiday, but he did not hesitate. He never had much doubt that his authority was sanctified. When he testified later about his reasons for acting as he did, he said that he had to protect his "moral control" over the railroads. "I feel bound in all honor," he said, "when I reorganize a property and am morally responsible for its management to protect it, and I generally do protect it; so I made up my mind that it would be desirable to buy 150,000 shares of stock, which we proceeded to do."[19]

It was an extreme understatement. The Morgan forces got their stock by luck and their rivals' miscalculation. Although he held a majority of all the shares, Harriman noticed that he did not have a majority of the common shares. On Saturday morning, May 4, he instructed Kuhn, Loeb and Company to buy a further forty thousand common shares and make his position impregnable. Schiff was, however, a devout man and at the synagogue. And when back in the office on Monday morning, he consulted with Stillman and decided to ignore Harriman's buying order. The stock seemed too expensive at 110, and a fortune had already been spent in getting what would be effective control of Northern Pacific in the opinion of most lawyers.

Harriman himself was sickening with appendicitis that Monday and could not intervene. Meanwhile, the Morgan brokers were swarming over the exchange, buying up the 150,000 shares they wanted and driving up the price of the Northern Pacific shares to 149¾. By the end of Tuesday's trading, they had acquired a bare majority of the common stock — and the possibility of retiring Harriman's dominant preferred shares by the vote of the common stockholders.

It seemed to be a stalemate. In fact, it was a debacle. This private war turned into a public catastrophe. By Wednesday it became clear that the shares bought by the Morgan brokers could not be delivered. So intense was the demand that there were not enough shares to meet it. It was worse than a corner. The cupboard was bare.

The result was Blue Thursday, the panic of May 9, 1901. The sellers of Northern Pacific tried frantically to cover their position. The price of the unavailable stock rose to 155 and eventually touched 1,000. To raise the money, most other stocks had to be dumped. Ironically enough, the value of Morgan's pet shares, United States Steel, halved to 24 because of the forced selling. Even so, his firm still stood to profit from the panic, joining a pool which made call money available at up to 60 percent. By noon that day, half of the commission houses were technically insolvent.

Faced with the ruin of Wall Street by their confrontation, the Harriman and the Morgan interests were forced into an understanding. Although Robert Bacon scented victory over the raiders who had caught him napping, Perkins advocated a compromise by which the enemies agreed not to call for immediate delivery of the Northern Pacific shares. When those who had sold short could obtain the stock, they should be allowed to settle for only 150, the price at the beginning of Blue Thursday. This wise decision ended the unnecessary panic, but it did not alleviate the anger and ruin of thousands of plungers. The speculative bubble Morgan had blown with his steel issues and Burlington raid was now punctured on the horns of the Northern Pacific.

Morgan's reputation was also punctured. Above all, he had been thought responsible, a powerful man who cared for his investors. Now he seemed to have promoted a panic for his own benefit, as bad as the open piracy before Black Friday in the days of Gould and Fisk. Both Harrison and Hill issued lame disclaimers. Harriman conveniently forgot his buying order to Schiff on the Saturday before the panic and declared, "Our holdings were all acquired prior to the supposed contest. . . . We had no hand in it." Hill was even more specious, washing his hands of all responsibility by equating Wall Street mania with Indian religious fervor. "All I can do is to liken it to a ghost dance," he said. "The Indians begin their dance and don't know why they are doing it. They whirl about until they are almost crazy. It is so when these Wall Street people get the speculative fever. Perhaps they imagine they have a motive in that they see two sets of powerful interests which may be said to be clashing. Then these outsiders, without rhyme or reason, rush in on one side or the other."[20]

On hearing the news, Morgan had gone to his firm's offices in Paris. For the Wall Street panic had sent a nervous tremor around the stock markets of the world, especially as the name of Morgan was the chief guarantee of the soundness of American bonds. Swarms of reporters fueled the great man's rage. He swore at the idiots and rascals who had upset his concept of community of interest, and he threatened to murder one member of the press. And when a reporter asked him whether some explanation from him was not due the public, he spoke a sentence that was a delight to his detractors: "I owe the public nothing."

The public, however, thought that it owed Morgan too much. Across the nation there were outbursts against his arrogance and irresponsibility. Within a month of his election to semidivinity as the founder of the new order of things with the United States Steel Corporation, he was reduced to the size of a vulnerable bully. And politicians in Washington took notice of the popular anger.

Here George Perkins came to the rescue. He was a gifted conciliator and excellent at public relations. With the blame for the fiasco landing on Bacon's broad shoulders, Perkins was the chief go-between at the series of meetings between the Harriman and Morgan interests, which bore fruit in the Metropolitan Club at the end of May. From that meeting, a statement was authorized and issued:

> It is officially announced that an understanding has been reached between the Northern Pacific and the Union Pacific interests under which the composition of the Northern Pacific Board will be left in the hands of J. P. Morgan. Certain names have already been suggested, not now to be made public, which will especially be recognized as representative of common interests. It is asserted that complete and perfect harmony will result under the plan adopted between all interests involved.[21]

If it was an official victory for Morgan and seemed to leave him with the power, it was also a hollow one. Harriman was put on the Northern Pacific board with two other directors friendly to the Union Pacific. Only Hill among the other directors was their opponent. Although Morgan still disliked "that little man," he had to admit him inside the pale. As a consequence, Hill thought up the scheme of a large holding company, to be called the Northern Securities Company. It would hold the stock of all his and Morgan's northwestern railroads "so that it could not be raided again as it had been." It would be capitalized at $400 million and be too strong to fall into the hands of the Harriman interests, which Hill believed "were anxious to destroy or restrict the growth of this country."[22]

Hill's fears influenced Morgan to set up the new combination. George Perkins and Francis Stetson were made to work on the formation of the new holding company in New Jersey. The idea might be financially wise, but it was politically stupid. The people of the Northwest were up in arms against this new octopus that might threaten to strangle their economy, especially after the scandal of May. Only as long as McKinley chose to ignore the trusts was Morgan safe. And McKinley was mortal like any other man.

Seen as a struggle between financial titans, the wars between Morgan and Hill and Harriman have a grubby grandeur. But their coming together was less the act of responsible men than an agreement to exploit the American people by restriction of competition. They could only be praised, as Hill's biographer praised them,

> because they were not actuated by a blind, vindictive desire just to crush and kill. They were big enough to see that the interests in their charge ought not to be made coppers in a game of pitch and toss. They had already accepted, not merely as a theory but as a conviction, the necessity of community of interest to a certain extent.[23]

The assassin Czolgosz, who shot President McKinley on September 6, also wounded Morgan's self-confidence. Many members of the press reported the effects of the bullets on him. One stopped Morgan as he left his office and told him the bad news. "What!" Morgan was said to have exclaimed and to have held onto the journalist's arm to steady himself. Then he hurried back into his office, where he was heard muttering, "Sad . . . sad . . ." William Allen White recorded a mythological story: Morgan heard of the tragedy and "whirled about once, like a man who is shot but feels no pain. An instant later the shock of the news got into his leather-covered consciousness; his face flared red, and he staggered back to his desk, where he sat ashen-gray, his head nodding and his jaw a-tremble."[24] Still another version had Morgan coming out of his office with a box of cigars under his arm, hearing the information, and then returning to his chair to trace out the pattern on the carpet for many hours with the point of his walking stick, forgetting for once that he was not smoking and saying nothing at all.

Such were the legends that Morgan's name now attracted, and there may be truth in all or none of them. What was certain was that, by morning, Morgan had rallied and was bullish about the President's chances of recovery. He could cope with the financial situation of the country. "There is nothing to derange it," he told the press. "The banks will take care of that."[25] When McKinley did die a week later, Morgan had to admit to reporters that it was the saddest news he ever heard. "I can't talk about it," he added, put on his hat, drove down to the dock and *Corsair III*, and steamed away up the Hudson to see his granddaughter by his favorite daughter, Louisa.

He had personal and political reasons for worry. He was being threatened with assassination himself. Carnegie's bequest to the United States Steel Corporation had been not only his equity, but the bitter labor relations after the Homestead strike as well. In the summer of 1901, the emerging Amalgamated Association of Iron, Steel and Tin Workers tried to take on the new trust and demand the recognition of union labor in all its works. Instead of Carnegie and Frick's strong-arm methods, Morgan and Elbert Gary broke the strike and the union by the old-fashioned use of scab labor and slow starvation. Finally, the union was forced to accept the principle of an open shop; as it declared, it had been "left almost entirely to its own resources to battle with the greatest combination of capital the world has ever known, while the trust with its immense money power to begin with was aided by every agency the public could furnish it with"; so it would have been suicidal to keep up such a contest.[26]

During the strike and after the assassination of McKinley, Morgan had to have police protection. A secret anarchist organization was suspected, dedicated to killing important figures. Several well-known Socialist "agitators" were questioned and brutalized by the police. Morgan appeared to be unconcerned, but was actually wary enough to live on his yacht for safety and not spend any nights in New York at all.

He was even more uneasy about the new President of the United States, Theodore Roosevelt, whom Mark Hanna had called a wild man and a damned cowboy, and others now called His Accidency. As governor of New York, Roosevelt had been, in Boss Platt's words, "a little loose on the relations of capital and labor, of trusts and combinations," and he had instituted a state franchise tax for corporations.[27] Morgan had not only organized huge steel and railroad trusts, but was now working on an international shipping trust. He sent along Roosevelt's old classmate Robert Bacon and the diplomatic Perkins to the White House to advise the new President about the necessity for the new trusts. Roosevelt personally admired Bacon and was about to recruit him into his Cabinet, and he learned later to depend upon Perkins; but at the meeting, he found that the two Morgan partners were arguing like attorneys for a bad case. At the bottom of their hearts, each of them seemed to know that. But as they represented "so strong and dominant a character as Pierpont Morgan," they would not admit the facts, even to the President of the United States.[28]

When Vice-President, Roosevelt himself had tried to come to terms with Morgan, and he now prepared to tread warily in the White House.

His first message to Congress fudged the problem of the trusts. Corporations ought to be controlled, but big business must not be upset. Labor unions should be protected, but they should not abuse their power. Mr. Dooley found Roosevelt's message far too balanced:

> "Th' trusts," says he, "are heejoous monsthers built up be th' inlightened intherprise iv th' men that have done so much to advance progress in our beloved counthry," he says. "On wan hand I wud stamp thim undher fut; on th' other hand not so fast."[29]

The White House had long been a school for straddle. Morgan was reassured. Holding office would tame the wild man as it had tamed every President in his lifetime except Abraham Lincoln. Quietly confident, he saw the *Columbia* beat off the challenge of *Shamrock II* in two straight races, then he set off on a special train for San Francisco with a large party of clerical and lay guests to attend the Triennial Convention of the Episcopal Church. The same railroad privilege was granted to Morgan for his religious duty as was granted to Hill on his dash to save the Northern Pacific. All trains, even the Transcontinental, were shunted aside to allow the Morgan special to make a record run across the American continent from coast to coast. Morgan liked to make personal use of what he owned. Manipulating money became real that way.

Before Morgan reached Oakland, Charles Crocker of the California banking family met him like a flunky and leased him his house. Because of local Socialist agitation, Crocker insisted that Morgan be surrounded by private bodyguards, even among the bishops. Morgan was not popular in the West. Surviving the conference speeches and the local agitators like Jack London, Morgan asked Bishop William Lawrence and his wife to join his party on his special train for a trip up to Oregon on an inspection of the Great Northern and Northern Pacific lines. It was apple time in Oregon, and an Indian summer promised prosperity and peace. Nature and the government seemed in harmony with Morgan's views.

On his return, he directed that the Northern Securities Corporation be formed; it was registered on November 13, 1901, in New Jersey with a board that included himself and Hill, Bacon and Baker. Morgan also made progress in acquiring two large British steamship lines that crossed the Atlantic. Already the king of the rails and the steel industry, he wanted to rule the waves. If the American government would not act, he would.

12

An Uncrowned Monarch

> Pierpont Morgan calls in wan iv his office boys, th' prisidint iv a naytional bank, an' says he, "James," he says, "take some change out iv th' damper an' r-run out an' buy Europe f'r me," he says. "I intind to re-organize it an' put it on a paying basis," he says. "Call up the Czar an' th' Pope an' th' Sultan an' th' Impror Willum, an' tell thim we won't need their sarvices afther nex' week."
>
> — FINLEY PETER DUNNE, *Mr. Dooley* (1901)

"GREAT is Mr. Morgan's power," the *Independent* magazine exclaimed in 1902, "greater in some respects even than that of Presidents and Kings."[1] The new President of the United States would not allow that. Theodore Roosevelt wanted to show Morgan that the White House was not the poor relation of Wall Street. In his first message to Congress, he had expressed his disapproval of men who sought gain, not by genuine work, but by gambling. He had noted the unnecessary panic caused by Harriman's raid on the Northern Pacific, and also Morgan's arrogant action in forming a new trust to protect his railroad empire from future raids.

Morgan was behaving as if he were above the law and superior to the White House. For forty years, capital had dominated government and the people. The rich had become too rich at the expense of the rest. The President would now listen to popular protest. Moreover, the New York aristocrat in Roosevelt was offended by the presumption of the new multimillionaires. "Of all forms of tyranny," he wrote in his autobiography, "the least attractive and the most vulgar is the tyranny of mere wealth, the tyranny of a plutocracy."[2]

Roosevelt acted in great secrecy without informing his Cabinet, some of whom would have informed Morgan. He conferred with Attorney General Knox and decided to prosecute the Northern Securities holding company under the terms of the Sherman Antitrust Law, which McKinley had honored by its disuse. The government had allowed itself to become impotent, unable to control large companies in interstate commerce. Now, on February 19, 1902, Knox announced that the federal government would be asking for the dissolution of the Northern Securities Company under the law. When Morgan was told, he became apoplectic. His lawyers assured him that he would win his legal case against the Attorney General, "an unknown country lawyer from Pennsylvania," even if he had to go as far as the Supreme Court. Morgan's associate James J. Hill was even more scathing about such interference in big business. "It really seems hard," he said, "that we should be compelled to fight for our lives against the political adventurers who have never done anything but pose and draw a salary."[3]

The effect on Wall Street was unsettling. Stocks slumped badly. Not since McKinley's assassination, the *Tribune* declared, had such a sudden shock hit the market. In Washington, Henry Adams was triumphant. "Our stormy petrel of a President," he wrote, "without warning, has hit Pierpont Morgan, the whole railway interest, and the whole Wall Street connection, a tremendous whack square on the nose. The wicked don't want to quarrel with him, but they don't like being hit that way. . . . The Wall Street people are in an ulcerated state of inflammation. Pierpont has declined the White House dinner."[4]

But Pierpont Morgan did not decline meeting the President. He stormed down to Washington to see Mark Hanna. With a senator in tow, they descended on the President and the Attorney General for what was termed a social call. The question of the suit against Northern Securities was broached. Morgan complained that he should have been told about it in advance.

"That is just what we did not want to do," the President said.

Morgan's reply displayed his total contempt for the power of the elected government.

"If we have done anything wrong," he said, "send your man to my man and they can fix it up." He meant that the President should send Attorney General Knox up to New York to do a deal with a Morgan lawyer like Stetson.

"That can't be done," Roosevelt answered.

"We don't want to fix it up," Knox said. "We want to stop it."

At last Morgan saw that the administration was in earnest. This trust was going to be busted, if Roosevelt had his way. Northern Securities had offended the antitrust laws too blatantly in the area of maximum public concern, the railroads. He must look to the rest of his business.

"Are you going to attack my other interests," he asked, "the Steel Trust and the others?"

"Certainly not," Roosevelt replied, "unless we find out that in any case they have done something that we regard as wrong."[5]

Morgan left. He realized that in the President he had found an adversary more difficult than Cleveland at the end of the Gold Crisis. The White House people were no longer in his pocket. In fact, he might be in theirs. Big business did best in secret and in the silence of the laws. And now a President was forcing disclosures in open court. The time was coming, as Morgan had said so truly, when all business would have to be done with glass pockets.[6]

For Roosevelt, however, Morgan's intrusion and way of treating a President was a disclosure in itself. "That is a most illuminating illustration of the Wall Street point of view," he said to Knox after Morgan had gone. "Mr. Morgan could not help regarding me as a big rival operator, who either intended to ruin all his interests or else could be induced to come to an agreement to ruin none."[7]

Fortunately, the President did not receive the denunciation that the angry Morgan penned in his hotel room that night. A Morgan lawyer had it suppressed. However great his financial power, Morgan could not dress down the President of the United States as if he were a rogue speculator like John W. Gates, soon to be dispossessed of the Louisville & Nashville Railroad and consigned to retirement in Port Arthur, Texas.

Roosevelt was firing only the opening shot in a war that any strong President would have to fight to prove his authority over the self-made symbol of American finance. Morgan had chosen to personify and aggrandize the trusts. He had to be Roosevelt's first target. It would be the test whether he was greater than Presidents and Kings.

"Morgan is not a conscious advertiser," one of his partners said, "but he has a positive genius for advertising." He was often on the front pages because of his pursuit of the biggest and the best. He had to have the most superb yacht and works of art, prize-winning dogs and horses. He headed or closed the subscription lists for Madison Square Garden and the Metropolitan Opera House and the New York Cathedral — the largest church in the country. Finally, it was recognized in New York that no public, charitable or sporting enterprise outside horse racing "could be started without going to him first and getting his sanction, for the reason that other people who were approached would always want to know what Mr. Morgan thought of it before committing themselves. It was equally so of business projects. Everyone wanted to be on the same list with him."[8]

This predominance in American financial affairs was translated by Morgan to the international scene. He seemed ready to alter the balance of world power. The American merchant fleet was in a bad way because of price wars and competition from the dominant British shipping lines. After his successful reorganization of the United States Steel Corporation, Morgan was approached on a transatlantic liner and asked to set up an international shipping trust. "It ought to be," he said, turning his opportunity into his morality.[9] What was good for him would be good for the United States.

The initial negotiations involved American, British and German shipping lines. Rumors of the proposed trust provoked intervention by both the British and the German governments. The Cunard Line was told not to deal with the Morgan group, as was the Hamburg-American Line. National security seemed threatened. But the American merged lines were allowed to acquire control of two old English shipping firms, the White Star and the Leyland, partly for $22.5 million payable in gold, and partly for stock and bonds from the $170 million capitalization of Morgan's new International Mercantile Marine Company.

The London and American press presumed that Morgan was trying to use his financial strength to buy up supremacy of the seas from Great Britain. Questions were asked in the House of Commons, to which the Prime Minister replied that Morgan had always been a friend of Britain and had offered to consult with the government on all points that might affect national interests. He had also paid an inflated price for what he wanted. The chairman of the Leyland Company frankly told his shareholders that the American offer was so extravagant that no management had the right to refuse it. "The vendors," the *Annual Shipping Review* declared in 1901, "made an exceptionally good bargain, which it is probable the purchasers will soon find out."

They did, but only many years later, when the English interests were able to buy back the whole trust for less than a third of the price that Morgan had paid for it. But for the moment, intoxicated by his success with the steel trust, Morgan persisted in his plan to capture the high seas for America. His son-in-law might state that Morgan only wanted efficiency, with one liner sailing nearly every day from New York with mail and passengers rather than three rivals sailing on the same date and none for the rest of the week. He might claim that Morgan wanted to make transatlantic sailings as simple as transcontinental railroad journeys.[10] But Morgan also wanted the ships to fly the American flag.

His involvement in sea power was a factor in the Kaiser's decision to send to America his younger brother, Prince Henry of Prussia, officially to see the launching of the schooner *Meteor*, one of the competitors in the New York–Hamburg race for an imperial cup. This was the first time that a member of a leading European royal family had visited New York since the Prince of Wales had come over forty years before. A magnificent "Captains of Industry" dinner, given by Morgan, entertained the Prince, who took back with him impressive reports of Morgan's wealth, declaring that the lavishness of American entertainment was far greater than the small beer he was used to as a royal younger brother.

Morgan's own proceedings were now princely. He continued the loan of the superb Garland collection of Chinese ceramics to the Metropolitan Museum of Art. It had been bought by Uncle Henry Duveen, who used it to bind Morgan to him as a client forever. He sold it to Morgan for a token profit of 15 percent, although he could have got a higher price for it in London from an industrial magnate, later Lord Leverhulme. He cast the bait deliberately. "I did it," he told a younger member of the Duveen family, "to make him a customer. I know that I will make him the best we ever had."[11]

He was right. After the deal was concluded, Morgan gave Uncle Henry Duveen carte blanche to complete the collection at any expense. It became the finest in the world. Within a few years, Morgan had acquired the exquisite Fragonard panels that now hang in the Frick Museum; the Mannheim collection of antiques, including a fan of Marie Antoinette's and a lock of her hair; and the Gutman collection of antique silver and bronzes from Berlin. He liked to buy up entire collections. "What's the use of bothering about one little piece?" he would say. In the opinion of the editor of the *Burlington Magazine*, "his successful raids upon the private collections of Europe were organized and carried out with the rapid decisive energy of a great general. He believed in military methods; he regarded rapidity and irrevocability of decision as more important than accuracy of judgment; he considered discipline more effective than a nice discrimination."[12] He was preparing to furnish the Greek Renaissance palace that Charles McKim was building for him off Madison Avenue, especially made from tailored stone blocks without mortar in the ancient style.

His traveling had also become a royal progress. He left by private train in March, 1902, for the Jekyll Island Club. It was an exclusive place off Georgia where millionaires could relax among the palmettos and magnolias, Cherokee roses and trumpet creepers, far from the intrusion of the poor and the press. Founded in 1888, it boasted a careful simplicity, a good golf course, a sulfur spring, a long shelving beach, terrapin, oysters, mockingbirds, oaks, Spanish moss, deer, turkey, duck, and eventually some wild boar, a present from the King of Italy to Morgan and loosed on his orders in the wilderness of Jekyll.[13] On the island, Morgan could talk in peace with his peers at the long after-dinner conversations where so much financial strategy was planned. On this occasion he conferred with the future president of the American Telephone and Telegraph Company, Senator Nelson W. Aldrich of Rhode Island, and his old friend Charles Lanier. Eight years later on Jekyll Island, a Morgan partner, Henry P. Davison, would hold a secret conference with Aldrich and three other bankers in order to submit proposals which would serve as the basis for the Federal Reserve System and end the need for Morgan's dominant role in American finance.

Yet he was still in the prime of his power and his glory. Leaving his winter paradise, he and his family party took the special train to Washington, where he still hoped to settle the Northern Securities business. Instead, he was served a subpoena to testify in a suit against his railroad companies. The hearing was public and the circuit courtroom was packed by the curious. Morgan had the press photographers banned. He was cross-examined by the counsel for the plaintiff and by his own counsel Stetson for three hours. He told his official story of the reasons for the formation of the Northern Securities Company. He wanted greater efficiency and no more stock-raiding. He was adamant that there was no price-fixing agreement between his merged lines or with other lines like the Union Pacific. There was no restraint of trade, nothing illegal at all.

If Morgan's evidence is assessed, he did not know, chose not to know, or lied under oath. Certainly he knew that Hill and Harriman were willy-nilly together on the board of the Northern Pacific, and that they had a community of interest with Harriman's Union Pacific. He had himself initiated gentlemen's agreements over price-fixing in his early railroad associations. Only in court did he deny his knowledge of such things. "Of course," his son-in-law wrote after the evidence, "everybody who knew Mr. Morgan believed him implicitly; but this did not stop those in political life from going ahead to destroy what he had accomplished."[14]

In point of fact, Morgan could not speak the truth, which was his best defense. Parallel railroads could not compete without destroying each other; they had to share whatever traffic there was at reasonable rates. The dilemma was: Should the government regulate the rates through the Interstate Commerce Commission, even if it meant setting them too low in order to keep the rural vote happy? Or should the railroads regulate themselves by their unofficial gentlemen's agreements, which might set the rates too high in pursuit of greater profits? Roosevelt was taking the first line, while Morgan always believed in the second. The historian of the Northern Securities case came out in Morgan's favor:

> Everyone who knows what is going on is aware of the fact that agreements which rest upon "what each was saying as he looked at his neighbor" have never ceased to exist, and that this form of agreement is the only guarantee against progressive anarchy in railway matters where the law forbids every other form. . . . The American public seems to be unwilling to admit that agreements will and must exist, and that it has a choice between regulated legal agreements and unregulated extra-legal agreements. We should have cast away more than fifty years ago the impossible doctrine of protection of the public by railway competition.[15]

In the end, the government suit against Northern Securities took three years to reach the Supreme Court, which decided by one vote in favor of the government and ordered the dissolution of the holding company. It was a symbolic victory for Roosevelt more than an actual one. Hill and Morgan still remained in control of the railroads and Harriman was considerably richer from his share of the stock. "Two certificates of stock are now issued instead of one," Hill said cynically. "They are printed in different colors, and this is the main difference."[16] He had put his mark on the surface of the earth, he went on to say — and nobody would wipe it out. Harriman was even less cowed. If the law allowed, he said, he would spread across the Atlantic as well as the Pacific Ocean, and go on as long as he lived, the "Colossus of Roads," to girdle the earth through China.

But the law now made it much more difficult at home. Roosevelt's symbolic victory signaled a real change in the climate of opinion. For the first time, the American government had attacked legally the control of American industry and communications by a few investment bankers. In the opinion of James Stillman and of his biographer, the dissolution of the Northern Securities Company marked "the close of the individualistic era in American business, for with it the domination over an industry by single men, such as Carnegie or Harriman, Morgan or Rockefeller, came to an end."[17]

Yet in 1902 hardly anybody saw that end coming. And certainly not Morgan. He continued on his royal way, still believing he would defeat the government in the courts. He did not stop acquiring railroads, once handing George F. Baker the single largest check yet issued in American

Sixteen-year-old Pierpont as a schoolboy at Göttingen, 1857

THE PIERPONT MORGAN LIBRARY

Junius Spencer Morgan, 1890

BROWN BROTHERS

Cragston, Pierpont Morgan's summer home at Highland Falls, on the Hudson

BROWN BROTHERS

Mrs. Junius Spencer Morgan, 1861

BROWN BROTHERS

The J. Pierpont Morgan home at 219 Madison Avenue

CULVER PICTURES

J. Pierpont Morgan, Paris, 1868

THE PIERPONT MORGAN LIBRARY

Mrs. J. Pierpont Morgan, 1902

BROWN BROTHERS

BROWN BROTHERS

A gallery of some of Morgan's friends and foes: Andrew Carnegie; James A. Stillman; George W. Perkins; Robert Bacon as a Harvard letterman;

BROWN BROTHERS

BROWN BROTHERS

eorge F. Baker; E. H. Harriman; John W. ("Bet-a-Million") Gates
hotographed at the track with his wife, his son Charles, and daughter-in-law);
y Gould; and James J. Hill

BROWN BROTHERS

BROWN BROTHERS

CULVER PICTURES

For most of his career, Morgan was a favorite target of political cartoonists.

BROWN BROTHERS

Morgan cut a fine figure as commodore and yachtsman.

BROWN BROTHERS

J. P. Morgan's magnificent yacht Corsair II

BROWN BROTHERS

The Morgan family's home at Prince's Gate in London

Morgan (second from right on the stairs) with distinguished guests at Nuneham Park, 1907. King Edward VII sits in the center.

Actress Maxine Elliott

CULVER PICTURES

Passionate about his privacy, Morgan resented a photographer's intrusion.

BROWN BROTHERS

Wall Street was thronged with desperate people in the panic of 1907.

The Morgan Library, designed by McKim, Mead and White, adjoined Morgan's Madison Avenue home.

In the West Room of his library, Morgan repaired for solitaire and convened many of his meetings.

J. P. Morgan at the Pujo Committee hearings, Washington, D.C., 1912

BROWN BROTHERS

Morgan with his daughter, Mrs. Satterlee, and his son, J. P. Morgan, Jr., arriving to testify before the Pujo Committee

BISHOP LAWRENCE

The Harvard Club of Khargeh, 1912. From left: Albert Morton Lythgoe, J. Pierpont Morgan, Herbert Eustis Winlock, Dr. Francis Parker Kinnicutt, William Lawrence, John Lambert Cadwalader

BROWN BROTHERS

The Morgan Bank building at the corner of Wall and Broad streets

business history: $23 million, by which he gained control over the Jersey Central line. He encouraged George Perkins in his efforts to organize the International Harvester Company, despite the fact that the farmers who bought McCormick or Deering reapers were prejudiced against Wall Street and especially against the house of Morgan.

Morgan was also encouraging Perkins's rise in the firm. Robert Bacon was exhausted and had been caught twice, once by the Harriman raid on the Northern Pacific and once by the government suit against Northern Securities; soon he would retire from the firm, broken in health, for two years of convalescence. Schwab was also in trouble with Morgan because of a gambling spree in Monte Carlo. Although he was betting within his means and along with Lord Rothschild, the New York yellow press announced that he was plunging heavily and breaking the bank. As Morgan had appointed him chairman of United States Steel, his notoriety might affect popular belief in the worth of the company's stock. Carnegie and Gary wanted Schwab dismissed; but Morgan was no hypocrite. He gambled himself in Europe and only made Schwab eat humble pie. "Steel Co. first — me second," Schwab wrote abjectly. "I'll do anything Mr. Morgan wants. He's my idea of a great man."[18] But Morgan did not forget the indiscretion; he forgave and blamed. A year later, Gary would supplant Schwab after Schwab had brought more discredit on the house of Morgan, and Perkins would fill the gap as he would fill Bacon's place.

If the younger partners felt the killing pace of the new trust business, the old Morgan felt it even more and paced himself wisely, sailing across the Atlantic in April on the White Star Line, which was to be part of his international shipping combine. For the first time, he ordered *Corsair III* to sail over to England. He intended to impress the kings and emperors of Europe even more than he already had. A contemporary cartoon by Donahey in the Cleveland *Plain Dealer* showed Morgan on a dollar throne, crowned and smoking his cigar, while the Kaiser blacked his boots and King Edward VII was his footman, holding up a silver salver for a tip. By Morgan on the throne, a sampler hung with the words embroidered on it:

J. PIERPONT MORGAN
Ruler of the Combined Continents
and Consolidated Islands
And the Profits Thereof.

"London and Berlin," Henry Adams wrote, "are standing in perfectly abject terror, watching Pierpont Morgan's nose flaming over the ocean waves, and approaching hourly nearer their bank-vaults."[19] His new incursion into England redoubled local fears. Not only was he buying up British shipping lines, but he was also burrowing underground by trying to finance the London subway system. And when he headed a syndicate of his own bank, the Rothschilds and the Barings, to take up half of a British government loan for £32 million, his shadow seemed to stretch further than the empire across the globe. Almost every day there were newspaper stories about his plans to acquire the national coal or steel industries. Street vendors sold a printed sheet for a penny, a license apparently signed by J. Pierpont Morgan for the right of one person to stay on earth.

Preparations for the coronation of Edward VII were under way. Now that Queen Victoria was dead and her sophisticated son reigned, the social scene was more lavish and relaxed. As Prince of Wales, he had always been a prince of the world in his ways. Morgan had met the new King socially at the German spas and had probably advised him financially, if not actually lent him money. For Edward had always lived beyond his means on expectations of coming to the throne, and he had cultivated the society of many international bankers. Now Morgan entertained royally at Prince's Gate and Dover House with his daughter Anne acting as his hostess. And he even put on a courtier's uniform to be presented to the King.

His new episcopal friend, Bishop Lawrence, also went along to the levee, wearing scarlet robes borrowed from the Archbishop of Canterbury over his trousers tied up with string above his knees. On arriving at Buckingham Palace, he found Morgan waiting there with three other important visiting Americans. Morgan was dressed in velvet, silver buttons, silk stockings and pumps, and a silver-hilted sword over which he was in constant fear he might stumble. The bishop and the great financier were both presented to the King, who was extremely gracious to them.[20] For in his forty years of traveling, apparently on pleasure while waiting for the throne, Edward VII had perfected a system of international intelligence through personal contact and social gossip. If Morgan threatened British financial or naval supremacy, the King would see that the American magnate stayed on his side before he visited the Kaiser at Kiel. The royal touch so often hid a diplomatic maneuver; there was an ironclad in the velvet glove.

The coronation was set for the end of June. Morgan's suppressed son

Jack had been appointed by President Roosevelt as a special attaché for the occasion. He was living in his father's shadow even more than his father had lived in Junius Morgan's. Jack's chief job was to act as liaison with the house of Duveen, which had been asked to help decorate Westminster Abbey for the ceremony; but so many ancient works of art had been sold to Pierpont Morgan that the Duveens wanted to borrow some of them back. Particularly important was a large Gothic tapestry that had belonged to Cardinal Mazarin, which Morgan had bought for £100,000 from the Duveen Brothers. He now was able to provide the backdrop for the British throne.

While waiting for the coronation, Morgan went across to Paris on his way to join *Corsair III* on the Riviera. It was probably then that he put to the international speculator George Kessler an incredible scheme to corner the whole of the champagne market. Kessler used to make more than a million dollars a year from the wine trade, and he claimed that Morgan offered to back him for half a billion dollars to create a monopoly on the most popular and expensive wine in the world. The champagne vineyards were all in a small area; money could buy anything; the price of the drink could be doubled or more; the profits of a champagne trust would rise higher than its bubbles. It was a heady idea, but impractical. "We were both ignorant babes," Kessler later admitted. There were sixteen thousand different growers in the region, too many even for a Morgan combination.[21]

Morgan relaxed on board *Corsair III* on its voyage to Venice and a subsequent cruise along the Adriatic. He was becoming the financial adviser to other kings, particularly the kings of Italy and Belgium. He enjoyed his status as a visiting potentate. On his return to London, the American Ambassador gave a dinner party for the King and Queen and for Mr. Morgan, who was seated on the King's right and was invited to the coronation ceremony in the Abbey. But on the eve, Edward VII was stricken with severe appendicitis and lay near death.

Morgan lingered in London, waiting for news of the only man he might have preferred to be if he were not himself. His wife once said that she would rather be the Princess of Rails than the Princess of Wales, but she spoke for herself. When the bulletins from the palace told of Edward's recovery, Morgan continued on his own royal way aboard *Corsair III* to visit the German fleet at Kiel. There the imperial German family was waiting to welcome such an international force on the financial scene. Morgan's court on board consisted of thirteen men and eight ladies and no relations. One of the ladies was the superb and famous actress

Maxine Elliott, whose long dark hair and liquid eyes, porcelain skin and full figure, made her seem one of the Italian beauties that Morgan liked to collect as works of art.

When *Corsair III* arrived at Kiel, Morgan was signally honored. Kaiser Wilhelm himself came aboard with his staff. After lunch, Morgan and the Kaiser paced up and down the deck. Twice was enough for Morgan, who hated exercise. He suggested that they should sit down. Nobody was allowed to suggest anything to the Kaiser, who was used to command. But he took it in good grace and sat down beside Morgan to discuss American politics and examine Morgan's shipping plans.

Next morning, the secretary-general of the Hamburg–American Line was waiting at the dock to act as their official host. While he saw that Morgan and his party were put on the imperial railroad carriage for the trip to Berlin, he was trying to find out more about the new International Mercantile Marine trust. During the next two days of sight-seeing, the imperial palaces in Berlin and Potsdam were opened for Morgan and his guests. The financier himself was asked to a private dinner by the Kaiser, who revealed his fears about socialism. Morgan looked as if he had never heard of the word. "I pay no attention to such theories," he said. When the visit was over, he made it clear to the American press that he had felt on an equal footing with His Imperial Majesty.

"I have met the Kaiser," he declared, "and I like him."[22]

While in Berlin, Morgan had also visited Dr. Wilhelm von Bode, the most famous art expert before the rise of Berenson and the director of the Kaiser Friedrich Museum. He made arrangements for von Bode to serve as his personal adviser and to authenticate certain works of art: von Bode had been the discoverer of the notorious wax "Leonardo da Vinci" bust of Flora. Morgan also asked von Bode to recommend to him any great collections that were for sale on the Continent. In point of fact, the Oskar Hainauer and Rodolphe and Maurice Kann collections would all go to Joseph Duveen for more than ten million dollars with certain pieces pre-selected by von Bode for Morgan's first approval.

Morgan and his party returned overland through Paris to London. Various members of his family came across to Prince's Gate to watch Morgan go off to his grand occasion, the postponed coronation. He filled in the time by acquiring the Bennett collection of incunabula for his proposed Library in New York; he also wanted to do in London what he had done in New York, and buy the mansion next door to house all the works of art that were burying him in 13 Prince's Gate. On August 8, he dressed in his court dress for the coronation, although not in the peer's robes that legend put upon him. At this apogee of the British Empire, Morgan was also at the zenith of his own position, the uncrowned monarch of international finance. And now he watched his contemporary crowned as King Edward VII. He was standing in the company of his aristocratic British friends, including the beautiful Candida Lady Tweeddale and Adele, the Countess of Essex, who was one of the many American heiresses who had crossed the Atlantic to gain a title. The Mazarin tapestry hung behind the altar itself.

Morgan had stayed away from America too long in the company of emperors and kings. Even his adversary, the new President of the United States, needed his return. There was a national financial crisis aggravated by a long-running strike by the anthracite miners. Morgan's chief banking rival, James Stillman, had cabled him to come back. Several New York banks were on the verge of failure, their assets mainly the watered and unsalable stocks of the new trusts. America's favorable trade balance with England had reversed itself with the ending of the Boer War. The United States was again a debtor nation, bleeding gold. Share prices were slumping. There would be a panic if money was not made available to the rural banks to finance the moving of the next harvest. Morgan had to come home.

He sailed on the *Oceanic* on August 20, 1902, and soon went into a series of conferences with Stillman. They decided to ask the government to put $25 million in securities into the rural banks. New York must be left to stew in its own juice. According to one witness, Morgan roared like a bull at the thought of helping Stillman and his friend Baker provide a money pool of another $50 million to shore up the city banks. Drained of that cash, he would not be able to support the price of his precious steel-trust shares, which would drop precipitously. Even so, he agreed to help in a national financial strategy.

The problem was to make Roosevelt agree to be rescued by Wall Street. When the intermediary Herman H. Kohlsaat saw the President, he saw a man whose face was a study. "He did not attempt to conceal his dislike for the big men in Wall Street, and said: 'By George, how I would like to get a chance to smash those fellows!' " But Kohlsaat replied: "The trouble is you would smash the whole country in the operation, and a lot of innocent people would suffer."[23]

So Roosevelt did as Grover Cleveland had done before him. He had to negotiate with Morgan until he could change the whole financial system. He did lend the securities to the rural banks, and he did value Morgan more for holding the line in New York and allowing his steel stock to fall as low as 8¾. In fact, he had to go to Morgan directly as McKinley had done in 1900, to help to solve the miners' strike. The great man was simply too powerful to ignore.

Morgan was being wrongfully blamed for allowing the coal strike to continue. The President had not asked for his intervention, and the country certainly would resent his intervention. To reporters he said that he was not the president of a coal company and that there was no need for him to do anything. And yet he would do something if he were asked by the right people. "I have not said that I will not interfere," he ended the interview, "or that I will interfere."[24]

His absence in Europe had not helped the confrontation. In October, 1901, Senator Hanna had foreseen the coming of the strike and had asked Morgan to intervene in case the Republican cause was again injured during the year of congressional elections. Morgan had seen John Mitchell, the leader of the coal miners' union, and had assured him that he would do what was right. But he had met strong opposition from the coal operators, even though he had some power over their obstinate and righteous leader, George F. Baer, through his stranglehold on the Reading Railroad in particular and Wall Street finance in general.

Unfortunately, during Morgan's stay in Europe Mitchell had called out 140,000 miners in support of fair wages, a shorter working day, union recognition, and the fair weighing of coal. Conditions were so bad in the mines (441 men had been killed in 1901 alone) that public sympathy was on the side of the strikers. There was little violence, Mitchell remained reasonable, and the men starved quietly. Then Baer was stupid enough to make a statement in defense of property rights that would have seemed backward in the heyday of the robber barons. "The rights and interests of the laboring men will be protected and cared for —" he wrote, "not by the labor agitators, but by the Christian men to whom God in his infinite wisdom has given the control of the property interests of this country."[25]

Morgan returned to a stalemate. The coal operators were proving intractable. It was for the government to intervene before winter came, not for a private person. Coal prices were rising from five dollars to thirty dollars a ton, although Morgan himself was arranging for some coal to be shipped from England and some given at a cheap rate to the poor. By October 3, Roosevelt felt forced to summon Baer and the coal operators to Washington to meet with Mitchell and other labor leaders. This was a de facto recognition of the union by the government, something which the operators had never recognized. It was a bitter and rowdy encounter, in which even Roosevelt lost his temper. Mitchell was the only person who behaved like a gentleman, proposing a presidential commission to arbitrate the situation. Baer behaved like a boor and a bully, telling the press outside that the operators objected to being summoned to meet a "common criminal, even by the President of the United States."[26]

This was more arrogance and stupidity than Morgan had ever shown. Two days later, Roosevelt wrote to a Morgan partner, his old classmate Robert Bacon. He praised Mitchell for his good behavior at the meeting. "He made no threats," he wrote to Bacon, "and resorted to no abuse. The proposition he made seemed to me eminently fair. The operators refused even to consider it." They had abused Mitchell and had been insolent to the President himself.[27] The implication of the letter was that Morgan should crack the operators' skulls together to let in some light. Only he had the power to do that.

Pressing his case four days later, Roosevelt asked Secretary of War Elihu Root to write directly to Morgan. Violence was getting worse with the approach of winter. The number of state militiamen at the coalfields had risen to ten thousand men. Acting as commander-in-chief, Roosevelt was prepared to send in ten thousand regular troops responsible only to himself. They would operate the mines and allow any citizen to take coal from them under his "common law" right for the preservation of his life in winter.

Roosevelt knew that his spurious doctrine hid the fact of state intervention, which would be anathema to Morgan and the coal operators. Morgan summoned Elihu Root to a conference on *Corsair III*. Root was an experienced and rich attorney who saw no conflict of interest in serving as a general counsel to J. P. Morgan and Company and acting on its behalf in the Northern Securities case, while sitting in Roosevelt's Cabinet. He claimed to Morgan that he was acting on his own initiative and was restraining the impetuous President from sending in the troops. Whether that was true or false, he drafted a plan for the settlement of the strike through a commission to be appointed by Roosevelt. The draft still exists in the Morgan Library, written on the yacht's paper under crossed pennants and the heading " — *On board the Corsair*."

Morgan then banged the coal operators' heads together, first at a meeting at the Union Club and later on *Corsair III* with Baer present. Summoning a special train to carry him and the signed agreement down to Washington, he went with Robert Bacon to confer with Root and Roosevelt. It was a strange encounter between the financier and the President after their confrontation of eight months before. But necessity was the mother of conciliation, and they both knew that much.

Specifically, the agreement signed by Baer and the coal operators accepted binding arbitration by a presidential commission, which would consist of a federal judge from the coal country, a military engineering officer, and an eminent sociologist. When Roosevelt took this proposal to Mitchell, the miners' leader wanted to add a Catholic bishop, because most of the coal workers were Catholics, and a high union official to represent that point of view. By now, Morgan had returned to New York, and Perkins had come down to replace him. But neither he nor Bacon on the long-distance telephone could get Baer and the other operators to budge an inch. They would not accept a labor leader on the commission. They refused to recognize the authority of such a breed. They sent back the Morgan partners to see the President and to tell him that the coal operators were adamant.

In this impasse, Roosevelt proved wilier than Root or the Morgan partners, when they came to see him. By the President's account, he conferred with Bacon and Perkins until two o'clock in the morning. They were "literally almost crazy." Bacon in particular was so excited that he caused the President concern; it was the beginning of the Harvard athlete's nervous breakdown through overwork in the service of Morgan. Both he and Perkins "grew more and more hysterical, and not merely admitted, but insisted, that the failure to agree meant probable violence and possible social war." They even preferred to see the Red Commune come than give way over the labor leader on the commission.

So the President came up with his "tweedledee" solution. If they would not have "tweedledum" as a labor leader, they should have "tweedledee," a labor leader who would officially be called an "eminent sociologist." This was the breakthrough. The operators could save face and insist that they had not recognized the union leaders except in an academic disguise. Whatever pressure Morgan had put on Baer remained a secret. The commission met and achieved a compromise, offering the union higher wages and better conditions, and accepting that the operators should keep an open shop. Both sides could claim a victory, and did. But the real victory went to Roosevelt, who was generous enough to acknowledge Morgan's help. He wrote to him, thanking him for the service he had done for the whole people. "If it had not been for your going in the matter, I do not see how the strike could have been settled at this time." The consequences that might have followed were "very dreadful to contemplate."[28]

The truth was that both Roosevelt and Morgan had to be forced to understand their interdependence. Neither could keep social or financial order without the other. Although Roosevelt wrote to Finley Peter Dunne that the whole thing had been a "screaming comedy," and that he now wanted to go to the circus or on a turkey shoot or bear hunt, he also admitted the danger of the situation.[29] It might have been so bad, the *Independent* wrote, that the entire army could not have held it in check. The potentate in the White House had to have the support of the potentate on Wall Street. Only between them could there be a quick settlement before a winter of arson and riot and blood.

By the end of 1902, some twenty men dominated American finance and industry. Through interlocking industrial and commercial trusts, banks and insurance companies, they were roughly grouped in two great combinations. The house of Morgan, the First National Bank under George F. Baker, the New York Life Insurance Company, and James J. Hill stood against the Rockefellers and Standard Oil, James Stillman at the National City Bank, Jacob H. Schiff of Kuhn, Loeb and Company, and Edward Harriman. There were important interests and families outside the two groupings, notably the Astors and the Vanderbilts, the Wideners and the Huntingtons and the Goulds. And there were raiders like the Moore brothers, who could still best even Harriman and take off him the Chicago & Alton Railroad. But essentially, in Frederick Lewis Allen's phrase, these were the overlords of creation.[30]

Yet creation implies destruction. By the beginning of 1903, there were more than four hundred trusts or major combinations capitalized at more than $20 billion. Too much new stock had been poured out too full of water. The market simply could not swallow it all. In Morgan's famous phrase of the period, the banks and underwriting syndicates were full of "undigested securities," which James J. Hill later redefined as "indigestible securities."[31] The situation was worsened by the manipulations of ruthless speculators, especially the Standard Oil financiers. As Henry Clews noticed at the time, the old robber barons like Jay Gould or Commodore Vanderbilt had faced failure or pitched battle. But the Standard Oil people had taken the speculation out of manipulation. They could drive Amalgamated Copper up to 130 and down to 60 as they wished. Their resources were so vast that, if they were to concentrate them, they knew they would win.

> With them the process is gradual, thorough and steady, with never a waver or break. How much money this group of men has made, it is

impossible even to estimate . . . and there is an utter absence of chance that is terrible to contemplate.[32]

There were overriding differences between the two great rival financial groups before the "rich men's panic" of 1903. They were matters of style and responsibility. The Rockefellers were morbid about secrecy, while Stillman himself was supposed to have visited the Sphinx in Egypt and made it speak first.[33] The Morgan group, however, kept itself in the public eye. It protested its avoidance of publicity only to promote itself more. As one critic wrote:

> The Standard Oil headquarters was an inaccessible citadel of silence. On the other hand, Morgan seemed to glory in the ostentation of publicity. Even if he did not, it was an indispensable requisite. In his threefold capacity of banker, railroad magnate and industrial trust organizer Morgan needed a certain amount of inspired publicity for the specific purposes of his undertakings. As a banker he had to advertise his financing of projects in order to dispose of the stock; the more power he was credited with, and the more extraordinary a financier he was extolled, the easier it was to induce a multitude of investors to put their money in enterprises sponsored by him.[34]

Morgan's ostentation spilled over into the way he actually exercised power. While the Rockefeller group preferred to take over by stealth and to pull wires behind the scenes, the Morgan men would seize control even when they did not have it. At one board meeting where a Morgan representative was seated, a young Bostonian industrialist refused to allow his firm to follow the Morgan line. They looked at him as if he were a leper. And while the old Rockefeller hardly appeared in public, Morgan at the age of sixty-six had never been more visible and potent. "Wherever Morgan sits on a board is the head of the table," Barron was told, "even if he has but one share."[35]

This basic difference of style was emphasized by a disagreement about responsibility. Stillman and the Rockefellers were in business to make money; if they had good causes, these were their private affairs. They usually kept clear of any commitment to social progress. But Morgan also seemed to revel in being a power broker for the Treasury, charity, and public works. He had a sense of his own importance in the present and future of the United States. Even if this sense was inflated in the Rockefellers' opinion, it was a motive in some of Morgan's actions. As he aged, he increasingly put his opinion of his country's interest above the making of more money.

When the clever young Nebraskan banker Charles G. Dawes visited Wall Street at this time, he came to a significant judgment:

> To talk an hour with James Stillman and another hour with George Perkins on the same day is to get a pretty clear-cut notion as to the ideas and policies which govern the two great rival camps in American finance. . . . The impartial judge must consider Mr. Morgan and his party to be the broader-gauged and higher-minded men. Stillman's talk was full of implications as to Morgan's financial strength to carry the enormous loads which he maintained are incident to the continuing business of the combinations heretofore brought out by Morgan. . . .
>
> On the other hand, George Perkins had no words of criticism. . . . He went into details showing the enormous financial strength of the firm and their ability to take care of themselves and their obligations — not stooping to criticism of others himself. He said, however, that it made Morgan furious to hear the reports of criticism brought in from so many of those indebted to him in various ways.
>
> From Stillman came the breath of innuendo — from Perkins nothing but the manly speech of a man who took pleasure and pride in being helpful and was above small practices.[36]

So it seemed to Dawes as a referee between both camps. When he later met Morgan himself, he was persuaded by the great man's "forceful and clear presentation of his views," compared with the "sneezes" he had heard from Stillman and George F. Baker. There was no question to him that Morgan was rightfully dominant. He acted as if he were. He made most men think he was. Even Stillman only dared to attack him by innuendo. The Morgan act had become the real Morgan.

The most famous photograph of the man was taken at this high point in his career. The young Edward Steichen was given precisely two minutes by Morgan to take the portrait. Morgan strode into the room exactly on time. He sat down on the chair that Steichen had arranged and put his cigar aside and stared into the camera, gripping the carved end of one chair arm. The lighting on the knob of the chair made Morgan appear to be grasping a naked blade. Steichen found that looking Morgan in the eye was like facing the headlight of an express train. One was either awed or terrified, depending on whether one was standing between the tracks.

The young photographer had the courage to click his shutter and to give the hypnotic Morgan a direction to swing his head around. Morgan did that, but sensitive about his nose, swung back to stare into the camera again. Yet his shoulders were more relaxed now, his glare less blazing. Steichen took a second picture and thanked his subject.

"Is that all?" Mr. Morgan asked.

"Yes, sir."[37]

Morgan left the sitting after the two minutes he had granted. He also left a portrait of self-will and dominance and defiance that is still awesome in its power. Even now, only a brave man would resist Morgan's image of himself.

13

Adversaries in Harness

We had, as was common, a sharp difference about President Roosevelt. I lost patience and said: "If you live long enough, you will fall on your knees and pray Almighty God to give you him again as President of the United States."

— W. S. Rainsford to J. Pierpont Morgan (1911)

In January, 1903, the Gridiron Club of the Washington press gave a dinner for rich men. Morgan accepted his invitation. As the club president said, the members had rounded up "money kings, captains of industry, monopolists, corporation cormorants, and malefactors of great wealth." The last phrase was taken from the lips of Theodore Roosevelt himself, when he opened his attack on the excesses of the financiers. On this lampoon night, however, skits were put on to show Morgan's power. In one, his partners were shown discussing next year's election. Their lines were these:

"The thing that worries the old man is what we had better do about a President."

"President of what? President of the board of aldermen?"

"No, President of the United States."

"Oh, I thought it was something important."

There was also a song about Morgan's rivalry with Roosevelt over hunting "bears" with a chorus sung to the tune of "Mr. Dooley":

With Mr. Morgan, with Mr. Morgan,
The greatest man the country ever knew!
Quite diplomatic and democratic
Is Mr. Morgan — organ — organ — ooh![1]

Morgan enjoyed his night at the Gridiron Club so much that he told Senator Mark Hanna next morning that he had had the time of his life. As he was encouraging Hanna to run against Roosevelt for the Republican nomination in 1904, he was staying close to the old political fixer from Ohio. But it was not to be. Within thirteen months, Hanna was dead. Morgan had to take a train to Cleveland to attend his funeral. Hanna was also an Episcopalian, and Morgan would always go to great pains to show his regret to God and men about the passing of the old guard.

With Hanna's death, the Republican "malefactors of great wealth" had no choice but to turn back to Roosevelt, who was running scared about his nomination and election. He held long conferences with Morgan now on financial matters. He consulted James Stillman on the currency question, appointed Frick to the Isthmian Canal Commission, and even saw John D. Archbold of Standard Oil. His third message to Congress changed emphasis, stressing that labor would be held as strictly accountable to law as capital. The *Wall Street Journal* approved, praising Roosevelt's courage and strength in making it clear that his policy was not directed against wealth.

There was a good reason for it. Roosevelt needed to raise his campaign funds for 1904. The wealthy answered his needs. More than three quarters of his war chest came from huge corporations and their owners; Harriman was responsible for collecting $250,000, Archbold for $125,000 from Standard Oil, and Morgan himself for $150,000. The truth about these donations did not come out until 1912, and Roosevelt could assure the American people in the interval that he had made no pledge or promise of immunity to any source that had contributed to his cause.

If these large contributions were meant to be political bribes, they proved bad investments. Elated by being elected with a large popular majority, Roosevelt bit the hands that had tried to feed him. Although only twenty-five suits against the trusts were initiated in the seven years of his administration, Roosevelt struck at the largest operators of all, particularly at Harriman's railroads and at the Rockefellers' Standard Oil. A fat contribution to his campaign seemed to invite a later prosecution. "Darkest Abyssinia," Archbold complained later, "never saw anything like the course of treatment we received at the hands of the administration following Mr. Roosevelt's election."[3]

Morgan was exempt. He had been the first and greatest sacrificial victim in the Northern Securities case, which the government had just won in the Supreme Court in 1904. The President seemed to appreciate Morgan's difference from the other plutocrats, his sense of duty to his concepts of how the United States should be managed. He basically agreed with Morgan about the need for capital to be responsible, but he disagreed with Morgan's contempt for unions and politicians.

The Harvard writer about cowboys who was from an old Philadelphia family, Owen Wister, once described his friendship with Roosevelt and illuminated the President's disagreements with Morgan. Wister traveled a great deal across the United States and acted as Roosevelt's eyes and ears in finding out what the public was doing and saying. The problem of a magnate such as Morgan was that, despite an occasional railroad junket in a Pullman car leased for his party, he knew nothing of America outside New England and was unaware of the millions of poor people affected by his reorganizations; in Rainsford's words, Morgan was like the water beetle in its perambulating diving bell, carrying its own atmosphere with it in a silvery bubble.[4] Owen Wister, on the other hand, could report to Roosevelt about the crippling effects of the Pullman strike or the two coal strikes. He knew both the people affected and the big operators like Baer and his friends. He admired Roosevelt's courage in confronting his natural Republican allies. As he wrote:

> Hands off! was what Big Business felt about itself in relation to the entire outside world; whatever it saw fit to do was, in its own eyes, right. It had come to resemble a good deal what a church was in the Middle Ages, a sanctuary in which you were safe from all hostile assault. Roosevelt, in bringing the Northern Securities suit, had violated the sanctuary, and his Coal Strike Commission was another violation; not even the Government of the United States must dare to call Big Business to order.[5]

Wister also saw what Roosevelt could see, that the American people were growing discontented with big business. Although they had always directed the American government to keep its hands off private commerce, they had not told the government to permit the wholesale plundering and overbearing insolence of the new breed of plutocrats. There was now "a vast popular and undiscriminating sympathy with the strikers, the sympathy of people whose means were modest, who were no more superior to the vice of envy than most of us are, and who were steadily coming to believe that if you are rich you are wrong."

Unfortunately, the Morgans and the Harrimans had grown up in a century of public encouragement to the unhampered man of ability and drive. But this climate of opinion was now changing to popular suspicion and spite. Their success was too great and made bitter enemies. "All of them did more good than harm; but all, born in the happy days of *laissez-faire*, and so taking it for granted that they could carry on their vast plans as they saw fit, were used to having their own way. When they were stopped, they were very naturally not pleased." They did not know what Wister knew, that the mere mention of the name of Morgan or Rockefeller across the country roused a black scowl of hate. Many citizens said that the government of the United States was situated in Wall Street. More of them were saying it each year. "Their hatred of Wall Street was excessive, but it was perfectly natural. They detested the arrogance of wealth, and they believed that all wealth was arrogant, and that to be rich was to be dishonest; any captain of industry was a public enemy."

As President, Roosevelt decided to lead this protest. To Wister, his decision to attack the rich and the trusts was a stroke of genius. He stole the thunder of the Populists and the Socialists. He put the plain people in the Republican camp. Of course, much of his assault on the plutocrats was a fireworks show. As he told Wister in private: "They had much better accept me. I am on their side. I believe in wealth. I belong to their class."

This was the truth behind his confrontation with Morgan himself at another Gridiron dinner. Secretly, Roosevelt needed Morgan and his resources both to pacify the two panics that took place during the administration and to provide the financial clout for an aggressive foreign policy in the Pacific and in the Americas. But publicly Roosevelt had to proclaim his independence of his necessary dependence on the chief symbol of Wall Street power. In the Gridiron Club that night, he was speaking about how the intransigence of capital and labor had unsettled the country. He had been forced to intervene in the regulation of railroad rates, in the packing industry, in canned goods, in the tobacco and oil monopolies.

Suddenly Roosevelt stopped speaking, walked over to where Morgan was sitting, and shook his fist in the financier's face.

"And if you don't let us do this," he shouted, "those who will come after us will rise and bring you to ruin."[6]

It was a fair warning from the President to the potentate. They were adversaries, but they were in harness together.

None of Morgan's partners were able to fill the dead Coster's shoes. Bad mistakes were being made in the reorganizations, and scandals were tarnishing the name of the firm, which was trying to do too much with too few people. The first scandal was Charles Schwab's second great indiscretion. Although president of Morgan's steel trust, he had privately bought, on money borrowed from Morgan, the independent Bethlehem Steel Company as a speculation. An angry Morgan had ordered Schwab to divest himself of this conflict of interest. Schwab unloaded it on the rocky new United States Shipbuilding trust, while gaining control of the whole trust through the voting power of his new bonds in it.

In fact, Bethlehem Steel was the Shipbuilding trust's only sound asset, as its shipyards were not competitive on the international scene. The underwriting of its new bonds was a failure. Its stock was not only indigestible, but left the underwriters inconsolable. It went into receivership and disintegrated. At the bankruptcy proceedings, J. P. Morgan and Company was said to have handled the Bethlehem Steel transactions for Schwab and to have held a special "insider trading" position on the sale of its stock in the trust. Morgan and his partners were accused of sharp practice. Characteristically, Morgan refused to defend himself, although he had been out of the country at the time. Meanwhile his many enemies hinted that the United States Steel Corporation would soon go the way of United States Shipbuilding.

After this scandal came the disappointment of the International Mercantile Marine. Morgan had paid too much for too little. He could not pour the leaky new stock onto a market swollen to bursting with water. For the first time, his prestige was unable to sell the stock to the American public, and the syndicate's underwriters were forced to carry the new shares. He could not control the oceans as he could the American interior. The British government gave the Cunard Line huge subsidies to build such ships as the *Mauretania* and the *Lusitania* in order to compete with Morgan's trust, while the Kaiser also gave government help to build up the German merchant fleet. With the feeling in Congress against Wall Street, Morgan could not get any government subsidies for his own ships. He was caught between the devil and the deep blue sea.

That year also, Morgan was plunging into another railroad morass that would sully his fame after his death. The New York, New Haven & Hartford Railroad was part of his nostalgia for his youth. He felt strongly that his intercontinental system should include the lines of his origins. Sentimentality clouded his business sense. The problems of the railroad seemed to demand no more of a reorganization than his many others. His error was to pick the wrong man as its president, the reckless and secretive Charles S. Mellen, born in Massachusetts and now president of the Northern Pacific. Although Mellen was always to assert that he wore the Morgan collar and was proud of it, he ran loose and expanded the line to the eventual ruin of its thousands of investors and of Morgan's posthumous reputation.[7]

These three miscalulations were made worse by the precipitate fall in the price of United States Steel common stock. J. P. Morgan and Company was short of cash because it had invested its assets in so many new combinations. It could not keep up the price of the steel shares. Even its regular syndicate members were feeling the pinch. The steel industry had fallen into bad times and could not meet the dividends on the stock of the new trust, which Carnegie himself called all air and water. Morgan seemed to be losing his grip. As *Judge* commented: "Mr. Morgan used to float better than he knew, and now he sinks better than he ever floated."[8]

All this loss of reputation was made worse by the "rich men's panic" of 1903. Henry Adams had seen it coming ever since the circuit-court decision in favor of the government in the Northern Securities case. "Wall Street has stood the blow altogether too well," he wrote. "Knowing what Pierpont Morgan and all the capitalists have been saying, and are thinking, I can only infer that there will be steady selling for an indeterminate time, with a possible panic in the end."[9]

Henry Adams was right in his inference. While the Wall Street men accused Roosevelt of destroying public confidence in the trusts by activating the Sherman Antitrust Law, he accused them of deliberately fomenting a panic, which was "due chiefly, almost solely, to the speculation, the watering of stock on a giant scale, in which Pierpont Morgan and so many of his kind have indulged during the last few years."[10]

Both complaints were correct. The creators of the new trusts depended on maintaining public confidence in the future in order to squeeze the water out of their stock over the years of prosperity to come. But when the President of the United States was calling wealthy men malefactors, he was also calling a trust a sort of sponge, if not a fraud. He was provoking a squeeze now from the public, which had to keep its hands off for some years if it wanted a fair return on its investments.

The swollen market was punctured in 1903. The capital value of Morgan's own billion-dollar steel trust fell to a mere $350 million; its share price would not recover for another two years. There was a run on the banks, several of which failed in the cities of the hinterland. Morgan himself was put under severe pressure. He held out by calculated ruthlessness. He issued an ultimatum. Anyone who had ever been helped by his firm had to rally around or else be forever excluded from the future dealings of the house of Morgan. He demanded that his associates stand up and be counted. Enough did out of fear for the future, even though they were not his friends.

By November, Morgan had raised $70 million in cash by selling off the best of his stock, such as the Bell and the Edison Electric shares. Suddenly, everything was for sale from the man who always advised others never to sell a first-class American share. "His determination," Barron was told, "was that he should have more ready money than anybody else in the United States."[11] He was determined to meet the next panic when it came, as it surely would.

Morgan had been caught short and had nearly gone down. He had been infatuated like the other plutocrats in great combinations for their own sakes, even when these exceeded fantasy in their projected profits. Now faced with government attack and public suspicion, he reverted to the traditional security in slump — hard money. In his vaults, liquid cash slopped around rather than watered stock. The panic itself had been brief and localized, a "rich men's panic" that hardly affected the country as a whole. In fact, it was only a hiccup in the steady breath of prosperity that blew across the land.

Another wind was blowing across America, a firestorm against the plutocrats who were running the nation's businesses and finances like arsonists who started blazes in order to be praised for putting them out. *McClure's Magazine* had set the match with Ida Tarbell's exposé of Standard Oil over nineteen issues. She revealed the Rockefeller monopoly's illegal and iniquitous practices, its greed and contempt for the public. The unraveling of the great conspiracy became a detective story that engaged the nation. When no injunctions came from the Standard Oil lawyers, the articles seemed to be the revealed truth. The muckrake had been set alight as the torch of liberty.

It was the first and best of the exposés. Lincoln Steffens and Ray Stannard Baker delved into corruption without digging too deep. Frank Norris and Upton Sinclair were too hysterical in their denunciations of the western railroads and the packing plants in Chicago. Although Sinclair's *The Jungle* was the first novel since *Uncle Tom's Cabin* to be a major force behind a radical political action, it was only a tract for the times that showed the direction of the winds of change.

None of these muckraking attacks directly concerned Morgan, except for one that is now forgotten. Thomas W. Lawson was a speculator who had been ruined in Wall Street and who decided to finance himself by a vendetta against the people he claimed had ruined him. He declared that his failure was not his own fault. His articles in *Everybody's Magazine*, later published in book form under the title *Frenzied Finance*, were a swingeing assault on Wall Street practices in general and on its two great groupings in particular. He knew of the connections between the investment banks, leading industries, deposit banks and insurance companies, which had grouped around Standard Oil and the house of Morgan, now called by Lawson the System.

Lawson accused the System of deliberately manipulating the steel-trust stock to take $760 million of the people's savings. He did not object to great fortunes honestly made, but to great fortunes made from financial tricks and legal evasions. The sooner the System realized that its doom was sealed and dug for the cyclone cellars, the sooner the American people would start on the strenuous housecleaning job ahead.

Lawson particularly publicized the most vulnerable point of attack in the Morgan group:

> One of the most colossal impositions ever perpetrated on the whole people of any nation is that formula which the "System" has so insidiously drilled into the minds of the American people during the last century, to wit: that they must do nothing which might disturb the "System" in its use at two to four per cent per annum of all the people's savings, deposited in banks and trust companies throughout the country; that if they do, there will be a Wall Street panic, and thereby all the people will be made to suffer great hardships. On the contrary, I know that if the people do what is necessary to shake off the "System's" strangling grip upon their savings, the "System" will suffer death, and everlasting profit and advantage will accrue to the nation.[12]

These reckless accusations by Lawson were tempered at the same time by John Moody's *The Truth About the Trusts*, which both justified and exposed their power. He set down in black and white the huge aggrandizement of the Morgan and Rockefeller groups. Moody, however, was a social Darwinist and believed that the rise of the trusts was inevitable:

> Instead of the growth of the Trust movement being an achievement to be laid at the door of Mr. Morgan or Mr. Rockefeller, or any other leader of men, it should be laid at the door of nature. For if anything in this world is true, the following proposition is:
>
> The modern Trust is the natural outcome or evolution of societary conditions and ethical standards which are recognized and established among men today as being necessary elements in the development of civilization.[13]

Whether attacked as a cancer or welcomed as a force for civilization, Morgan's financial control had been thoroughly exposed. His secret systems were becoming a commonplace in the marketplace. His weak spots were being revealed to his enemies and to reformers. Through Perkins, the house of Morgan was particularly linked to the New York Life Insurance Company. It was one of many insurance companies with assets that were being handled during the speculative boom as if they were gigantic sponges for soaking up watered stock. In every one of his promotions, Morgan would allocate a block of shares to each insurance or trust company connected to him. He did not request or consult, he assigned. In that way, the savings of the nation were available for his schemes.

Despite these flagrant abuses, the insurance companies might have escaped investigation if an internecine squabble had not broken out. The young socialite James Hazen Hyde had inherited most of the Equitable Life stock from his father and was wasting it on a dandy's life-style. He was credited with the remark, "I have wealth, beauty and intellect: what more could I wish?"[14] An effort was made by the president of the Equitable to remove his influence on the company's policy. The noise of the battle, the thunder and stink of the charges and the countercharges, reached Pulitzer's *World*, which started a campaign for an insurance investigation. Hyde was induced to sell out his holdings in the Equitable to a streetcar magnate, who was induced in turn to sell out later to Morgan. "It was," as Morgan finally testified without giving off any light, "a desirable thing for the situation to do that."[15]

The desirable thing for the situation was to add Equitable's capital assets to those of New York Life as a cash source for Morgan's schemes. But this was the undesirable situation which the newly appointed state investigating committee wanted to remedy. It was fortunate in having as its investigating attorney the incorruptible and lethal Charles Evans Hughes, whose courtesy hid an instinct for the gut of the matter. Over the following months, Hughes relentlessly examined the officers of the insurance companies, particularly George Perkins, whose double job in New York Life and in J. P. Morgan and Company made him extremely vulnerable to allegations of conflict of interest. He appeared both forthright and stonewalling in his answers. Yet as his biographer pointed out, he gave the impression of considering himself above the law; legal restrictions, he seemed to be saying, only applied to people who were dishonest, which he was not.[16]

Although Perkins was not convicted of any crimes, the public outcry against him made him resign from New York Life. The investigating committee presented its report, recommending sweeping changes in the laws governing insurance companies. Although Perkins lobbied at the state legislature against these recommendations, the lawmakers had to protect the savings of the voters. Reform was in the air, and even Perkins's cash could not prevent the ending of unrestricted personal use of insurance funds. The companies were regulated, the policyholders protected just in time to prevent their ruin before the next panic.

Indicted twice for "larceny" because of a hidden campaign contribution to Roosevelt and for "forgery" because of a secret sale of railroad bonds, Perkins was persecuted during the next two years, further tarnishing the reputation of the Morgan partners. Even though he was acquitted on both specious charges, he had been dragged for so long through the gutters of New York that he made his associates look as soiled as he appeared to be. One contemporary cartoon in the New York *Evening World* showed a huge "Wall Street Speculator," Morgan, dressed as Bill Sikes, pushing a tiny "Oliver" Perkins through a small window to steal the "Policy Holders' Dough" from New York Life.[17] It was a sample of the mud that was spattering Morgan from all directions, even in New York, where he had recently been revered as the demigod of fortune.

Perkins was again instrumental in bringing the house of Morgan into a scandal. The pioneers to Alaska had been followed by the Guggenheim mining and smelting interests. Even more important than the Klondike gold strikes were the discoveries of huge deposits of copper near the Kennecott glacier. The Guggenheims went through Perkins to Morgan in order to finance a twenty-million-dollar railroad from the ore site to the coast.

So began what Wall Street was to call "the Second Purchase of Alaska." The Morgan-Guggenheim group also bought up steamship lines, coalfields, fisheries and canneries. They seemed to be trying to make an economic colony out of the new territory. A struggle slowly developed between two members of the Republican administration: the pro-Morgan Secretary of the Interior Ballinger and the anti-Morgan Pinchot, whom Roosevelt had made director of the Forest Service. Ballinger said that the Alaskan resources could and should be exploited by a great financial group such as the Morgan-Guggenheim combination, while Pinchot said that the resources should lie underground for the future benefit of the American people. The quarrel between the two men led directly to Roosevelt's rift with his chosen successor, Taft.

Morgan money had set the battle lines for the first political confrontation in American history between the opposed forces of exploitation and conservation. The bad publicity was intense, with Morgan again cast in the role of the rapacious ravager of the people's heritage. In America, the old era of personal financing was ending, the new era of regulations beginning. But overseas, there were no such controls. Out of the United States, Morgan was free to do as he pleased — and seem a patriot as often as not.

Theodore Roosevelt needed Morgan over the taking of the Panama Canal. If he wanted businessmen at home with glass pockets, he also wanted business done abroad with concealed weapons. In hidden dealings, he acquired the "rights" of the Panama Canal Company of France through American dummy corporations set up by the bankruptcy expert and reorganizer William Nelson Cromwell. The United States government agreed to pay $40 million for these "rights," and the President arranged for the cruiser *Nashville* to be off Panama when an insurrection broke out that led to the creation of a republic independent of Colombia. After recognizing the new republic with suspicious speed, Roosevelt claimed that the population had risen literally as one man. "Yes," replied a senator from Tennessee, "and the one man was Roosevelt."[18]

Later, Roosevelt admitted to taking the Isthmus and starting the building of the canal across it, leaving Congress to debate not the issue, but him. To finance the new republic created in American strategic interests, he sent the leading conspirator, Jean P. Bunau-Varilla, now designated as an envoy extraordinary, to see Morgan personally. Morgan agreed in November, 1903, to act as the financial agent for the Republic of Panama. He advanced $100,000 immediately for running expenses and contracted to cash the $10 million indemnity which the United States was to pay for the right to hold the Canal Zone in perpetuity. Of this sum, Morgan and Cromwell would see that $6 million was invested in mortgages on good New York real estate. There was no point in wasting dollars in the smallest of all the Central American republics.

More important for Roosevelt and Morgan was the payment of $40 million to the stockholders of the French Panama Canal Company and the American dummy corporations. The Treasury check for the full amount was the largest ever signed. The purchase of Alaska from Russia had only cost $7.2 million, while the Louisiana territory had cost $15 million and the Philippines $20 million. Morgan sailed to France to oversee personally the transfer of $3.5 million in gold bullion. He made up the rest of the amount by foreign-exchange transactions in London and Paris. In all, the $50 million paid for the Panama Canal Zone was the most expensive land purchase of foreign territory in American history.

By acting as Roosevelt's bagman in the taking of the Panama Canal,

Morgan showed his patriotism and his insensivity to criticism. The huge payments to the French company's stockholders were inexplicable; its "rights" were soon due to lapse. Morgan himself took only the small fee of $35,000 for handling the transaction, while Cromwell claimed $800,000 and was finally awarded one quarter of the amount. The New York *World* and the Indianapolis *News* ran a series of articles asking, "Who Got the Money?" These irritated Roosevelt so much that he insisted on bringing suit against each newspaper for criminal libel of himself and Cromwell and Morgan. After many years of litigation, the Supreme Court ruled in favor of the press.

By his precipitate and bold action, Roosevelt proved himself a man in the mold of Morgan. Both would take full personal responsibility. Both would act decisively in a time of crisis. Roosevelt began using Morgan more and more as an instrument in his aggressive foreign policy. During the next eight years, the firm of J. P. Morgan and Company would finance railroads in Panama, government loans in Bolivia and Argentina, and the refunding of the foreign debt of Honduras. The Monroe Doctrine was being interpreted in a different way, and American finance was being used as a weapon to repel European penetration of the Americas.

More significant was Morgan's intervention in China. In 1902, the International Banking Corporation was formed, which was eventually taken over by the National City Bank. It was an offshoot of the Standard Oil and Harriman interests and had sixteen branches across the Far East and Central America. Harriman's ambitions were now global. He had bought a Pacific merchant fleet, and he wanted railroad concessions in China, Manchuria and Russia to complete a route around the world. During the Russo-Japanese War, his financial consortium had joined together with Morgan in floating $130 million of Japanese war loans, thus giving themselves influence with the victorious imperial government.

Harriman now engaged in negotiations to refinance the South Manchurian Railroad and to get an interest in the Trans-Siberian road. Nationalistic elements in Japan and in Russia killed off Harriman's interventions. Balked, he turned to the Chinese government of Dowager Empress Tz'u-hsi, proposing a new road through northern China to link the Trans-Siberian with an ice-free terminus on the Pacific. The road would provide China with a counterweight to Japanese influence in Manchuria and would promote American influence in the Far East.[19]

Morgan had always felt personally competitive with Harriman. He had his own transcontinental network of railroads and an Atlantic merchant fleet to serve as the basis of a world communications system. In

1905, he sent his son and George Perkins to Russia to negotiate a new Russian bond issue and the supply of rails from the steel trust to renew the tracks of the Trans-Siberian road. A loan of $350 million was agreed on, but the first Russian Revolution broke out, and the negotiations had to be abandoned. Perkins and young Morgan escaped by chartered steamer to Stockholm, from where Perkins cabled Morgan that he had changed the government of Russia and had separated Norway from Sweden. If there was anything else that Morgan thought needed attention, he should cable Perkins in Paris.[20]

Morgan's failure to anticipate Harriman in Russia was counterbalanced by a success in China. He had long been the financial adviser of Leopold, King of the Belgians, whose ruthless exploitation of the rubber industry in the Congo was becoming an international scandal. King Leopold had formed a Franco-Belgian consortium to build a railroad from Peking to Hankow. He had also secretly acquired control of the American-owned China Development Company, which had originally been backed by the Standard Oil interests to run communications systems in China and to build the railroad from Hankow to Canton and on to Szechuan.

The Chinese administration had expressly forbidden one European interest from constructing the whole line from Peking to Canton. It wanted to divide and rule the competing European and American powers, which were trying to divide and rule China. So King Leopold conferred with Morgan on one of Morgan's trips to Europe and arranged to sell him a majority holding in the China Development Company. He could then claim to the Dowager Empress's government that an American group still controlled the railroad concessions that ran on from Hankow.

Informed of the manipulations of the King of the Belgians, the Chinese government threatened to cancel the railroad concessions altogether. King Leopold appealed to Roosevelt to intervene on behalf of the American and Belgian interests. The State Department warned the Dowager Empress's government that Washington would not tolerate such "spoiliation" by Peking, when other European powers had been granted large concessions in the area. The Chinese administration replied that there was great popular feeling against foreign interference; memories of the Boxer Rebellion were still fresh in many minds.

In this difficult diplomatic situation, Roosevelt decided to confer with Morgan, who cut short a holiday in Europe and returned to meet the President at Oyster Bay. There Morgan offered to waive the concessionary rights of the China Development Company provided that the Chinese government would indemnify the stockholders if this would help American diplomacy in China. Although Roosevelt wanted to keep American control over the railroads, he accepted Morgan's solution. He assured Morgan in private that "in every honorable way the Government will stand by you and will do all that lies in its power to see that you suffer no wrong whatever from the Chinese or any other power in this matter."[21]

This was hardly the letter of one adversary to another. Roosevelt would have preferred Morgan to keep the concession and build the Hankow railroads, but it was too difficult. Because of the Chinese Exclusion Act curbing immigration to America, there was already a boycott of American goods in China. Morgan's duty was to protect his stockholders even at the expense of long-term American strategy. Roosevelt understood the financier's decision and took pains to praise him publicly, stating that he had consulted with the administration and had "shown every desire to do what American interests in the Orient demanded."[22]

As Morgan withdrew, Harriman advanced once more. He appealed to China's wish for independence from the Japanese control of southern Manchuria by pressing again for a rail link between Chinchow and Aigun to connect with the Trans-Siberian. The death of the Dowager Empress, a combination of the Russians and the Japanese against the project, and Harriman's own death in 1909 aborted the grand design. It was the last American attempt to put an iron girdle about the earth.

The rivalry between the Morgan group and the Harriman and Standard Oil group in the Far East was finally settled by both participating in the American share of the financing of the Hukuang Railroad. Originally the road was to have been financed by the Germans and the British and the French, but the American government insisted on a strict application of the open-door policy and a quarter share in the financing with the other three great powers. The Secretary of State asked the house of Morgan whether he could count on its help in perfecting the financial planning. He was told yes. The house of Morgan organized the necessary syndicate, which included its major rivals, in order to present a united front for American finance in China.

In 1910, Morgan and the International Banking Corporation would secure the rights to the Chinese currency reform loan of $50 million. This time, however, reverse pressure to participate would be applied by the three European great powers. Reluctantly, the American government would direct Morgan to yield and to allocate one quarter of the loan to each of the interested parties. By that time, Taft would be President of the United States and fulsomely praise Morgan for his assistance in getting the loan and in helping American commercial interests in China.

Effectively, the house of Morgan was a powerful instrument in the "dollar diplomacy" of the Roosevelt and Taft administrations. Financial power was being used as the spearhead of diplomatic and military power. The Morgan balance sheet was the pilot boat of Roosevelt's Great White Fleet around the globe. The flag was following the foreign trade that Morgan was financing. The United States became the fourth aggressive imperial power after Britain and France and Germany, while Spain and Portugal tried to hang on to some of their colonies, and Italy sought to acquire a patch of Africa.

Roosevelt made one significant appointment to show his diplomatic alliance with Morgan abroad. He appointed Robert Bacon as Assistant Secretary of State. Bacon had been retired for two years while he recovered from his collapse from overwork as a Morgan partner and enjoyed his millions. When called back to America to serve in Roosevelt's foreign maneuverings, he was the perfect tool for dollar diplomacy, an experienced banker respected by both Morgan and the President. However much Roosevelt might denounce malefactors of great wealth in America, he used them as he needed them in his policy overseas. The big stick he carried when he walked softly had a knob of gold.

On the whole, Morgan's assistance to American foreign policy polished the reputation that was tarnished at home. One of his ventures, however, discredited him. He was part of an American syndicate with the Rockefellers and the Guggenheims to exploit a rubber concession, granted in the Congo by King Leopold. The New York *American* printed lurid and damaging stories about the atrocities employed to bring in the rubber. Morgan found himself with a group of clergymen signing a petition to the American government, asking it to intervene with King Leopold and insist on immediate reforms in the Congo. It was one of Morgan's rare pieces of public relations.

14

Panic, 1907

> The very word "panic" denotes a fear so great as to make those who experience it to become for the time being crazy; and when crazy with fear men both say and do foolish things, and, moreover, always seek for some one to hold responsible for their sufferings. . . . Surely, you can hardly believe that all this is due to my action in enforcing the law against wealthy wrong-doers.
>
> — THEODORE ROOSEVELT (1907)

"IT is difficult for me to understand why there should be this belief in Wall Street that I am a wild-eyed revolutionist." So Roosevelt wrote to Jacob Schiff, the head of Kuhn, Loeb and Company on March 28, 1907. He had just seen Morgan, who was trying to arbitrate between the President and the angry Rockefellers and Harriman. Morgan had recommended that Roosevelt hold an open White House for the railroad magnates, and Roosevelt had agreed to meet them even though he could not see any advantage in it. "Sooner or later," he informed Schiff in his letter, "I think they will realize that in their opposition to me for the last few years they have been utterly mistaken, even from the standpoint of their own interests."

Roosevelt was correct. By giving a few teeth to the Interstate Commerce Commission in the Hepburn Act and by instituting antitrust suits against the more notorious combinations, such as Harriman's railroads and Rockefeller's Standard Oil companies, Roosevelt appeared to be attacking the men of great wealth whom he was actually defending. He was leading popular prejudice as a means of blunting its retribution. Moreover, he saw himself as a judge more than a scourge. "I wish to do everything in my power to aid every honest business man," his letter to Schiff went on, "and the dishonest business man I wish to punish simply as I would punish the dishonest man of any type." He did not wish to punish past wrongs, but to prevent present abuses.[1]

There had been a short sharp panic that March, and Wall Street was blaming it entirely on the President's hostility to big business. This had destroyed public confidence in the financial leaders of the nation and in the shares they were issuing. In point of fact, Roosevelt had little to do with the underlying causes of the two panics of 1907. The bumper harvests of the two preceding years had again led to overspeculation on the New York stock market; foreign investors had begun to take their profits and withdraw their capital. All over the world the stock exchanges were troubled, from Chile to Egypt, from Tokyo to London. The British banks in particular had begun calling in their loans; the reparations for the San Francisco earthquake had absorbed much of the cash available in the United States.

The result was that huge new issues of railroad bonds could find no takers on the New York market. Harriman and the other railroad magnates had already issued $12 billion worth of stock in their enterprises, of which the railroad companies held more than one third themselves. But there was a limit to public tolerance of new issues and manipulation of the old ones. Harriman himself had been accused by Roosevelt of being an "undesirable citizen" and a "wealthy corruptionist." War between the White House and Wall Street could not have been more open.

The rich had counterattacked, creating for themselves the first brief panic in March. Rockefeller had predicted bad economic conditions to come after January, 1907. His words of doom increased the slide in prices — the dealers were experienced in bear markets. Roosevelt refused to stop his public attacks on the railroad tycoons even at the price of depressing stocks and shares. The fault was theirs: they were both financiers and "conscienceless speculators" who were choosing to bring their destruction upon their own heads. Their only hope of survival was to accept government regulation of their worst practices. "It is an act of sheer folly and short-sightedness on the part of the railway men," Roosevelt wrote again at this time, "not to realize that I am best serving their interests."[2]

Yet the public quarrel between Roosevelt and Wall Street continued. The magnates seemed almost to want to provoke a slump in order to accuse the President of having been responsible. Even though a panic would only happen because of the old causes — overspeculation and stock-watering and the flight of foreign capital — Roosevelt was the scapegoat because he had dared assault the unaccountable sanctuaries of big business. He was even resigned to misunderstanding. "When hard times come," he informed the writer Hamlin Garland, "it is inevitable that the President under whom they come should be blamed. There are foolish people who supported me because we had heavy crops; and there are now foolish people who oppose me because extravagant speculations, complicated here and there with dishonesty, have produced the inevitable reaction."[3]

Short of calling off his campaign to reform the worst abuses in business, Roosevelt did actually do what he could to prevent panics on Wall Street. The first slump in share prices in March was ended when the Secretary of the Treasury refused to make the customary withdrawals from the New York banks and deposited $70 million of customs receipts in New York to help the money shortage there. Yet these were only temporary mitigations. If the overspeculation did not stop or international capital did not return, there would be another panic soon.

Morgan was now seventy years old and slowly handing over his business to his son Jack, who was often recalled to New York and aided by Perkins and the steady Charles Steele. It was a changeover of the generations. At the National City Bank, James Stillman was preparing Frank Vanderlip to be his successor, while Henry P. Davison was being groomed to take over from George F. Baker at the First National Bank, only to be snatched away by Morgan himself. Vanderlip and Davison, and the urbane and discriminating Thomas W. Lamont, soon to join Morgan, were the three chosen successors for Wall Street's triumvirate of money power, the farm-bred Vanderlip as cool a calculator as Stillman and Davison more in the Morgan mold — "fair-minded, extraordinarily capable, jovial, a real prince."[4]

Yet something in the conditions of the summer of 1907 held back the old men from calling up the younger ones too quickly. Stillman postponed his retirement for a year. Morgan left on his usual long voyage to Europe, but he did not hand over control to his namesake. Although a middle-aged man, Jack Morgan was not going to be trusted sooner or treated better than Pierpont had been by Junius.

During the summer there were rumors and alarms. The Westinghouse Electric Company was failing. The New York street railway trust went into bankruptcy. The eastern-seaboard shipping trust financed by Charles W. Morse also collapsed; and as Morse was a specialist in "chain-banking," the buying up of one trust company with the stock of another *ad infinitum*, the overextension of the market was clear to the cautious. Three billion dollars was withdrawn in cash over the next months, while the city of New York was unable to sell its bonds — for the first time, not the last.

In the fall, Morgan came back to the United States to attend the Triennial Convention of the Episcopal Church. These were his favorite grand and ritualistic occasions. In 1904, he had made all the arrangements for the visit of the Archbishop of Canterbury, who had declared that Morgan had carried him and his party so efficiently everywhere that they had not felt American soil. In 1907, Morgan invited onto two special railroad cars a party of three bishops and their wives, a Mrs. John Markoe and a Miss Townsend. In honor of the father of his country, he planted a mulberry tree at Mount Vernon on the way, and then proceeded to the Episcopal convention at Richmond, near where British settlers had first landed three hundred years before.

Although Morgan dutifully attended the lengthy debates and ceremonies of the convention, he returned daily to his railroad cars to attend to his business affairs. Messages bombarded the banker in his sumptuous office on wheels. In Bishop Lawrence's words:

> As the Richmond Convention drew to an end, telegrams were delivered to him more frequently than usual. If one came during a meal, he tore it open, read it; then putting the palms of both hands on the table, a habit of his, he looked straight ahead with fixed eyes and deep thought for a few minutes. One day a member of the party said, "Mr. Morgan, you seem to have some bad news." He shot his eyes across the table at the speaker and said nothing. No question of that sort was asked again.

The bishops were so busy in their councils that they were unconscious of the financial crash ahead. The convention was due to end on Saturday, October 19, and Morgan's special cars were to be attached to a train on the evening of Sunday. Bishop Lawrence's diary went on:

> As I was going out of the door to the House of Bishops on Saturday morning, Mr. Morgan called me into his room and said . . . "They are in trouble in New York: they do not know what to do, and I don't know what to do, but I am going back." . . . We went by the evening train. Still, there was no suggestion of care or anxiety on his part, indeed rather the contrary: he was in the best of spirits. Held at Washington for an hour at midnight, he sat on the rear platform smoking until the train should start.
>
> Sunday morning, as we ran into Jersey City, we went into Mr. Morgan's

> car for some bread and coffee before arrival, and found him sitting at the table with a tumbler turned upside down in each hand, singing lustily some tune which no one could recognize.[5]

On arrival, Morgan put his guests into cabs. He himself went straight to his Library on Madison Avenue. It became the night nerve center of his holding operation for the next week. He did not want to excite further rumor and speculation by being seen working late at his office downtown.

The collapse was provoked by a young speculator called F. Augustus Heinze, who believed that he had a corner in United Copper shares and persuaded Charles W. Morse to back him with his "chain-banks," particularly the respected Knickerbocker Trust Company. Heinze had also acquired control of the Mercantile National Bank, which was part of the Clearing House banking system. Unfortunately, the corner in copper was an illusion. Heinze and Morse were unable to meet their obligations, even with the resources of their banking connections.

The Clearing House system provided cash for any member that was temporarily short of liquidity. The Mercantile National applied for help on Wednesday, October 16, and was found to be heavily involved in the copper corner and in Heinze's other murky dealings. Soon the Knickerbocker Trust was also found to be in trouble. Heinze and Morse were forced to resign along with the president of the Knickerbocker, Charles T. Barney, who shot himself shortly afterwards. The newspaper headlines about the resignations merely increased the panic on Wall Street.

On the Sunday evening of Morgan's return to New York, he conferred in his Library with the leading financiers in the city. He thought over the situation, slept well, and proceeded to his office to consult his partners and supervise the "housecleaning in various financial institutions. Those men were eliminated," in his son-in-law Herbert Satterlee's words, "who were already discredited or might soon be heavily involved and perhaps thrown into bankruptcy."[6] Morgan was always pirate enough to clear the decks before action.

That evening, Morgan returned to Madison Avenue, where he was staying with Satterlee and his daughter Louisa in the house next to his own. He was suffering from a bad cold and was prepared to let the Knickerbocker sink as unsalvageable. Those who did wish to save the trust company with its seventeen thousand depositors and liabilities of $35 million met at Louis Sherry's restaurant, the man who had been privately catering for Morgan on his special railroad cars at the

Episcopalian convention. As this was one of the more popular restaurants in New York, the Knickerbocker conference over dinner became a town meeting. The trust-company directors and rescuers might as well have shouted the news from the rooftops. Waiters brought down the bad tidings to the diners downstairs. One by one, they slipped away to Harriman's new experiment, the Night and Day Bank nearby. Checks drawn on the Knickerbocker were cashable throughout the early morning, and many were cashed.

By Tuesday morning, the panic was out of control. A line outside the doors of the Knickbocker Trust stretched around the block. Frank Vanderlip, whose bank would steady the panic and survive it, has left a description of the fear which every banker knows when a run on his institution is becoming a stampede. He was haunted all his life from his experience of that October:

> Just fancy yourself as a banker — and discovering outside your plate glass façade an ever-lengthening column of men and women, all having bankbooks and checks clutched in their hands. Fancy those who would be best known to you, the ones with the biggest balances, pushing to the head of the line — there to bargain excitedly with the depositors holding the places nearest the wickets of the paying tellers. Even that won't give you a hint of what a banker's dread is like unless you heighten the effect with a swarm of hoarse-throated newsboys, each with his cry pitched to an hysterical scream; and then give the hideous concert an overtone of sound from the scuffling feet of a mob.[7]

The Knickerbocker directors were terrified enough to run around to Morgan after breakfast on Tuesday. He refused his help. "I can't go on being everybody's goat," he is reported to have said. "I've got to stop somewhere."[8] The run continued until the Knickerbocker was forced to close its doors at noon upon presentation of a check for $2 million which it could not meet. The fearful mobs of depositors now began to descend on certain other trust companies and banks. The National Bank of America was collapsing under the pressure and would close the next day. And still Morgan did not move.

He was waiting for Wednesday morning to be called to command, even by his rivals and enemies. Frick was the first to come to his office to offer his support, and then Harriman, and then James Stillman with the news that $10 million of Standard Oil money would be loaned to the banks without interest charges. Stillman's visit was followed by Morgan's old friend Baker, also pledging his aid. Morgan himself asked Secretary of the Treasury Cortelyou to come up from Washington to New York for a conference that night at the Manhattan Hotel. Roosevelt's man offered at least $30 million of the government's surplus funds to be deposited with the leading banks and doled out to the trust companies so that these could meet their obligations. Furthermore, government restrictions on the banks themselves would be lifted temporarily to allow them to borrow as much as possible from other sources.

After the meeting had broken up at two in the morning, George Perkins made a mistake. Reporters had been besieging Morgan's home and his office, but they had got nothing from him. Now the Secretary of the Treasury issued a reassuring statement, and Perkins was reported as saying that yet another institution, the Trust Company of America, was the "chief sore point" of the crisis. He had named a name. The damage was done. The fear-stricken mob descended on the Trust Company of America next morning, and the $11 million collected to meet the emergency there was drained in a few hours of business.

Since four o'clock that Wednesday morning, Morgan's experts had been sifting through the evidence of the Trust Company of America's records to see if it was worth saving. By noon its president had arrived at Morgan's office, demanding help to dam the ebb tide of withdrawals. Morgan declared that he had called in the heads of the other trust companies to see whether they would put up a common pool. When they arrived at his office, they would not immediately commit themselves to helping a sinking sister. Each company was too fearful for itself.

By early afternoon, the Trust Company of America only had $800,000 left. Its securities were being brought into the Morgan building in boxes for inspection. Morgan was consulting his experts, who had still not finished their examination of the company's records. Their interim opinion was that the company was probably sound, if it could meet the run on it. Morgan made one of his usual abrupt decisions. "Then this," he said, "is the place to stop the trouble."[9] With Stillman's and Baker's support, he checked through the list of the securities in the boxes and sent around cash to the embattled company. When the first money came in from Morgan, its reserves were down to $180,000; but by the end of the day, it held over $3 million secured on the collateral of its securities held in the Morgan building.

Weeping from a heavy cold, Morgan showed his ruthless streak late that afternoon, when another run began on the Lincoln Trust Company. He said to a known gossip that if any member of the Stock Exchange sold short and helped to promote the panic, he would be "properly attended to" after the panic was over. The bears hesitated, fearful that Morgan would do just that. He could be, in Vanderlip's words, "savage when he was out of patience, and, when he was crossed, unrelenting."[10]

That night, Morgan went to a meeting of the trust company presidents and insisted that they should finish the business of that noon. The trust companies should save themselves by their united efforts. It was their problem. During the long discussion that took place after his demands, Morgan fell asleep, his unlit cigar in his hand. He woke, demanding the subscription list. The trust presidents bowed to his imperiousness and put up $8.25 million of the $10 million he asked for the Trust Company of America. He declared that he and his associates would make up the rest. They were already guaranteed by the government funds that Perkins was confirming with Cortelyou the same night. And even Rockefeller came to their support in the morning, depositing $10 million with one trust company alone.

Morgan's unpopularity was briefly forgotten. He had again become what he had been during the Gold Crisis, the symbol of strength and hope to New York City. Shouts of "There goes the Old Man . . . the Big Chief!" followed him as he slowly drove to his office in his brougham, pulled by a solitary white horse on that Thursday morning. "He might have been a general at the head of a column going to the relief of a beleaguered city," his son-in-law wrote.[11] He was more like Kutuzov in *War and Peace* at the Battle of Borodino, an old man on a white horse who knew that the enemy was breaking through everywhere and could not do much about it, but also knew that he had to give the impression that he had it all under control. As it was, he was an old man in a slow coach, trying to prove for the last time in American financial history that one person could stop the "panics" that were a characteristic of the greedy and wasteful system that had made him rich.

That morning the crisis had shifted from the trust companies to the floor of the Stock Exchange. There was no money available to finance the buying of shares. No sales were being recorded even though prices shed ten points at each quotation. The western banks were calling in their deposits from the New York banks, and the Pittsburgh Stock Exchange had shut its doors. The president of the New York Exchange went to see Morgan and told him that he would have to close at half-past one, not at the usual hour of three o'clock. Morgan told him not to close one minute before the due hour. By two o'clock, he had summoned all the presidents of the neighboring banks, including Stillman and Baker. Once again they obeyed his call, as if mesmerized by his powers of instant decision. He told them that unless they could provide $25 million to lend to the Stock Exchange within the next fifteen minutes, fifty firms would collapse. By the time Morgan had added up the pledges, he knew that he had $2 million more than he needed. His chief emissary announcing this sudden salvation in the Exchange had his coat torn off his back by the relieved brokers mobbing the money post, which provided loans for meeting obligations.

But there was no staunching the financial wounds. Millions bled away in minutes. Three more banks had suspended payments in the afternoon. Morgan felt that he had to break his golden rule of silence to the press. As he left his office early that evening, he turned to the reporters, who were expecting their daily nothing. He spoke slowly and significantly. "If people will keep their money in the banks," he said, "everything will be all right."

It was as simple and true a statement as a commandment from a mountain. Morgan proceeded to a conference at his Library that night with the presidents of the other banks and trust companies. It was a form of psychological warfare. He put them in the East Room with the rare Bibles and medieval illuminated manuscripts to add to their sense of awe and responsibility, while he sat alone in the West Room playing solitaire. A banker would occasionally proceed from the East Room to the West to tell Morgan of some idea. Morgan would not look up from his cards. "No, that will not work," he would say. When the bankers had gone away many times without further comment, his new librarian, the young Belle da Costa Greene with the alluring pug-dog face and lidded green eyes and tiny waist, would ask her silent employer why he did not tell them what to do. She believed in the myth of the great commander as they did. But he answered like Kutuzov: "I don't know what to do myself, but some time, some one will come in with a plan that I know *will* work. And then I will tell them what to do."[12]

A plan emerged. During the Civil War and during previous panics, Clearing House certificates had been issued to serve in lieu of currency. Morgan did not like the idea. He and Stillman and Baker were all cash rich, and the Clearing House certificates would enable their weaker rivals to remain in business. But the device had Stillman's support. And as Vanderlip noted of his chief, Stillman had an eye for the future, as if he were looking into a crystal ball. "Often the proposal that Mr. Stillman uttered quietly was the thing that Mr. Morgan executed; but Stillman was above the struggle, rather than in it."[13] Finally, Morgan agreed to the plan. At least it would work.

Friday was nearly as bad as the day before. There were more bank and trust company failures, bringing up the total in New York and Brooklyn alone to eight. The Trust Company of America and the Lincoln used every device to pay out their clamoring depositors slowly. Many of these had stood in line all night and now met tellers with palsy in their fingers. The Stock Exchange needed more relief. Morgan again allocated rescue loans to his banking associates, but he could not settle for what he wanted. Some bankers even risked his wrath by delivering less than his assessments. He sent over $13 million to the money post of the Exchange, $2 million short of its needs. Business tottered to a close and the brief truce of the weekend, while Morgan was castigating the fainthearted who were still clinging to their last reserves. "You ought to be ashamed of yourself," he told one of them. "What is a reserve for if not to be used in times like these?"[14]

His son-in-law and biographer, usually short on drama, has left one inimitable account of him at the time of his last and greatest appearance in a crisis. Morgan was returning home from the Clearing House to his office:

> With his coat unbuttoned and flying open, a piece of white paper clutched tightly in his right hand, he walked fast down Nassau Street. His flat-topped black derby hat was set firmly down on his head. Between his teeth he held a paper cigar holder in which was one of his long cigars, half smoked. His eyes were fixed straight ahead. He swung his arms as he walked and took no notice of anyone. He did not seem to see the throngs in the street, so intent was his mind on the thing that he was doing. Everyone knew him, and people made way for him, except some who were equally intent on their own affairs; and these he brushed aside. The thing that made his progress different from that of all the other people on the street was that he did not dodge, or walk in and out, or halt or slacken his pace. He simply barged along, as if he had been the only man going down the Nassau Street hill past the Subtreasury. He was the embodiment of power and purpose.[15]

The presidents of the savings banks now met and decided to protect themselves by requiring sixty days' notice from their depositors before funds could be taken out. It cut down the flow of panic money. During the respite of Saturday and Sunday, Morgan and his cohorts took every opportunity to calm the troubled waters. Bishops and rabbis were asked to preach confidence to their congregations: one Brooklyn clergyman prayed for "that magnificent and praiseworthy leader, J. P. Morgan."[16] President Roosevelt was recalled from a hunting trip to claim that credit would be restored and that prosperity lay ahead. Stillman arranged that $8 million in gold should be shipped from London, while Morgan arranged for the shipment of another $3 million in bullion. Further lines of credit were extended to the two battered trust companies. Morgan was so weary by Sunday morning that he even missed morning service at Highland Falls.

By Monday morning, the panic seemed to be contained. Yet like a smoldering forest fire it broke out in another direction. The city of New York was threatened with default and needed $30 million to meet its payrolls and short-term debts. It could only offer 6 percent, while Morgan was lending at 10 percent to the Stock Exchange and some call money had reached the rate of 50 percent. Thomas W. Lamont has recorded the occasion when the mayor and the city officials went cap in hand to Morgan like the burghers of Calais with halters around their necks. They did not approve of his power in the city, but they needed to abase themselves to survive.

Morgan had considered the problem for forty-eight hours. At the meeting in his Library, he discussed the matter for fifteen minutes with the city officials in front of Stillman and Baker and Stetson. Then he picked up a pencil and began to write on his Library paper. After another fifteen minutes he had drafted a rough contract. He passed it to his banking associates and to his attorney. It was satisfactory in outline and substance. This performance of Morgan's was unique, the display of a sort of financial genius — the saving of the city from disgrace under pressure.

"Neither Mr. Morgan nor his banking associates knew then just where the money was coming from for the fulfillment of the contract," Lamont recorded, "but before the next twenty-four hours had passed they had completed their plans, and the city's credit was saved at a time when banking and corporate structures all over the country were falling to the ground." They worked a sleight of hand by which the big banks agreed to take another $30 million worth of Clearing House certificates — a confidence trick by which $30 million more could be put into circulation and lent to the city of New York. It is likely that J. P. Morgan and Company had overstretched its finances by this time. But as a senior Morgan partner, Charles Steele, told Lamont later, Morgan himself "was almost recklessly prodigal of the firm's resources, if he thought the utilization of them could be made to help stem the tide of disaster. He seemed to care not a whit what losses he and his partners might suffer, if only the situation could be saved. And at no time throughout the entire crisis did he harbor any thought other than that the difficulties must, and finally would, certainly be overcome."[17]

The refusal to admit defeat was Morgan's greatest quality. Yet he would not continue to help people who did not help themselves. The run on the two trust companies continued. Their delaying tactic was to dole out money so slowly that sometimes only three customers a day received any cash in the hand. They did not go out to sell their remaining unpledged securities or to raise money internationally; they merely provoked the wrath of the state superintendent of banks, who bluntly told them to pay quicker or shut their doors altogether. "We hadn't any use for their management," Perkins said later, "and knew that they ought to be closed, but we fought to keep them open in order not to have runs on other concerns."[18]

The following Saturday night conference in Morgan's Library finally dealt with the matter of the trust companies. The previous pool contributed by the others had all drained away. Morgan put his ultimatum. Either the other trust companies raised a further $25 million between them, or he would let them all fail. The trust company presidents were put in the West Room, the bankers in the East Room, while Morgan retired to Belle Greene's small librarian's office to puff at his cigars and play his solitaire. One legend insisted that he actually locked everybody inside like cardinals at a conclave until a decision should be reached.

Lamont himself attended the conference as an "experienced errand boy." It would last until quarter to five in the morning. He described the scene:

> A more incongruous meeting place for anxious bankers could hardly be imagined. In one room were lofty, magnificent tapestries hanging on the walls, rare Bibles and illuminated manuscripts of the Middle Ages filling the cases; in another, that collection of the Early Renaissance masters — Castagno, Ghirlandaio, Perugino, to mention only a few — the huge open fire, the door just ajar to the holy of holies where the original manuscripts were guarded. An anxious throng of bankers, too uneasy to sit down or converse at ease, paced up and down the lofty chambers and through the lovely marble hall.[19]

Morgan went on playing cards by himself, letting the place and the hour, anxiety and fatigue, do the work of resolution. Another witness to the occasion, the malicious James Stillman, was now being forced to act as Morgan's lieutenant. Later on he claimed a leading role for himself, saying that Morgan had been unwilling to go on helping the trust companies at all because he said he had done enough and would not waste any more time unless he got what he wanted out of it. Stillman then claimed that he argued patiently with Morgan and the other bankers until dawn, and that he quietly gained the day, "incredibly tactful, incredibly patient."[20]

In hindsight, this may have seemed so to Stillman. But at the time, the last decision was indubitably Morgan's. Without him, many of the trust companies would already have collapsed. And he was prepared to wait until the very waiting itself gave him what he wanted. At dawn, he appeared in the West Room in order to declare he would settle for a simple signature from each banker and each trust company president that his institution would contribute an amount based on its remaining resources and computed by Morgan's experts. In Lamont's words:

> Mr. Morgan waved his hand invitingly towards the paper. "There you are, gentlemen," he said.
>
> The bankers shifted from one foot to another, but no one stepped forward. Mr. Morgan waited a few moments. Then he put his hand on the shoulder of his friend, Edward King, and gently urged him forward. "There's the place, King," he said kindly, but firmly, "and here's the pen," placing a handsome gold pen in Mr. King's fingers. Mr. King signed. The ice was broken. They all signed. Mr. King had been neither more nor less hesitant than the others. It had simply fallen to his lot to lead off when the crucial moment came.[21]

The worst problem of all surfaced at the same time. And then Morgan confused at last his formidable sense of responsibility with his advantage. He used the opportunity to make his political adversary Roosevelt pay for the harm he had done to Morgan in the Northern Securities case. The big brokerage firm of Moore and Schley was in serious difficulties. If it went bankrupt, it would cause a worse panic in the market. Schley also happened to be the brother-in-law of Morgan's friend Baker of the First National Bank. Unfortunately, the firm had been speculating and owed $25 million, a sum impossible to raise at that time. Its chief asset was a majority of the shares of the Tennessee Coal, Iron and Railroad Company, a competitor of United States Steel that had its own enormous iron-ore and coal deposits. The public still had confidence in the steel trust bonds, but not in Tennessee Coal, Iron and Railroad stock. If the bonds of the first could be exchanged for the stock of the second, Moore and Schley could pledge the steel bonds, and Morgan's pet trust would become even stronger. For $45 million of its own paper, it would acquire a major source of raw materials for its products, a reserve worth a billion dollars a few years later.

The problem was the antitrust activities of Theodore Roosevelt. Elbert Gary and Frick took a special night one-car train to Washington to see the President. He and Elihu Root met the two men from the steel trust early next morning. According to Gary's account of the interview, he told Roosevelt that the United States Steel Corporation could acquire a controlling interest in Tennessee Coal, Iron and Railroad at a price in excess of its market value. This would be of great benefit to financial conditions and would save from failure an important business concern. Unless the President objected, the steel trust would buy.

Gary further defended the acquisition by saying that it would still leave the trust with only 60 percent of all American steel production. He did not mention the lucrative raw-material sources of Tennessee Coal, Iron and Railroad. He also said that he was against the steel trust having a monopoly in its lines or increasing its relative capacity. Roosevelt made a decision as quick as Morgan usually did. He replied that while he would not and could not legally make any binding promise or agreement, "from all the circumstances as presented he certainly would not advise against the proposed purchase."[22]

From the White House, Gary telephoned Perkins at the Morgan office block. The good news from Washington was relayed to Morgan himself and to the stock market. The bankers and the brokers became bullish. It appeared that Roosevelt might stop his attacks on the trusts and the wealthy — the cause of the panic in the opinion of Wall Street. Although economic conditions remained difficult for some months to come, the worst was over.

Once the panic had subsided, voices were raised saying that Roosevelt had been deceived by Gary. First, the President had thought that a large trust company would fail, not merely a leading brokerage house. Second, Gary had said that the steel trust had not wanted to buy its rival; but in fact it had exploited the panic to snap up a valuable competitor extremely cheaply. Gary had mentioned no names in his presentation, and the President had thought it just as well not to ask for any in case he might appear to be conniving with the house of Morgan. "It was necessary for me to decide on the instant before the Stock Exchange opened," Roosevelt testified later in 1911, "for the situation in New York was such that any hour might be vital."[23] He had never since doubted for one moment the wisdom of his quick action.

The truth was that the panic of 1907 had frightened him almost as much as the leading financiers. Because of worsening business conditions in August, he had stopped an antitrust suit against Morgan's and Perkins's International Harvester Company. He did not want to aggress against the only man who might be able to quell a panic in New York. Willy-nilly, he had to recognize the stature and importance of the monarch of Wall Street. As William Allen White wrote:

> The panic did menace the security of the nation. It was charged that Roosevelt made terms with J. P. Morgan, the elder. He probably consented to certain consolidations that Morgan was planning, but the gun was in the President's ribs. If he did connive with Morgan, it was because he had to.[24]

With the President disciplined for the time being, Morgan could devote himself to tidying up the pieces after the panic. The crisis had forced the two opposed great groups on Wall Street into an uneasy alliance. Stillman had moved to back Morgan, and Perkins went to see John D. Rockefeller, Jr., with a bold plan. He told Rockefeller that the house of Morgan would put up a final fund of $20 million to bail out the Lincoln and the Trust Company of America if the Rockefellers would match that amount. The knowledge of such a large sum in the trust companies' vaults would end the run on them and the panic. The President of the United States, Perkins added craftily, had already commended Morgan for his wisdom and public spirit. Why did not the elder Rockefeller join with Morgan, win the goodwill of millions of Americans, and make a favorable impression on the President?[25] Perkins knew that the $29 million fine levied on Standard Oil that August by Judge Landis still rankled in the Rockefellers' minds.

The elder Rockefeller would not bite. He would not work with Morgan and curry favor with the President. He would rather be right and rich than patriotic. So Morgan alone went ahead, raised a final $20 million for the two trust companies, put them both under the control of his friends, and absorbed the Tennessee Coal, Iron and Railroad Company in his steel trust. Gold bullion was flowing in from Europe—$10 million worth on the *Lusitania* alone. After many weeks of concentration and effort and lack of sleep, Morgan would begin to relax. Vanderlip recalled one of the final meetings during the crisis. It was in the office of an uptown bank, where Morgan had taken the chair:

> Mr. Morgan's utterances usually came with a force that suggested his words were literally fired from the remarkable, cannon-like cigars that he

> smoked habitually. He was a connoisseur of wines and in tobacco, too, his taste was aware of equally subtle gradations. He smoked only the tobacco of certain favored crop years. It was Havana tobacco, but it was rolled in shapes never sold in any cigar store. Morgan cigars had the form of a Hercules club, bulging thickly at the outer end, and they were absolutely poisonous for all but the most experienced smokers. . . .
>
> On this night, Mr. Morgan was listening as a report was made on the contents of the portfolio of the bank we were considering. That astonishing brain of his would take into itself a welter of facts and then, after consideration, he would speak, and we who listened would know that we were hearing wisdom. Suddenly I saw that the hand holding his cigar had relaxed on the table; his head had sunk forward until his chin was cushioned on his cravat. His breathing had become audible. The weary old man had fallen asleep.
>
> Some one there, with a touch on the arm, silenced the one who was talking; another reached forward and lifted from the relaxed fingers, as one might take a rattle from a baby, the big cigar that was scorching the varnish of the table. Then we sat quietly, saying nothing whatever. One who went for a drink of water walked on tiptoe. The only sound that could be heard was the breathing of Mr. Morgan. It seems to me now that it was a long while before he awakened. When he did consciousness returned abruptly; in a second he was wide awake and our conference was resumed with no reference being made to Mr. Morgan's nap.[26]

So Wall Street now waited on the wise old Morgan, and Morgan proved himself the master of the Street. It was an extraordinary performance and a Pyrrhic victory. Although Morgan had triumphed, the cost had been too great. The panic had finally proved that the financial health of the United States could not be left in the hands of one aged man, however strong, however imperious. What would happen when Morgan was gone? There was nobody to fill his place, nobody to dominate as he did.

Morgan and his partners began talks with Senator Aldrich, which were conducted at a secret conference on Jekyll Island three years later. Their aim was to create in America a system of central government finance and currency control on the European model. The new guard of Henry P. Davison and Frank Vanderlip were the more important members of the conference; they were the hidden hands of Wall Street, which was not meant to be making its own bridle and bit. The Aldrich bill was not passed by Congress, but another version of it was approved by the Woodrow Wilson administration in the year of Morgan's death. The Federal Reserve Act of 1913 was the eventual consequence of President

Jackson's destruction of the Second Bank of the United States at the time of Morgan's birth. This vacuum in the power of Washington over the economy for the length of Morgan's life had allowed him to act as the private warlord of the banking system.

His last victory in 1907 was to make his future role unnecessary. He became the master of the abuses that had allowed him to flourish. As one western newspaper wrote, Morgan stood firm until every speculator had made his way to safety. But his holding of the Street did provoke some reform, particularly in the trust companies, although not enough to stop the worst crash of them all twenty-two years later.

The immediate effect of the panic of 1907 was to bring Morgan's rivals to heel, or at least to some sense of responsibility. Stillman found that there were advantages in an alliance with Morgan, as did Schiff of Kuhn, Loeb and Company. If the Rockefellers stayed away, their prestige and power had suffered badly during the panic, and they chose not to meddle with Morgan in the future. Even Harriman, who had now become America's chief scapegoat, saved the ill-fated Erie Railroad from bankruptcy in April, 1908, by personally advancing it $5.5 million while Morgan was absent in Europe. This prompt action probably prevented another panic during the period of convalescence. The most unregenerate of the great speculators was shaken enough by the events of 1907 to be capable now of maturity.

Unwillingly, Harriman and Stillman and the rest had to recognize the supremacy of Morgan. Until the government could pass legislation to exert more control, the aging Morgan ruled Wall Street and its raiders. A threat of ostracism from him was enough to hold the line. "Where there had once been many principalities," Frederick Lewis Allen wrote in *The Lords of Creation*, "there was now one kingdom, and it was Morgan's."[27]

The President of the United States had to concede that much. He had tried himself to bring Morgan to heel, and he had failed. Yet his complaint against the existence of such people was just. "Our big financiers," Roosevelt said after the panic was over, "are for the most part speculators, which is not true of the European big financiers."[28] Moreover, Roosevelt echoed his countrymen in withdrawing their respect and admiration from "the huge moneyed men to whom money is the be-all and the end-all of existence; to whom the acquisition of untold millions is the supreme goal of life, and who are too often utterly indifferent as to how these millions are obtained."[29]

Morgan did not feel socially responsible for the welfare of the workers or the poor, except when a rector like Rainsford brought him a particular charitable proposition. Making money had been the be-all and the end-all of too much of his existence until his last decade on earth. But the ending of a lifetime spent in the countinghouse seemed to goad him on to the gratifications that his long business hours had often denied him. He pursued women and art as if to deny his age and his looks, as if he would live forever. As he once said to a rival too weak to splurge on a tapestry in Rome, "Always resist everything, Stillman, except temptation!"[30]

15

A Discriminating Collector

> Morgan's inclination ran to the highest beauty, with intelligence. Here, too, he was a discriminating collector. He loved to visit the great, and his importance and tremendous personality made him a welcome visitor; but his greatest pleasure was to be compared to the great art-protecting princes of the Renaissance. It is more than likely that his open contempt for the value of money where art purchases were concerned was somewhat of a pose in the manner of Lorenzo the Magnificent.
>
> — James Henry Duveen (1936)

Like Cyrano de Bererac, Morgan was famous for his nose. More and more, it looked like an overripe pomegranate. In his early life, this affliction made him silent and withdrawn. In his middle life, it made him brusque and aggressive. In his later life, he learned to live with it, commenting that he could not appear in the streets without it. Morgan's nose had become international folklore. As he said himself, "It is part of the American business structure."[1]

In their classic study of English schoolchildren's language, the Opies found that a song was still being sung on playgrounds twenty years ago:

Johnny Morgan played the organ,
Jimmy played the drum,
His sister played the tambourine
Till father smacked her bum.

It was a joke rhyme based on the music-hall comic John Read's song "Johnny Morgan," published in 1877.[2] But by the time it reached the ears of the young Edward Fowles, who became one of the heirs of the Duveen antique business, "Johnny Morgan" had become associated with the actual J. P. Morgan and his most famous feature. The playing children used to sing to the tune of "Coming Through the Rye":

Johnny Morgan's nasal organ
Has a purple hue . . .

The ditty ended:

You could see his nasal organ
Coming through the dye.

When young Fowles met J. P. Morgan for the first time in Uncle Henry Duveen's gallery, he found himself choking on the memory of the playground rhyme as much as at the awful sight of Morgan's nose. He was hardly able to open his mouth and tell the great man that the art dealer was out.[3]

James Henry Duveen's first encounter with the notorious nose was even worse. As his first major transaction on his own, he had bought a set of superb early Kang-He black vases. Morgan had heard of them and had sent for the young dealer, who recorded the meeting in his *Collections and Recollections*:

> I had heard of Morgan's disfigurement, but was not prepared at all for what I saw. No nose in caricature ever assumed such gigantic proportions or presented such appalling excrescences. If I did not gasp, I must have changed color. Morgan noticed this, and his small, piercing eyes transfixed me with a malicious stare. I sensed that he noticed my feelings of pity, and for some seconds which seemed centuries we stood opposite each other without saying a word. I could not utter a sound, and when at last I managed to open my mouth I could only produce a raucous cough. He grunted. Then I produced a large photograph which I had brought.
>
> "This is a picture of the vases about which I wrote you, Mr. Morgan."
>
> He made a vicious grab at the print, glanced at it and rapped out: "How much?"
>
> "Twenty-two thousand pounds."
>
> "Much too dear."
>
> Turning his back on me, he walked away. It was devastatingly final, but I was never more relieved in my life to be in the open air again after that nightmare of an interview. I thought that his obvious unwillingness to consider the vases was a revenge for my pity.

On another occasion, the art expert Wilhelm von Bode was taking his elder daughter around Morgan's collection at Prince's Gate. She had previously been taken by her father to see a Ghirlandaio masterpiece, *Grandfather and Grandson*, in which an angelic small boy nestles lovingly near his repulsive grandfather's disfigured and enormous nose. Morgan himself was showing the von Bodes around, when his own grandson ran into the room and leaped into his arms and kissed him.

"Ghirlandaio, father," Miss von Bode said.

"What's that about Ghirlandaio, miss?" Morgan said, glaring at the girl.

Wilhelm von Bode had to intervene quickly. He claimed that he and his daughter had just been talking about the portrait of Giovanna Tornabuoni, whose young beauty was the subject of another Ghirlandaio masterpiece just acquired by Morgan.[4]

As he aged and grew into his dominance, Morgan learned to use his disfigurement as his most potent weapon. He was overpowering in bulk and height, something that already put businessmen and art dealers in awe of him. But their pity for his nose further weakened them, so that he could easily exploit their feeling with his abrupt demands. The size and the nose were allied with a burning stare from small eyes that blazed like twin laser beams from beneath heavy brows. Morgan's presence was irresistible, and he used it to break down resistance in what he wanted in business, but also in collecting women and art.

If Morgan's first rule was discretion, his second was indiscretion. But in that order. He was notorious for traveling with beautiful women on the *Corsair* or in his private railroad cars while his wife stayed at home. Yet he bought a conspiracy of silence. No reporter dared to name names for fear Morgan might buy his whole newspaper from behind his back. No editor risked printing names in case of a libel suit. And no mistress would speak out and lose her golden goose. Morgan had the power to ensure the privacy enjoyed by his contemporary, Edward, Prince of Wales, in pursuit of the same satisfactions. And like the Prince of Wales, he did not forgive those who broke his rules. When Charles M. Schwab, whom Morgan had just made president of the steel trust, went on a scandalous junket to Monte Carlo, Morgan dressed him down like a bad servant for daring to sully the reputation of a Morgan company, even by association.

"But all I did," Schwab said, "was what you have been doing behind locked doors for years."

"That, sir," Morgan replied, "is what doors are for."

With the double standard of the Victorian gentleman, Morgan put his wife first, as long as she stayed in the home and in her proper place. A neighbor who knew him well said that Morgan was a great gallant, but that few knew of his wife's beauty and charm. One who did was the actress Mary Anderson de Navarro, who found Mrs. Morgan amusing, even about her husband's passion for collecting. "Why," she said, "Pierpont would collect anything from a pyramid to Mary Magdalene's tooth."[5]

Morgan believed absolutely in the purity of the home and partition outside it. The women of his family were hardly ever allowed in the Drexel building. That was a male preserve; in fact, George Perkins was forced to keep his woman secretary across the street. Only when Morgan was beginning to retire was she allowed to occupy a cubbyhole inside the Drexel building, where the old man could not possibly see her. As for the various *Corsairs*, they were understood to be Morgan's pleasure ground, an understanding shared by the wives of the other plutocrats who owned yachts. Mrs. William B. Astor once admitted that she had never set foot on her husband's boat, and then she added: "Dreadful confession from a wife, is it not?"[6]

It was usual at that time. It was better for a wife to hear nothing of her husband's private amusements. Mrs. Morgan was a wife in the proper mold. In later life she disliked the limelight as much as her husband enjoyed it. She often disappointed him by her shyness. She would refuse to wear the Worth gowns he bought her, and she would frequently decline to go with him to great formal occasions. In a way, she could blame herself for his notoriety with other women. She did not choose to compete.

As the *Corsair* sailed north each year up the Atlantic coast, Morgan's morality would follow the latitude. Winter at Jekyll Island was a domestic affair, a time for family matters and after-dinner conversation with other rich men. By the time the *Corsair* had reached Newport for the season, Morgan was already entertaining New York actresses — Lillian Russell was one — on his yacht in between the business conferences. He was notorious there among the great hostesses of Ocean Drive for choosing to stay aboard with his lady friends, only coming ashore to fish at the Graves Point Fishing Club at the cost of five hundred dollars an hour. Knowing his reputation, Mrs. Astor once offered to give a party for Café Society rather than the usual smart Newport set. Who would be there? "Why," she said, "J. P. Morgan and Edith Wharton."

When finally the *Corsair* would sail up to Bar Harbor in Maine, where the Morgan partners shared summer peace with Pulitzer and the Standard Oil men, Morgan would confer with them, distribute hundred-dollar bills to the local bishop, and spend the night at one of two houses on High Street. In each of them an aging actress lived. Because of Morgan's visits, the street was called Rotten Row. A local painter, A. E. Gallatin, was so annoyed at Morgan's buying only antique canvases instead of his modern art that he blew the gaff. "Morgan not only collects old masters," he said, "he also collects old mistresses."[7]

Morgan was faithful over the years to those women whom he knew to be discreet. Before 1900, no names were publicly mentioned with his. But with the death of Queen Victoria and the accession of King Edward VII, whose frequent indiscretions were common knowledge in the closed circles of English society, Morgan became more open about appearing with his favorites. "His *aventures galantes*," according to James Henry Duveen, "partook of the splendor and ostentation of King Solomon. He had various agents in the pursuit of these conquests, just as he had in his pursuit of collections. In fact, one great and noble collector was his boon companion in these adventures, and was said to act as his *ministre de menus plaisirs* (light diversions) in England and France. Morgan's inclination ran to the highest beauty, with intelligence. Here, too, he was a discriminating collector."[8]

Even in America he began to appear with his women in public places, where he could count on lips being sealed. The Philadelphia beauty Mrs. John Markoe, who traveled with him in a private car to the Episcopalian convention of 1907 along with a group of bishops, also accompanied him on his Nile trip of 1912. She was a relation of Dr. James Markoe from the Manhattan General Hospital, who was Morgan's personal physician and in charge of the Lying-In Ward in the hospital, endowed by Morgan for pregnant women. Several doctors there, it was said, married Morgan mistresses passing through, especially as he was known to distribute *dots* of one hundred thousand dollars at each of their marriages.[9] He liked his women to be respectable.

Morgan's other open association was with the popular actress Maxine Elliott. She was a close friend of both Morgan and King Edward VII, whom she captured at Marienbad in the last years of his reign. Her bright beauty and talent were allied to a mind like a ticker tape. Helped by her influential friends, she made enough money to build her own theater in New York. She always denied that Morgan had given her the money for the theater, and her friend Alexander Woollcott confirmed her story in *While Rome Burns*. Certainly Morgan could have given her enough inside information to make her own fortune without having to pay for her services.

Morgan probably met Maxine Elliott through Charles M. Schwab, who was her neighbor and friend. As she worked on the stage in both London and New York, she would join Morgan on transatlantic trips. She once told a friend she had been on the *Corsair* when Morgan met the Kaiser, and that she had driven under the Brandenburg Gate with the German Emperor. She also declared that she had made Morgan remodel his yacht for her because she found his arrangements ridiculous. "He had the cabins on a lower deck where there was no light, and the dining saloon on the upper deck. I had him change the whole thing so we could dine below, where we needed no outside light, and all the sleeping cabins could have proper portholes."[10]

In 1908, when Maxine arrived in New York for the opening of her theater, reporters noticed that Morgan was also traveling on the same steamship from England. She was asked about her friendship with him and his financial interest in her building. For once, he agreed to meet the press to preserve his official reputation. "The only interest I have in Maxine Elliott's theater," he declared, "is that I'd like to get a free ticket on opening night." But he had to pay off the blackmailing *bon viveur* Colonel Mann to keep Maxine's name from being linked with his in *Town Topics*, the leading scandal sheet of the time.[11]

Morgan's discretion and taciturnity, indeed, spread the legend of his conquests. His appreciation of beauty in art was matched by his obvious delight in beauty in people. The young men in his office were always famous for their Anglo-Saxon good looks. And Morgan's penchant for the company of bishops and actresses obviously led to jokes about them and him. Even the divine Sarah Bernhardt came to call on him at his Library; her principal interest was in Morgan himself.[12]

Those who are silent about their sexual adventures usually achieve the greatest credit for them. Morgan's dominance in business was widely believed to make him irresistible to women, despite his age and his nose. Power can be an aphrodisiac, but not to the extent that gossip ascribed it to Morgan. His biographer in 1930, John Winkler, put down the surviving legend about the great man's sexual adventures in veiled, charged prose:

> Let the world tell tales of a luxurious mansion on Forty-sixth Street, just off Fifth Avenue; of parties aboard his yacht; of Lucullan banquets in a private apartment at the Fifth Avenue Hotel where favors to the ladies were bracelets and necklaces of diamond and pearl. Many women knew Morgan as a generous patron. In a way, his very defiance of convention was a protection. . . . His adventures in romance were many and varied. But they were never tainted by open scandal. His women were as loyal, and worshipful as the associates he chose in business.[13]

His taciturnity covered his tracks. He wrote few letters, except to his father when Junius was alive, and these he destroyed. Love letters from him do not exist. If they were written, they were returned or bought back and destroyed. He never felt the need to boast or to confess. Who would wish to be a Don Juan if he could be a Morgan? Except in one case, there is no record of his technique as a lover. And that record was kept in a family beyond even Morgan's control, a family now famous for its many indiscretions.

In 1900 in London, Morgan met the famous Lady Victoria Sackville. The illegitimate daughter of a Spanish dancer and Lionel Sackville-West, she had served as her father's official hostess at the British embassy in Washington at the age of eighteen. Queen Victoria herself had approved of this extraordinary arrangement, and Victoria Sackville-West had been the toast of Washington during the 1880s. She had returned to England to marry her first cousin, Lord Sackville, and to be the chatelaine of the great house of Knole. In later years, she became the mistress of Sir John Murray Scott, the secretary and heir of Sir Richard Wallace, and the man who persuaded Lady Wallace to leave her dead husband's great collection to the nation in 1900 — at least, the pieces he did not remove for himself.

That was the year Lady Victoria met Pierpont Morgan. She was immediately attracted to his power and magnetism, noting that she even liked his gigantic nose. (She was not like the notorious English peeress, mentioned by James Henry Duveen, whose debts of £200,000 were to be paid by Morgan; but after his down payment of £15,000, she had welshed on the bargain with the remark, "I just cannot bear the thought of being kissed by that nose.")[14] In fact, Morgan's ugliness drove him to conquer beautiful women, and his urge to possess drove him to collect them, as if they were illuminated manuscripts or rival railroads. He was constantly on the attack, as Lady Victoria's diary disclosed, and he loved mixing business with pleasure, art with flesh.

She was ready to be courted after 1909, when Sir John Murray Scott had a stroke; he would die within three years, leaving a legacy worth half a million pounds to Lady Victoria. And after 1909, Morgan was ready to court her, after losing Maxine Elliott to King Edward VII at Marienbad. When Lady Victoria met Morgan again, she was pleased to find another wealthy protector, who might take Sir John Murray Scott's place in her life and use his fortune to help keep up Knole. Although Morgan was in his seventies, she was mesmerized by his aura of power. He had bought Gainsborough's *Miss Linley* for £36,000 from the Knole collection, and he invited her to Prince's Gate, apparently to discuss further art deals. Her diary for July 8, 1911, records:

> We sat on a long sofa, yards away from each other! It was most awkward. He asked me what and why we had to sell anything. I said, "Lloyd George's super tax and land tax and the death duties." He answered, "Damn Lloyd George . . . I want to help you. What have you got to get rid of?"
>
> "Tapestries."
>
> "I don't want any tapestries, let me come down to Knole and look around."
>
> "No, Mr. Morgan . . . it is a case of take it or leave it."
>
> He thought for a few moments and said, "Well, I'll take your tapestries to help you. How much do you want for them?"

They soon agreed on a price of £65,000. On the way to the door, Morgan folded Lady Victoria in his arms, saying, "I hope you don't mind." She was utterly astonished at such a sudden approach. Twelve days later, he came to Knole and was delighted at what he had agreed to buy, particularly a tapestry called *The Seven Deadly Sins.* Ten days after that, he came to dinner at Knole. The diary reads:

> I had a long talk with him in the garden. He told me many of the bothers of being very rich, but the great thing to have was personality, which he has to an infinite degree. He has a wonderful personality, I have not met anyone as attractive . . . he is full of life and energy; a wonderful man.

After that, Lady Victoria went regularly to Prince's Gate. She had to see him hurriedly between business meetings, but she was fascinated by watching him decide what to do about his worldwide financial empire. When he left England that autumn, she waited for his return in May of 1912 on his way to Egypt. The diary for May 20 reads:

> I called on busy Mr. Morgan at Prince's Gate. He was arranging a loan with ten men, for China, but he gave me half an hour all the same. He came in like a whirlwind and crushed me, saying he had longed for this moment, that he had told nobody of his return, but wanted to see me at once. . . . I can think of nothing else. That man has such marvellous personality and attraction for me.

She wrote this despite a quarrel over the Gainsborough portrait, *Miss Linley*, which she could not bear to see hanging in Prince's Gate and not at Knole. She offered to buy it back from him, when she had the money. He refused to part with it at any price. She accused him of liking *Miss Linley* better than her, but he replied

> that I was the only woman he loved and would never change. He is very careful not to get me talked about and told me so, and said it would be too dangerous to come to America this winter. He keeps on saying that there is nothing better in the world than the affection he has for me. How can he find time to come as he does, beats me, as I know he is so busy. I won't talk about MISS LINLEY or money with him; I hate it. Our friendship must be free from any sordid motive.

Two days later, Morgan visited Lady Victoria alone. He told her that he had cared for her ever since he had met her, but had not dared tell her. He confessed how much he had been in love on the day when he had talked to her in the garden at Knole. He swore he would always love Lady Victoria, even if she fell ill or became ugly.[15] And so he left her for his last voyage to Egypt and his death the following March in Rome. At seventy-four, he was behaving like the impractical, romantic young man he had been at the time of his marriage to Mimi Sturges, sweeping an experienced and sophisticated peeress of fifty off her feet as if she were a young girl.

His death was timely for his private love of her. She was in the storm center of a great scandal in 1913, reported everywhere. The heirs of Sir John Murray Scott sued her for undue influence over her benefactor and for the return of the half-million-pound legacy. She was cross-examined for two days by F. E. Smith, the most brilliant barrister of his time; but she was one of the few witnesses who ever defeated him. She persisted in treating him as if he were a cad whom she had to tell off at dinner. She did her best to embarrass him socially, and she succeeded. She won the case and kept the legacy for Knole. But Morgan would have hated the notoriety.

This last late love affair of Pierpont Morgan is the only one on record. It showed his latent romanticism and his aggression. He liked to use his power, to crush and dominate the women in his life. After his long repression by his father and by Victorian morality, he was greedy for the experiences he had missed in his young manhood and long apprenticeship. With the urbane manners of Edwardian society, whereby the rich and powerful were allowed their clandestine liaisons with each other, Morgan came out of the display cabinet, but not as far as the press. Arrogant as always, he thought he was immune from publicity, because he had the power to suppress it. And except for Lady Sackville's diary, he was successful. But even with such elaborate caution, no man can hide everything forever.

Morgan's frantic acquisition of what was probably the greatest collection made since Lord Hertford and Sir Richard Wallace's was done openly and overseas. He used the profits of his investment banks in New York and London and Paris to buy up works of art on an unprecedented scale for Edwardian times. As he rarely bothered to distinguish between the private and the public, the books of his firms were said not always to balance at the year's end because of his personal extravagance. His lavishness was imitated by the Duveen brothers, who needed Morgan bank guarantees for millions of dollars to acquire large collections; he himself used to pledge his credit at his banks for payment a year ahead to cover the millions of dollars he spent with the dealers on every European trip. In April and May of 1906 alone, he contracted to pay three-quarters of a million dollars in Paris on *objets d'art*, which he supplemented by buying heavily in Rome and London during the summer. When his son-in-law asked him why he was spending so much and storing it all in Prince's Gate, he replied that he was making trouble for his executors.

He was fondest of his collection of miniatures, more than two hundred exquisite pieces by Holbein and the Hilliards and the Coopers and lesser artists. His executors did, indeed, have to sell them during the Great Depression because he left behind so many treasures and so little cash. He did, though, ensure in one way the permanence of his collections. He had learned from the Duveens the elegant flattery of the private catalogue, and he hired the English expert Dr. George C. Williamson to prepare eight sumptuous catalogues of the wide varieties of his hoard. Only twenty copies of each were ever printed, and of the first two, one was sent to the King of England and the other to the President of the United States. The sixth of the catalogues comprised his collection of rare watches and was so thickly encrusted with gold and silver leaf that it appeared as rich as the watches themselves. It lay beside Morgan's bed during his dying in Rome. It was, he declared, the most beautiful book he had ever seen.

He seemed to have a premonition that, however fast he garnered beautiful things, they would not survive his passing. It was a race against death to accumulate all the best property for sale in the world. When Dr. Williamson was asked to start on the catalogues without any limit on expense, Morgan hesitated to give his reasons for commissioning the work. "If anything happens to the originals," he said and paused — "if they should ever be dispersed, students can work as though they had the originals in front of them."

Morgan's lust for the best in the fastest time sometimes created forgeries to meet his demand. James Henry Duveen told the story of a rock-crystal cross that was manufactured because Morgan was searching for a perfect example. "Strategy, tact, intrigue and methods far worse came into play to satisfy the commands of this Croesus."[16] The original cross of the sixteenth century was in ebony and was re-created in crystal with all its authentic gold and enamel trappings. It was simply too beautiful to be true, and when Dr. Williamson was asked to check its authenticity, he had to refuse a bribe and report back to the disappointed Morgan.

Uncle Henry's nephew Joseph, later Lord Duveen of Millbank, became the chief exporter of the treasures of Europe for the pleasures of America. While Morgan was sporadic and voracious on his annual pirate expeditions, Joseph Duveen constructed a perfect reproduction of Louis XV's Ministry of Marine on Fifth Avenue as a display palace for his wares. The very rich did not have to take a liner across the ocean anymore to see the more expensive and available Gothic tapestries and Renaissance altarpieces and Georgian portraits of English countesses. If Morgan was the supreme raider, Joseph Duveen was the prime merchant of the irreplaceable. With its emigrants, Europe was also exporting its heritage to educate them in what they had lost.

And all for money. As Joseph Duveen used to say, "When you pay high for the priceless, you're getting it cheap."[17] But the European countries were beginning to count the cost of losing their patrimony. When there was a public outcry against his looting, Morgan soothed international feelings by lending his major pictures to the Victoria and Albert Museum while they were in London, presenting to the Louvre a bust of Saint Martin and two of forty-three exquisite Byzantine enamels he was exporting from France, and returning to the Italian government a superb medieval papal vestment that he had not known was stolen from the cathedral at Ascoli.

Joseph Duveen wore no mask of discretion over his urge for acquisition. He was even prepared to flout the Kaiser to make a good investment. When the most distinguished private collection in Germany came up for sale, he journeyed to see Oscar Hainauer's widow and made her an offer three times the size of that made by Dr. von Bode, who wanted the collection for his imperial master. The angry Kaiser first asked the chancellor to issue a decree blocking the export of works of art, but von

Bode pointed out that the German museums were still buying treasures from abroad. If one country prevented the export of some of its masterpieces, it might provoke retaliation elsewhere and end the free trade in art works. The Kaiser gave way, and the Duveens and Morgan were allowed to plunder unrestricted in Europe, although not by the United States Customs.

Because of the revenue service at home, Morgan had kept the bulk of his collection in his twin adjoining houses at Prince's Gate. The display was so magnificent that even King Edward VII came to see it. He walked around, noting that many of the pictures acquired by Morgan used to hang in the country houses of his friends. On one visit, he criticized Morgan's taste, asking him why he had hung Lawrence's portrait of Nellie Farren, the Countess of Derby, in a room with a low ceiling. "Because I like it there, sir," Morgan replied, putting the King on the same level of familiar equality as he had put the Kaiser.[18]

If the plundering of Europe by Morgan and the Duveens helped to educate future generations of Americans, it irritated and diminished the Old World cultures. Lord Duveen would end by endowing the Tate Gallery magnificently, but as Osbert Sitwell pointed out, he had left few Georgian pictures to hang in the empty gallery he had endowed. Morgan himself might have had to leave the bulk of his collections on loan in English museums if he had not managed to help change the revenue laws of his home country. As early as 1903, he had consulted with the Secretary of the Treasury about bringing his treasure trove back to America for exhibition at the Metropolitan Museum — so long as there were no customs duties to be paid. Six years later a law was passed that works of art more than twenty years old could be imported into America without paying duty; the law was later changed to fifty years and then abolished.

This was the signal for the transfer of the Morgan hoard across the Atlantic; but it also provoked an attack by the customs on the Duveens, who had royally ignored their regulations. Ironically, Uncle Henry had been an adviser to the New York Customs about how much tax to put on his rivals' imports; he had exaggerated their value and underestimated the worth of his own antiques; now he was betrayed by a disaffected bookkeeper. The customs demanded $10 million from the Duveens and eventually settled for $1.4 million.

Stretched as always by their vast purchases, the Duveens did not have the money; but Morgan sent for Uncle Henry's lawyer and showed his usual benevolent autocracy. "Get him off," he ordered, "get him off."

When told how much it would cost to get him off, Morgan arranged for a check for the full fine to be paid over immediately by the First National Bank.[19]

An inspired quirk of the law had made legal what the Duveens had anticipated. Morgan himself had flouted the law when it had blocked his desires. But as he wished to display his collections at the Metropolitan Museum and in the Pierpont Morgan Library, he had to wait for his opportunity. And after 1909, the full extent of his magnificence and munificence slowly went on display. Stimulated by the threat of the rising death duties in England, Morgan could satisfy his final ambitions: the creation in New York of "a greater museum than anyone at that time dreamed it was possible to realize, and a library which would go down in history as comparing favorably to the Vatican, the Laurentian Library in Florence, and the most sumptuous assemblages of rare books in Paris, London, and Vienna."[20]

The catalogues of his many collections cannot be discussed within the scope of this book except as illustrations of the extraordinary avidity and quality of his tastes. The greater part of the four thousand items eventually donated to the Metropolitan Museum remain on display in the permanent collection, and any visitor to the Pierpont Morgan Library may still gauge the sense of grandeur and hierarchy that lay behind his passion for collecting. He preferred objects that derived historically from an ecclesiastical or royal or aristocratic period, beautiful things that were invested with the ordered values of the ages in which Morgan would liked to have ruled as a pope in Rome, a Burgundian duke, a Florentine prince or a belted earl in the House of Lords.

His particular gift as a collector was to combine the comfortable with the spectacular. The two great rooms of his Library to east and west could be inhabited as well as appreciated. His friend Bishop Lawrence wrote the most accurate evaluation of his style of life in Prince's Gate, where his mother's china pug-dogs were still displayed near the Sèvres and the Limoges, the Turners and the Romneys.

> I doubt if any private citizen ever lived in as comfortable splendor as did Mr. Morgan. Some may have had more comfort, others more splendor, but his was splendor with comfort. It is a question open to debate whether he had a right to live in this way.
>
> I never knew a man to whom in expenditure the question of dollars was of less interest nor one who so naturally surrounded himself with all that was richest, most convenient and artistic. He reached the climax of his abilities just as the financial world was flowing into great masses, and

> working in the midst of this, masses of wealth flowed towards him. They came quickly and increasingly. His mind was intensely occupied with many things. He did not have time nor probably interest to enter into the philosophy of the use of wealth. . . . With a good conscience, he followed the traditions of his forebears and the habits of the best citizens.[21]

Bishop Lawrence explained the catholicity of Morgan's styles of collection in terms of passion and surfeit. Once there were no more samples of the best of a particular genre to be acquired, Morgan gave up the chase to begin the pursuit of another variety. On one occasion he told his sister Mary Morgan Burns, "I have done with Greek antiquities; I am at the Egyptian." He wanted the more elegant examples of everything for sale; but once he had them, he forayed in another period with the order and splendor that suited his Episcopal creed.

After he had become the president of the Metropolitan Museum in 1904, Morgan's ambition was not only for the enrichment of his monumental Library, but also for the ennoblement and education of the citizens of New York through their leading display case of antiquities. His problem was that he tried to run the museum like a fiefdom, and that the other trustees and even the curators were not prepared to act as villeins. As the Great Gatsby discovered, Americans were occasionally willing to be serfs, but were always obstinate about being peasants. Although Morgan's imperiousness usually carried the day, he could be confronted from time to time, if never confounded.

Every triumph seems to provoke a chosen enemy, and Europe's riposte to Morgan's splendid piracies was to send over the aesthete Roger Fry. Beloved by Virginia Woolf, Fry was a precious, vain and modish art critic, desperate to keep afloat his *Burlington Magazine* in London. His reputation as an expert was almost as great as Bernard Berenson's, and he cost less; he did not demand a 25 percent sales commission from the Duveens for authenticating Italian works of art. Fry knew of the boom in old masters across the Atlantic and hoped to fleece the American millionaires without compromising his disapproval of them. When Morgan asked him to come to New York in 1905 to act as second-in-command to Sir Purdon Clarke at the Metropolitan Museum, he jumped at the chance.

On his arrival in New York, he made an immediate display of his expertise. He found Morgan's Chinese ceramics collection marvelous, but the pictures at the Metropolitan a nightmare. "The blatant forgeries done by any hack Royal Institute man that Agnew could lay hands on are enough to make you stagger," he wrote back to his wife, "and all these things have been accepted without a murmur."

Fry was summoned by Morgan onto his private railroad car to go to Washington and visit the President. Like von Bode's daughter, Fry compared Morgan's appearance to Ghirlandaio's portrait of the disfigured grandfather with the lovely small boy. "He behaves not as a host," Fry commented, "but exactly as a crowned head and everyone else behaves accordingly." Morgan joked that the Englishman would become an American, which Fry did not accept. His attitude toward Morgan was both damning and fawning. He noted that the financier's huge cigar was called the Regalia de Morgan, and that the whole thing was "regal and yet how infinitely provincial." Morgan overwhelmed Fry with a largesse of promises, backing for the *Burlington Magazine* and a free hand for purchases for the Metropolitan Museum. Fry felt

> like a courtier who has at last got an audience, and, as though, for a few minutes I wielded absolute power. I think I behaved tactfully and indeed why should I not be able to manage, for they've not got anything but money to intimidate you with. There's precious little distinction or cachet about the whole lot, so one ought to be able to hold one's own. Really, he strikes me as a big man all the same and too big in his ambitions to be low or mean or go back on his word.

In this preliminary euphoria, Fry saw himself as the arbiter of the immense art boom taking place in America. He was exhilarated by the bigness of the job and his own confidence in the future. Then he fell into the trap of greed that Morgan's luxurious style spread as a lure about him. Fry tried to renegotiate his proposed salary, increasing it by half. Morgan became furious with him because, in Fry's words, "he had made up his mind that things were to be just as he'd said and that no one could dispute his dictates." He was running the Metropolitan Museum as he ran the board of any of his reorganized companies. He tried to break Fry's resistance by withdrawing his offer of help for the *Burlington Magazine*. In writing home, Fry complimented himself on his own courage:

> Above all, I don't regret that I stood up to Morgan. If I hadn't, my postition here would have been intolerable. He's not quite a man; he's a sort of financial steam-engine and I should have been in the position of watching the cranks work and dancing attendance. I wanted if we came to be in a position of complete independence, able to help him by advice without looking to him for any returns. But he likes to be in a position of being surrounded by people he has in his power to make or unmake. . . . He's much too much a God Almighty.[22]

Fry's letter was a little disingenuous. Morgan was the power behind the rapid rise of the Metropolitan Museum, and as long as he was alive, he would interfere with its salaried officers. There was no question of independence in those jobs. But a kind of compromise was effected. Morgan gave Fry some money for the *Burlington Magazine* and retained him as a European adviser and curator of paintings for the Metropolitan. Fry returned to London, where his presence on the Morgan payroll made him even more vitriolic against his benefactor. He not only bit the hand that fed him, but asserted his master was blind.

Fry now claimed that Morgan did not need anything but flattery; he did not wish to listen to what art critics said; he wished them to confirm his personal judgments. "All he wants experts for is to give him a sense of his own wonderful sagacity."[23] Morgan, in Fry's view, was too swollen with pride and with his own power to allow other people their rights. Even his artistic choices were finally damned by Fry with the jibe "a crude historical imagination was the only flaw in his otherwise perfect insensibility toward art."[24]

It was the final flutter of the butterfly crushed by the buffalo, not the sneer of the aesthete condemning the Philistine. Morgan had a long experience as a ferocious collector with an eye for the good work and the main chance. "*Entre nous* he's a brigand like all these great businessmen," Fry complained to his wife. "Business is warfare is their acknowledged motto, so one has to be pretty sharp." That is what Fry particularly hated: Morgan's success in getting what he wanted in art as well as business. Yet Fry failed to judge himself for doing in New York what he affected to despise in others. "The money pours in here like anything," he wrote home. "I charge £20 for an opinion on a picture and have already had to give it on quite a lot."[25]

Despite his sniping, Fry followed as meekly as a towed boat in the wake of Morgan's plundering trips to Europe. He agreed with the financier's decision not to purchase a Degas, possibly *Le Viol*, because its subject might offend the "Comstockians" of New York despite its beauty; in his early days, Morgan had supported the Society for the Suppression of Vice, which had allowed Comstock to impose his prudery on the city. Fry also complained to his wife that Morgan would not help the Metropolitan Museum acquire anything that did not redound to his glory. Finally, after four years of lip service, he lost his post over a superb Fra Angelico *Virgin and Child* from the collection of Leopold, King of the Belgians. Fry had reserved it for the museum. A few days later, Morgan himself saw the picture in Paris and bought it for his private collection. With the occasional bravery of the man who despises himself for what he is doing, Fry decided to write to Morgan, telling him that the French art dealer had sold the Fra Angelico only because he believed that Morgan was completing the purchase that Fry had made on behalf of the museum.

The letter infuriated Morgan, who called it the most remarkable letter he had ever received.[26] He made his anger known in the museum, which terminated Fry's contract with six months' notice. He would not tolerate any examination of the nice line he trod between being a private collector and a public benefactor. He wanted to enjoy a work of art himself before it might hang as a Morgan loan or gift in the museum so largely developed through his support.

Morgan's indulgence of his tastes in women and art, and his ruthless pursuit of the most desirable, were part of a grand style that he felt was his earned due. He would have to account to God in the end, but he usually felt secure enough to be able to balance those accounts, all in all. His was the semidivine right of the Edwardian gentleman to take what he pleased to the glory of the senses and with the connivance of his conscience.

At a dinner party one evening at Prince's Gate, an English lady turned to Morgan's friend Bishop Lawrence, saying how interesting the collections were in Morgan's house. "My dear madam," the bishop replied, "the most interesting thing in this house is the host." He was right, and his reasons for saying so explained the admiration of the few people who ever pierced the financier's armor of arrogance, which so repelled Roger Fry. While staying at Prince's Gate, the bishop had cause every day to marvel at some characteristic in the titan at home.

> He was in some ways as simple as a child, most emotional, most bashful, masterful, courageous: a genius in his instinct for things beautiful; with a brain that drove him ceaselessly on in his search for beauty and his desire to acquire the best. His dominant characteristic was his intuition of truth: his eye and mind seemed to pierce and consume shams and lies.[27]

So searching in exposing the truth of others, Morgan hid his own. He was two things to all men: admirable to the few people who knew him, dreadful to the masses who did not. Solitaire was his usual card game, and his silences explained nothing.

16

Going Down and Going Up

Another story James Stillman told himself, concerned a visit he paid his friend in London. Having heard that Morgan had arrived in England unaccompanied by any member of his family, he went around one hot June morning to find his friend alone eating strawberries in the garden. The two had some talk and then a pause fell, and Morgan asked:

"What brought you here to see me, Stillman?"

"Oh," said the other slowly, in that quiet way of his — "I thought you might be lonely! Whereat," the narrator continued, "Morgan jumped up from the table and ran around and kissed me on the cheek! I was very much amused. We ate up all the rest of the strawberries!"

— James Stillman to Anna Burr (about 1912)

As the old magnates of American finance declined toward their dying, they closed ranks, forgave one another, and groomed their successors. Harriman even sent for Morgan in the last fortnight of his life. All the trains on the Erie Railroad would put off passengers by request at Harriman's flag stop at Arden as they would at Morgan's daughter's flag stop at Sterlington, the other side of the smart resort of Tuxedo. Morgan descended from the train at Arden and went to see his ailing rival in his house on top of the mountain. Harriman was lying in a lounging chair, wrapped in a blanket as if he were on an ocean voyage. He said he wanted to settle some things with Morgan. The two old men talked of their differences. Morgan said that he understood all perfectly and prayed for Harriman's recovery: everything was forgiven and forgotten.[1] Then he left to have the next train flagged down at Arden and to go back to New York.

James Stillman also gave up his long rivalry with Morgan and drew close to him. The lesson of the panic of 1907 was evident. Combine or perish. It was stupid for the Rockefeller interests to fight with the Morgan interests when the temper of the time was working against all trusts and large accumulations of money power. Stillman was now imitating Morgan and visiting Europe for the greater part of every year, leaving his banking decisions more and more to Vanderlip as Morgan was leaving his to his son and Davison. Only Baker still held present sway over the First National Bank, filling Morgan's place during his long absences as the new Sphinx of Wall Street.

"If anything happens to me," Morgan had told Baker as he sailed away after settling the panic, "I want you to know that my association with you has been one of the most satisfactory parts of my life."[2]

After Harriman's death, there was much to be done in consolidating the financial triumvirate of the three surviving old magnates. Morgan and Baker bought up Harriman's controlling interest in the huge Guaranty Trust Company and his holdings in the Mutual Life Insurance Company. Morgan also bought from Ryan, the streetcar tycoon, control over the scandal-ridden Equitable Life. This gave the house of Morgan the power over the larger trust or insurance companies of New York, which were soon to swallow up six lesser trust companies. Stillman and the National City Bank were given their piece of Mutual Life and their place in the gigantic combination in order to assure their cooperation. As Morgan telegraphed from London to Stillman in Paris in June, 1910, he was delighted to be sailing back with him on the *Adriatic*, "for from present indications we shall need each other over there."[3]

The truce between the previous rivals was such that Morgan bought stock in Stillman's National City Bank and his son Jack became a director of that organization. The cooperation and proliferation of harmonious interests spread. Forbidden by the comptroller of the Treasury from holding stock in other banks, both Baker's and Stillman's banks set up affiliates to avoid the ban. The device was, in the words of Frederick Lewis Allen, a masterpiece of legal humor, also "a body-blow at the principle of disinterested commercial banking; for although of course the affiliate did not directly involve the funds of the depositors in its various ventures, inevitably its existence invited bank officials to serve two masters."[4]

So the closing ranks of the old magnates seemed to create a money trust in New York. By the time the Pujo Committee met in 1912, the triumvirate would control or influence nine major banks or trust companies with assets of a $1.5 billion: the First National, the National City, the Chase National and the National Bank of Commerce, along with the Guaranty, Astor, Liberty and Banker's Trust companies, and the Farmers' Loan and Trust. It was the last accord of the dying chiefs, mellowing with age and handing over peace pipes to their heirs rather than tomahawks.

The newer men like Vanderlip and Davison did not have to struggle for mastery over the great financial machine. Their work, as John Moody wrote, was to perfect it and keep it well oiled; consequently, a less spectacular season set in on Wall Street.[5] The Morgan partners could rise above the rough and tumble of the old days and polish the image of the firm until it shone with a deep golden glow like the reliquaries in the Morgan Library. Without a hint of irony, Thomas Lamont told the story of how Morgan invited him in 1910 to leave Baker's bank and join the Morgan firm. Morgan told the young banker that he had already settled the matter with Baker. "Then, not given to the practice of uttering moral sentiments aloud, he turned and twisted in his seat a moment.

" 'You know, Lamont,' he said, 'I want my business done up there,' holding his hand high over his head, 'not down there,' pointing to the floor."[6]

Such a new-minted image of piety had its disadvantages, and so did Morgan's reputation as the savior from the panic of 1907. Good business on earth was not the easy way to make one's peace with heaven. Soon after Lamont arrived to join Davison as a partner, he found himself part of a rescue operation ordered by the grand old senior partner for the sake of salvation rather than profit. Andrew Carnegie, retired to his castle in his native Scotland, had injudiciously allowed a new trust company to bear his name; it was, as wits said, conceived in sin and born in iniquity.[7] It borrowed heavily from two small institutions, the Twelfth and the Nineteenth Ward Banks with thirty thousand small depositors between them. As the Carnegie Trust plunged into insolvency, it threatened to drag down the small banks with it. A run began on them. Morgan was telephoned in his Library and listened to the bad situation of the banks.

"What is the character of them?" he asked.

"Mostly East-siders, working people, small tradesmen, dressmakers, persons whose little all is on deposit."

"Well," Morgan replied," some way *must* be found to help these poor people. We mustn't let them lose all they have in the world. Suppose that, at worst, we were to gurantee the payment of these deposits in full. You say the total is only $6,000,000. That means that the firm can't lose more than $6,000,000, doesn't it?"

Morgan may have treated the possible loss lightly over the telephone, but he did not mean it. He meant for Davison and the other partners to work day and night to lessen the damage. It seemed to them that Morgan's new righteousness had allowed some people to think that his firm's main business was to save lost banking souls. After the usual vilification in the press that the house of Morgan was gobbling up more banks, the partners managed to check the run and come out with a loss of $190,000 and hundreds of hours of their time. Morgan grandly put the burden on Davison's shoulders.

"Whatever you think is right," he said to Davison, "I will approve, but, whatever happens, don't let those poor people lose their money."[8]

The new image of the firm led to a rift with the tarnished George Perkins, who was asked to leave by the end of 1910.[9] On three occasions while he was abroad, Morgan took offense at what Perkins was doing in his name at home. Perkins had authorized the sale of $20 million worth of U.S. Steel bonds to a Morgan enemy; he had contradicted the old man's orders about the Studebaker Company; and he had made a deal with the Goodrich rubber company which Morgan refused to back. Perkins was also running a private fund within the house of Morgan for his friends; the capital value of the invested money was increased four times within five years. Furthermore, Perkins was growing closer and closer to Morgan's adversary Theodore Roosevelt, whom Morgan had never quite forgiven for the antitrust cases. On hearing that the former President was shooting big game in Africa, Morgan said, "I hope the first lion he meets does his duty."

Joseph Pulitzer, always looking for a muckraking story, was unable to find one on the new Morgan partners. On March 8, 1911, he instructed the editor of the *World* to dig into the matter. Why had there been so many partners since Junius Morgan had died? Coster, Bacon, Fabbri, Burns and Perkins were all dead or gone. "Morgan has had bad luck in his partners either dying or making a fortune so quickly that they retire. He is always hunting for partners." To Pulitzer, J. P. Morgan and Company was a government and a machine like Tammany, but one that used up its bosses at a dreadful rate. In fact, Pulitzer even wanted Morgan to spend twenty-four hours in jail to prove to the country that the rich could also suffer under the law.[10]

Pulitzer never got his story because there was not much of a story to get. All was hidden in 1911 under the cover of cooperation, truce and no recrimination. The fighting had moved from Wall Street to the temporary Morgan offices, where the partners were huddling and waiting for the new pink-marble Morgan building to rise on the rubble of the old Drexel one. There was a disagreement between the Stillman group and the Morgan–Baker group, but nobody heard of it until the later memoirs were published. Morgan, indeed, was now displaying such magnanimity that he was capable of taking the other side against his own. When Vanderlip became worried that the house of Morgan was inflating the National

Bank of Commerce into a greater organization than his and Stillman's National City Bank, he visited the old man in his Library to complain about the actions of the Morgan partners.

"You should trust me to do what is right," Morgan told him with his new Biblical vocabulary. "I would cut off my right hand before I would injure you or Mr. Stillman."

When there was later a question of Kuhn, Loeb and Company's coming into the syndicate behind the growth of the National Bank of Commerce, Vanderlip protested and was supported by Morgan against his own son and Davison and Baker.

"I am ready to put my arms around you," Morgan impulsively told Vanderlip, "for the stand you are taking about Kuhn, Loeb."

He then persuaded his partners and friends to drop their plan and support the preeminence of the National City Bank, for so long their opponent. As Vanderlip recorded:

> Never did a voice so gruff sound as sweet to me. I knew in that moment the full flavor of victory. Mr. Morgan was on my side! I grew to love him then and there. He was a great gentleman. What he thought was fair as between friends was the course you could know he would follow. Nevertheless, he was in his own soul, in his ego, a king; royalty. There were royal prerogatives and he knew how to exercise them. I do not mean to suggest that he surrendered; it simply happened that when he found that something in which he had acquiesced was displeasing to friends, he changed his mind and did it heartily.[11]

The new magnanimity of Morgan was not only his careful diplomacy in the cause of harmony. Old age seemed to be breaking through the crust of his arrogance. The sensitive and romantic nature inherited from his Pierpont ancestors and shown in his first marriage to Mimi Sturges was displayed more and more in his dealings with other men and women. His family had almost exclusively known of his softer side, his grandchildren adoring him for his love and concern, his daughters relying on his support and generosity. Now his son Jack was being ridden only half as hard as his father had been ridden by Junius Morgan. Once the old man even said that he thought his Harvard-trained and sophisticated son would be more effective than himself in the changing times.

The metamorphosis in Morgan's character in his old age was noticed even by his acquaintances. Morgan had grown close to William Laffan, the proprietor of the New York *Sun* and the coauthor of the Morgan catalogue on Oriental ceramics. Laffan was also a trustee of the Metropolitan Museum and a pioneer of its department of Egyptian antiquities, encouraging Morgan to sponsor extensive archaeological diggings and spending Morgan's money for the museum at a million dollars a time. To him, Morgan was "a whale of a man," and on his death in 1909, Laffan's trusted editor at the *Sun*, Edward Mitchell, came to know Morgan better and wrote of him in his two guises. On first impression:

> Mr. Morgan was dynamic both in intelligence and in will. . . . The boldest man was likely to become timid under his piercing gaze. The most impudent or recalcitrant were ground to humility as he chewed truculently at his huge black cigar. The lesser monarchs of finance, of insurance, of transportation, of individual enterprise, each in his own domain haughty as Lucifier, were glad to stand in the corridor waiting their turns like applicants for minor clerkships in the anteroom of a department official, while he sat at his desk in his library room within, looking hastily through the pile of newly bound volumes which the binder had sent for his inspection, giving a three-seconds glance at some treasure of printed or manuscript literature which was to go instanter to the shelf or safe in that incomparable storehouse, probably never to be seen again by the eyes then contemplating the acquisition. It was his possession now and Mr Morgan was pleased.

Yet once Mitchell knew more of Morgan, he had wholly to re-create his ideas of the old man. He found a courtesy in him that approached amiability, and a regard for others in matters big and small as genuine as his passion for the possession of a Caxton or a Ghirlandaio, and "a magnanimity that could either oversee or overlook." In conclusion:

> Mr. Morgan would have paid half a million of dollars to add Dido's brooch to his collection, if satisfied of the genuineness of the object. At the same time there was in his inmost heart the tender kindness that would have impelled him, as I verily believe, to give away his Ur-Engur to a loved child, if he was convinced that the loved child really wanted Ur-Engur for a plaything.[12]

Ur-Engur was the oldest inscribed effigy yet known in the world, and one of Morgan's more cherished possessions. His son-in-law confirmed his generous streak, saying that when Morgan had acquired a collection of jewels or bibelots, and one of them was admired by a relative or a friend, he was apt to say, "If you like it, keep it."[13] Though most of his wealthy friends like Baker became richer than he was because they never gave much away, Morgan was the exception to the mercenary golden rule: The rich have riches because they keep them.

Morgan's sentimentality and generosity remained hidden to most people, who only saw the image of a huge portly plutocrat with a grotesque nose, dressed in an aristocratic velvet-collared overcoat and a silk hat so large that it would have fallen onto the shoulders of a man whose head was of average size. He would also wear an old-fashioned wing collar with an ascot tie and a gold watch chain stretching across his white waistcoat, while his Chinese imperial Pekinese Chun would yap by his side. He had given up the breeding of his prize collies from Cragston in 1907 when they failed for the first time to win first prize in the Westminster Kennel Club Show at Madison Square Garden, just as he gave up breeding prize Guernsey cows when the herd was decimated by tuberculosis and could no longer walk off with the awards from the state fairs. He hated to lose in public.

By his habitual refusal to speak to reporters and his open lust for acquisition, he had made his own false image as the secretive center of a vast money conspiracy. In point of fact, he was so mobbed with demands for charity or for business rescue deals that his best defenses were his truculence, his absence and his silence. Unlike most other multimillionaires, he did not develop a retinue or a foundation to give away his wealth through expert advice. He had the confidence of his own choices in art and charity.

A leading concern of his was to commemorate his father, who had certainly endowed him with his heritage and talents. Before committing himself to his Library and the Metropolitan Museum, Morgan had developed the Wadsworth Atheneum in Hartford. When its new building was completed, he donated works of art to the Connecticut museum, above all Benjamin West's *The Raising of Lazarus*, which had hung for many years in Winchester Cathedral in England. Because Junius Morgan had also been a merchant in Boston, Pierpont gave a million dollars to the Harvard Medical School for the construction of three new buildings in the name of his father. When they were finished, he went to Boston to stay with Bishop Lawrence and inspect what had been done. He only gave them a glance and then walked up to the plaque to Junius Morgan. He read the simple inscription, wet his thumb, rubbed it on the stone, and said, "I think that grain is fine enough. Now, let's go back." When he heard that night that he had acquired all the Caxtons from the Amherst collection, his commemoration cup was full.[14]

Only the best monuments would do for Junius and for himself. He was also pleased with belated recognition by the academic community. Yale presented him with an honorary doctorate in 1908 in recognition of his services in the panic of the year before. To receive it, he made a special trip across the Atlantic to New Haven, grumbling that he wished Yale would give him the degree in a more worthy city. Still, he soon endowed a chair there. Seeing this, Harvard was not slow to follow, giving him an honorary doctorate two years after Yale. He shared the platform with Theodore Roosevelt, who had just returned from his hunting trip to Africa, where the lions had failed to do their duty. President Lowell cited Morgan as follows:

> Public citizen, patron of literature and art, prince among merchants, who by his skill, his wisdom and courage, has twice in times of stress repelled a national danger of financial panic.

No comment was made on his large gift to the Medical School, although Lowell might well have remembered that president of a new college who was asked how he would endow the institution, and replied, "By degrees."

Business on Wall Street occupied Morgan less every year. He was more occupied with his passport to posterity and the hereafter. On a trip to Egypt in the winter of 1909, he had been impressed by the excavations of Albert Lythgoe, who was in charge of the interests of the Metropolitan Museum there. Two sites were being examined. At Lisht, south of Cairo, the temple-pyramids of Amenemhat I and Sesostris I were being freed from the sands. Moreover, at the oasis of Khargeh in the Libyan desert, early Christian monuments and cemeteries were being uncovered. Morgan was fascinated by the complexity and organization of the works at Lisht, where 350 bucket boys were toiling under the whips of overseers in clouds of dust, revealing brilliant murals beneath the acrid ground.

On the six-hour trip by special train to Khargeh, through a gray limestone ravine, onto the weird plateau of the Libyan desert, he was struck particularly by its eroded melancholy. Except for two terse questions about the desert, he sat plunged in thought throughout the journey in a wickerwork armchair in the little saloon. He would eat only an egg and a piece of bread for lunch. From time to time, he would write out a cable and give it to an attendant, who would see that it was sent back by telegraph from one of the little huts on the line. He smoked his interminable black cigars, and no one dared disturb him.

When finally the train reached the date palms and the irrigated fields of the oasis, the huge extent of the ancient Christian burial ground at the end of the abomination of desolation was balm to Morgan's soul. He decided to continue financing the two digs, as if there might be some ancient mysery or lost wisdom connecting pyramid to cross to time. He also arranged a meeting with the local potentate, the Omdeh. Although the two old men could not talk to each other, each recognized in his opposite "a man of force and importance, and so they sat down very contentedly and enjoyed the view together in silence."[15]

Three times, Morgan had an audience with Pope Pius X in Rome. The first time the supreme pontiff saw the financier, he was struck dumb with astonishment at Morgan's presence or, as his interpreter claimed, at Morgan's nose. Through policy or embarrassment, Morgan himself remained silent. When the silence became painful, the interpreter suggested a phrase to the Pope to welcome Morgan's visit. The Pope agreed to the phrase, which was translated to Morgan. It was his turn not to reply until the interpreter suggested a suitable answer. He also approved it. Once the ice was broken, a conversation took place about mutual interests in pictures and books, and at the future audiences there was no shyness on either side. Morgan finally asked the Pope for his autograph.[16]

Morgan did seek out popes and kings, bishops and omdehs, as if their exalted position near God and on earth confirmed his own. He also loved Egypt and Rome for the grandeur of their religious monuments, the immutable pyramids and Vatican City. He would have bought the Sistine Chapel if he could; he wished that he might have a bed to sleep there under Michelangelo's sublime frescoes.[17] Unable to achieve such religious splendor, he had become the leading layman in the American Episcopal Church. His pew in the old Trinity Church in Newport was known as the Parlor Car and was covered with crimson damask; in it, Morgan and his wife sat in two large, padded armchairs. He was particularly prominent at the Triennial Convention of 1910 in Cincinnati, where there was no financial panic to disturb him. A special car took his private party there of four bishops and four ladies, while Louis Sherry catered for them all in a hired mansion. Morgan knew the legislation he wanted and lobbied for it through friendly bishops for the full nineteen days of the convention, as if he could prove his fitness for the afterlife by his concern over the laws governing his temporal church.

His rector and confidant Rainsford knew well the religious nature of the aging Morgan. He saw the sure and limited essence of the financier's faith, which was built on gold bricks rather than the rock of ages. As Rainsford testified:

> Religion we think we can afford to treat as an individual matter only; while the truth is, it is above all other interests in our lives the one part of ourselves that so treated withers in disuse. It was meant to be leaven, not a gold brick. Its very nature and property is expansion. This divine property Mr. Morgan found it hard to see. His mental qualities drew him strongly to the ecclesiastical side of the Episcopal Church's life. Its very archaic element, its atmosphere of withdrawal from common everyday affairs of men, answered to some need of his soul. The floor of the convention, the association with men who were, by virtue of their office, guardians and exponents of a religious tradition, beautiful and venerable, had for him an attraction stronger than any other gathering afforded.[18]

Yet even the respect of a convention of bishops was not the final judgment of society or of God. Harriman's death had been greeted with public indifference or enmity, though his life had been passed as a puritan except for his rapacity over money. But when King Edward VII died in 1910, his people wept in the streets for a beloved monarch, whose self-indulgent love of beauty and worldliness had been matched by his tolerance and brilliant diplomacy for his country. Morgan hoped to be judged as Edward was, for his public contributions rather than his private life; but he had the misfortune to be the leading magnate in a progressive America, not a king in a permissive London. He had outlived the appreciation of his age, and he did not know the outcome of heaven.

17

Death in Rome

> I am simply unable to understand the value placed by so many people upon great wealth. . . . I am delighted to show any courtesy to Pierpont Morgan or Andrew Carnegie or James J. Hill, but . . . the very luxurious, grossly material life of the average multimillionaire whom I know does not appeal to me in the least, and nothing could hire me to lead it.
>
> — THEODORE ROOSEVELT (1908)

> I've got to go up the hill.
>
> — J. PIERPONT MORGAN'S LAST WORDS (1913)

WHEN King Edward VII died, Morgan was in Paris. He crossed the Channel to attend the state funeral and the private luncheon for the grieving royal family after the burial. It was a signal for the ending of the stable world of the Edwardian age, when a few distinguished and indefatigable old men had kept together a tracery of international diplomacy and finance. Time after time they had prevented the collision of the thrusting western nations, greedy for the resources and the trade of the globe. As they died off, they left lesser men to fill their places without the prestige or experience to prevent class war and the First World War.

For Morgan, premonitions of the end kept on coming to him. His health was worsening, his sight and memory slowly failing, his great body shrinking onto its frame. In 1911, he went to Belfast in northern Ireland for the launching of the pride of the White Star Line in his International Mercantile Marine trust. The liner was named *Titanic*, and Morgan selected his personal staterooms aboard. Afterwards, he took the *Corsair* to visit the Kaiser again at Kiel. There he presented the German Emperor with a letter written by Martin Luther, an embryo charter for the Protestant church; the Emperor decorated him with the order of the Red Eagle. In a regatta, American yachts sailed against German yachts and were victorious. Despite this omen, the Kaiser's diplomacy was aimed at detaching American finance from the English cause in case of a conflict to come.

Returning to America, Morgan heard the result of the government's suit against Standard Oil, which had caused the Rockefellers to withdraw from speculation in Wall Street and had allowed Stillman to become a friend. The government officially won its case, but the Supreme Court only declared the great oil trust guilty of an unreasonable restraint of trade. The nine wise men refused to consider combination a crime, only its excesses. Morgan himself found the verdict very satisfactory. It had caused the Rockefellers problems and seemed to leave his own trusts in the clear. To him, the ten railroad systems and five industrial combines under his control were all reasonable and responsible, especially the ingot of his eye, United States Steel.

Yet unreasonably, Morgan felt no fear of the President, William Howard Taft. When Taft had been nominated at the Republican convention of 1908, Morgan had declared, "Good! Good!" Two years later, in conditions of such secrecy that they seemed like "some criminal conspiracy," he had conferred with Taft at the summer White House.[1] He felt safe from persecution by the administration, but he misjudged the temper of the time against the trusts. No President running for a second term could afford to ignore popular opinion, even for a favored magnate.

The progressive movement was gathering momentum. Roosevelt was threatening to run again and lead the radicals. Two thousand muckracking articles attacking big business had been published in the past decade. The unions were growing in strength, particularly complaining against the seven-day workweek and occasional twenty-four-hour shifts at United States Steel. The savior of the panic of 1907 was again becoming the scapegoat of the reform movement of 1911. Congress ordered an investigation of the steel trust, although its chairman, Elbert Gary, had tried to keep its books open and its finances clean — the only good corporation in the business.

Taft offered Morgan a compromise, a voluntary breaking up of his large combines, a reform from within. But Morgan refused. He felt that he had nothing to be sorry for. He stated that the steel trust was not in restraint of trade. It was legal and upheld the rights of its competitors. Perkins, who was still on the board of the steel trust, even claimed that it was run better than a government department could run it, and that Morgan had given the authority over it to tens of thousands of shareholders. This was true public ownership.

It was also untrue public relations. As Henry Davison had to admit later to the Pujo Committee, he could not recall a single case in which the stockholders had ever been able to oust the management in any of Morgan's railroads — or in any of his trusts. Morgan controlled his companies by personal fiat. The authority lay within him, not with the investing public. Taft knew this, and he also knew that the demand for reform was sweeping the country. And hell hath no fury like a President scampering for office.

In October, 1911, Taft allowed his administration to bring a suit to dissolve the United States Steel Corporation. This action involved serving a summons on Morgan, who was at home on Madison Avenue with a bad cold. He took the summons at the door and returned to sit with it in his lap by the fire. He sat in silence for ten minutes. Then he said:

"Well, it has come to this."

It had come to the beginning of his final persecution, as both houses of Congress and all three leading presidential candidates, Taft and Theodore Roosevelt and Woodrow Wilson from New Jersey, tried to ride the reform tide. In four years in the White House, Taft brought double the amount of antitrust suits that Roosevelt had in seven. He attacked two more of Morgan's trusts, the International Harvester Company and the American Telephone and Telegraph Company, which was forced to divest itself of Western Union. The legal persecution of the old financier would not end until he had been indicted for conspiracy in a transaction to do with the New Haven Railroad. At that time, he was reported to have wept and said: "To think that after all these years I have been branded by my own government a criminal, fit only to be thrown into jail."[2]

Most of the government attacks would prove futile. After nine years of litigation, the United States Steel Corporation would be cleared by the Supreme Court. The other suits caused some internal housecleaning, but little external regulation. The chief victim was Morgan himself. His belief that he was America's financial guardian and savior, the permanent keeper of the gold standard, was eroded, if not destroyed. Rainsford knew of Morgan's emotional nature, his long hours of despair and depression, which were due to overexertion and nervous collapse. But he also knew of Morgan's basic intellectual conviction that he was fighting the good fight for America and for God.[3] As another Morgan observer put it:

> While he may not have created conditions, he certainly knew how to make the most of them and he was absolutely honest in his belief that the money of the country was safer in his hands than if left lying around for others to take a whack at it. Neither did it occur to him that there was anything wrong with a system that made such a situation possible. That he

was a despot he did not deny. He qualified it by the adjective "benevolent." And he was sincere in his belief that his despotism was a good thing for the country.[4]

Yet this private belief appeared retrograde and irrelevant as the political storm rose during the election of 1912. Perkins, turned away from the house of Morgan, became Roosevelt's backer and banker; and, when Roosevelt lost the Republican nomination to Taft, Perkins encouraged him to split the party and run on the Progressive ticket. Morgan was disgusted by Taft's attack on his trusts and even more horrified by Woodrow Wilson's calls for a return to open competition through new laws and regulations. If he could support anyone, it would have to be Roosevelt as the least among evils. Perkins collected campaign funds from Stillman and Gary, but nothing directly from the house of Morgan. Ironically enough, he was believed to be Morgan's agent within the Progressive party, something he no longer was. And even more ironically, the congressional Clapp Committee called Morgan to Washington to testify about his contributions of $150,000 to Roosevelt in 1904 and $30,000 to Taft in 1908. Morgan was glad to be able to say that he was giving no candidate any money that year.

Roosevelt ran ahead of Taft, but allowed the election of Woodrow Wilson by splitting the Republican party. Now there was no stopping the persecution of Morgan and his peers. Catastrophe had already been signaled by the sinking of the *Titanic* on her maiden voyage. Morgan had not been occupying his chosen staterooms; but John Jacob Astor IV, P. A. B. Widener's son George, and Benjamin Guggenheim were among the notables drowned in the disaster. Morgan's shipping line was accused of cutting costs on its safety precautions and was blamed for the tragedy, although the iceberg that sank the ship was clearly an act of God.

Morgan was further depressed by the refusal of New York City to appropriate funds to build a special wing on the Metropolitan Museum for his magnificent collection on loan there. From a political point of view, it was no time to vote money to the rich. Yet Morgan was embittered. He had saved the city's credit in 1907, and now the city was asking him to pay for the resting place of what might be his greatest gift to its citizens. Aggrieved, he made a mistake in his wishes for his reputation after his death. He left his collection to his son, not to the Metropolitan Museum. He had kept everything his father Junius had collected, including both London houses. He did not foresee that Jack

Morgan might feel obliged to disperse much of what had been gathered together so obsessively.

His depression was made worse by the prevalent conspiracy theory of 1912, that a Money Trust existed under his leadership which was the chief financial power in the United States. From the outside, Morgan's systems of industrial combinations, affiliate banks, and interlocking directorates did look like a gigantic spider web with the magnate crouched in the middle of the trap for the unwary. "The maker of tables and graphs was able," a Morgan partner admitted, "by using concentric circles so to speak, to extend his interlocking directorates at will and almost indefinitely."[5] The Morgan partners alone held seventy-two directorships in forty-seven large financial or industrial corporations worth more than $10 billion; if the partners in the Baker and Stillman groups were linked to them, more than $22 billion of capital seemed to be under the control of Morgan, his associates and his lieutenants. For those who wanted to see a conspiratorial Money Trust, the evidence could be drawn from the facts.

From the inside, there was no conspiracy, but only a cooperation of like minds in search of more efficiency and public welfare. To people like Henry Davison, Morgan was the man who had cleaned up the cutthroat competition of the robber barons in favor of the great cartels necessary to keep down prices and provide better services in the more complex modern world of industrial advances and international financing. Interlocking directorates in the right hands helped the economy; they were not a conspiracy against the general good. When accused by Charles Evans Hughes of buying shares for the New York Life Insurance Company and selling them for J. P. Morgan and Company at the same time, Perkins had claimed that he had bargained with himself.

Yet this point of view was impossible to defend outside the closed financial circles of Wall Street. Those who cried conspiracy convinced the grass roots, always looking for a whipping boy on whom to vent their anger about their social ills. And here the magnates' lifelong refusal to explain anything told against them. Even the loyal Vanderlip blamed the honorable but mistaken silence of Morgan and Baker and Stillman. They would not have seemed conspirators if they had talked more to reporters and had been more open in their financial dealings. In Vanderlip's opinion, good publicity was the remedy for the public's misunderstanding of Morgan's motives.[6] But the old man stuck to his injured pride and stubborn silence.

Because of his extreme privacy, his examination by the Pujo Committee at the end of 1912 promised to be a great public show, the climax and exposure of his fifty years of business life. He approached the ordeal in suffering and chagrin. As one of his partners wrote:

> For years it had been an axiom of the financial world that the chief reason for Mr. Morgan's power was the complete trust which the financial community had in him — a trust not in the infallibility of his judgment, which was human like other men's, but in the integrity of his motives and the straightforwardness of his dealings. Therefore, to have the very foundation of his character and dealings assailed cut him to the quick. It was in vain that his friends pointed out that these charges were being pressed by men unfamiliar with actual conditions in the world of affairs, and urged on by a kind of popular clamor that was largely manufactured. I think Mr. Morgan realized these facts as fully as his friends did. But that knowledge seemed not to lessen his sense of mortification and melancholy.[7]

The counsel for the Money Trust investigating committee had decided to make a Roman holiday of Morgan's appearance. Newspapermen and photographers with flashbulbs besieged the committee building, waiting for the arrival of the gloomy Morgan. "I do not mind a fair hearing," he told his friend Bishop Lawrence. "What I dread is that they will ask me questions to which I cannot give full answers and that people will not understand."[8] The queue of people wanting to see or hear him extended along the hall down the steps outside and around the block. His son-in-law, who was present with fifteen other Morgan partners and lawyers and friends, wrote that the lines reminded him of people trying to get into a World Series baseball game.

During the two days of interrogation by Samuel Untermyer, the counsel for the committee, the old financier acquitted himself well, either denying flatly that there was a Money Trust and that he had any real power, or else asserting that character was the only essential for a banker or businessman. He had, he said, given a man who had come into his office "a check for a million dollars when I knew he had not a cent in the world." It was not good business, he said, but it was the way he did business. He was willing to take the criticism or the credit for all he had done.

When he left the committee room, he found himself victorious and defeated. His claim that character was the basis of credit became the theme of hundreds of sermons and editorials; but Untermyer's insinuations about a Money Trust were reported as admissions by Morgan that he did control tens of billions of dollars. What he had said and what he had denied were both reported as the truth. His legend was already stronger than his testimony. The fact that he had personally curbed the panic of 1907 made it appear that he did control a Money Trust, even though his friend Baker said that Morgan's power at that time had now expired.

By persistent and ruthless questioning of Morgan's partners and other bankers, Untermyer did succeed in showing that too few men had too much power in New York over the financial institutions of the nation. Even the sphinxlike Baker was finally trapped by Untermyer, who demanded whether the banker thought it a comfortable situation for a great country to have wealth concentrated in such a few hands.

"Not entirely," Baker said.

The Pujo Committee failed to prove that there was a Money Trust, but it succeeded in demonstrating the small circles of power in Wall Street. And while those circles persisted in believing that their little band was responsible and good for the country, much of Congress and the American people saw them as conspirators. It was like looking down the same telescope from a different end. The American public saw a microscopic group of plotters plundering the national finances for their own profit; the Morgan partners saw a few men of enlightened vision enlarging the national wealth for the good of all.

Henry Davison, who was examined after Morgan, put the theory of banking responsibility at its strongest. "I know," he testified, "that J. P. Morgan and Company could do no wrong, if their endeavors and the circumstances permitted them to do as they wanted to do." He amplified his spoken testimony with an open letter to the congressional committee, taking issue with the very reason for its existence. He claimed that it was set up to investigate a wicked Money Trust that was imaginary. If the panic of 1907 could have been engineered by a few powerful men, what would their motives have been? To lose money for themselves? Such a belief was incredible, abhorrent and harmful. "We believe," Davison wrote, "that the whole frame-work and language of the Congressional resolution under which you are acting implies a conception impossible in sound theory, and wholly impossible in practice; such theory being that a comparatively small group of men, chiefly centered in New York City, can and do obtain such complete mastery over the financial machinery of one hundred millions of independent people that they have power to cause this whole country incalculable distress."

Davison knew that international trade was already too great and diversified, and that the wealth of America was spread too broadly across the continent, for a Money Trust to control the nation from New York, even if the Morgan partners had wanted to do so. There were ten banks in London, five in Berlin, and four in Paris of the size of the three larger banks of New York. How could Morgan control these? Every year, America's own resources grew and fell into more hands; its energy and abundance would end the concentration of wealth by giving more to more people. The real financial problem was a weak central banking system, which had forced the house of Morgan into taking too much responsibility in a time of panic. Davison had already worked with Senator Aldrich and other bankers on the basis of a national banking system to fill the vacuum in currency control, a gap which had so often been plugged unwillingly by Morgan and his lieutenants.

"Something has got to be done," Aldrich had said after the last panic. "We may not always have Pierpont Morgan with us to meet a banking crisis."[9]

What depressed Morgan and angered Davison was the assumption by much of Congress and the grass roots that big bankers were villains. Political power was, after all, just as concentrated in Washington as financial power was in New York. Admittedly, all power was dangerous in evil hands. "But to us," Davison wrote for the Morgan partners, "it seems as little likely that the citizens of this country will fill Congress with rascals as it is that they will entrust the leadership of their business and financial affairs to a set of clever rogues."[10] What America needed was a strong and scientific banking system to prevent future panics and make Morgan's oversized role an anachronism.

Although the Pujo Committee failed to prove that the Money Trust existed, its findings did persuade Wilson to push through Congress the Federal Reserve Act and the Clayton Act, which forbade interlocking directorships in banks. Neither the new President nor Congress would allow the Morgan partners to be so overtly powerful in so many boardrooms at the same time. They had proliferated too much. The time of concentration was over.

These were the initial successes of the Pujo Committee. Its next triumph was a form of poisoning, the slow dying of Morgan. Despite his good performance in front of Untermyer, Morgan appeared tired out to his family. His energy had totally deserted him. He made plans to go to Egypt again that winter, hoping that the desert air and the antiquities would revive him as they had done the previous year. His business friends were shocked at the change in him, the loss of his abundant will to live and take.

"The Pujo Committee Investigation killed Morgan," the financier F. H. Prince flatly declared to C. W. Barron in 1913. "Morgan was a very sensitive, shrinking man and all his exterior bluff was simply a protecting coating."[11]

The old man was not dying of a broken heart, but of a broken image. The new Humpty-Dumpty had been pushed off his Wall Street, and he could not put the pieces of his shell together again. He had depended for his self-respect on the high opinion of him held by men of influence, if not by the masses. He had twice been thanked by a President for saving the economy of his country. Now he was publicly accused of trying to ruin it.

He wanted to do one last great public service to right the record, if he were allowed to do it. When George Harvey, the editor of *Harper's Weekly* and a backer of Woodrow Wilson, called on him in his Library before he set off on his last voyage, the editor was moved by the sight of the old man sitting under his Renaissance ceiling from Lucca and in front of his red brocade walls from the Chigi Palace in Rome. Morgan looked like a great *condottiere* who had been denied a last campaign because his age had turned against him. Harvey quoted to him Walter Scott's patriotic lines:

Breathes there the man, with soul so dead,
Who never to himself hath said,
This is my own, my native land.

Morgan repeated the last line and offered himself as a sacrifice to his adversaries for the last time.

"When you see Mr. Wilson," he said to Harvey, "tell him for me that if there should ever come a time when he thinks any influence or resources that I have can be used for the country, they are wholly at his disposal."[12]

There was no call for him. He slipped away on the *Adriatic* at the beginning of January, 1913, avoiding reporters and farewells to his family. Senator Aldrich was on board, and Morgan's self-esteem was raised a little by talks on the banking laws to come. At sea he heard of the success of the exhibition of part of his collection at the Metropolitan Museum. And when he reached Egypt, he was asked to lunch by Lord Kitchener at the English residency. That bull of a man had a carapace and a mustache even more aggressive than Morgan's. He told Morgan bluntly that he would not permit any more looting of the best antiquities from Egypt by the Metropolitan archaeological teams. For once, Morgan was too weary to argue. New restrictions seemed to thwart him everywhere.

The winter before, he had also lunched with Kitchener, who had been cordial and easy. Morgan had then felt energetic and dominant and secure, accepting delivery of his new dahabieh, the *Khargeh*, a luxurious, one-hundred-and-thirty-foot, open-decked launch with a glass room in the bows. Sailing the boat for Luxor, he had pointed out to his guest Bishop Lawrence the exact spot where Moses had been hidden in the bulrushes of the Nile.

"It doesn't look it now," he had told the bishop with his fundamentalist certainty. "Critics may say there never were any bulrushes or any Moses, but I know that there was a Moses and that he was hidden in the bulrushes, for there is the spot. It must be so."[13]

His sense of security and energy had made him lead his guests to chaffer over artifacts, scramble from tomb to tomb in search of murals, scour the Coptic cemetery in the desert oasis, and even found the Harvard Club of Khargeh with six members, five of them who had been to college there and one who had recently been awarded a doctorate. "We are all Harvard men by work or honor," Morgan had happily declared. He had then returned home to be damned by his work to national dishonor.

In 1913, his previous enthusiasm and drive was sunk into morose silence and dissatisfaction. The new dahabieh was too slow and took too long to press up the Nile toward the Sudan. The weather was unusually cold, the chef and the waiters unsatisfactory, the boat overcrowded with guests and friends and Metropolitan Museum Egyptologists. At Luxor, Morgan felt too ill to visit the Valley of the Kings. He agreed to drive across the desert to a fresh archaeological site, but the journey exhausted him. On the voyage farther up the Nile to Aswan he was weak and restless and depressed. The overland trip by railroad to Khartoum was canceled, and Morgan's boat hurried back downriver to Luxor, where he was struck down by nervous indigestion. He thought he might die in an alien land and insisted on getting back to a Christian country to meet his Maker.

Once back at Shepheard's Hotel in Cairo, Morgan was plagued by reporters and medical advice and despair. He managed to pay a last visit to the Sphinx before sailing on the *Adriatic* to Naples. A train took him to his usual suite in the Grand Hotel in Rome, where he was again blockaded by newspapermen and sellers of antiques. He had wanted to buy two triumphal Roman columns for the entrance of the new Morgan office building in New York, so that he might walk between them on his way to his office like an emperor returning from a victorious campaign. But he did not have the strength to negotiate in the bedlam of news gathering and greed about him. The London *Daily Mail* reported:

> The Grand Hotel, where J. Pierpont Morgan is staying may be compared to a closely besieged fortress. There is not an art dealer or antiquary in Rome who is not making desperate efforts to approach the banker with the offer of some "extraordinary bargain." . . . Waves of amateur art dealers, most of whom carry mysterious bundles, sweep upon the hotel from early morning to late at night and are repulsed with the regularity of surf on the beach.[14]

There was nothing organically wrong with Morgan, only a settled melancholy and the loss of his will to live. He drove out sometimes with his daughter Louisa and her husband Herbert Satterlee to visit the Villa Aurelia, which had been acquired by the American Academy in Rome, an institution also endowed by Morgan. He hated being coddled like an invalid; but he trembled with nerves as if he were breaking down or frightened. An American psychiatrist found him mentally and physically exhausted as a result of his long exertions at work, play, traveling and collecting.

On Easter Sunday, he went to the American Church; but he fidgeted and complained during the sermon, insisting on leaving the service early. He took sedation, but was unable to escape from his nervous depression. He stayed in his suite in the Grand Hotel during the next few days and nights, unable to eat, starving to death. His mind began to wander back through his life. At times he thought he was a boy in Hartford, a youth in Vevey, a family man at his home in New York. Just after midnight on Monday, March 31, he pointed at the ceiling and said, "I've got to go up the hill." He fell unconscious and did not wake again. He had worn out.

18

The Rich Are Different . . .

> I have known, and known tolerably well, a good many "successful" men — "big" financially — men famous during the last half-century; and a less interesting crowd I do not care to encounter. Not one that I have ever known would I care to meet again, either in this world or the next.
>
> — Charles Francis Adams (1890)

> I commit my soul into the hands of my Savior, in full confidence that having redeemed it and washed it in His most precious blood, He will present it faultless before the throne of my Heavenly Father; and I entreat my children to maintain and defend, at all hazard and at any cost of personal sacrifice, the blessed doctrine of the complete atonement for sin through the blood of Jesus Christ, once offered, and through that alone.
>
> — From the last will and testament of J. Pierpont Morgan (1913)

When Morgan died, nobody could replace him. "There will be no successor to Morgan" the *Wall Street Journal* declared. "He was the last of his line" the New York *World* admitted. "Now Wall Street is beyond the need or possibility," the New York *Times* pronounced, "of one-man leadership." His death did not affect prices on the stock markets of the world because he had outlived his personal power over them. As Elihu Root said, Morgan's life had seen America emerging from its provincialism to world influence in industry and commerce, and he himself had been the first, the commanding and controlling figure in this amazing development.[1] Yet the change was too great for its chief creator to control. He was almost superfluous. Now groups must take the place of a single man.

With his going, even his opponents recognized his greatness. William Jennings Bryan, the new Secretary of State, directed the American ambassador in Rome to arrange for the return of Morgan's body in honor. A memorial service was held in Westminster Abbey with the choir singing Morgan's favorite hymns. To his funeral service in New York, wreaths were sent by Kaiser Wilhelm and the kings of England, Belgium and Italy. The Chicago and New York stock exchanges closed as a mark of respect, while business in Hartford ceased totally during his burial by the side of his father.

His last will and testament showed an absolute faith that his sins on earth would be redeemed by the atonement of Christ, and that he would be received in heaven. It was as if he could command divine mercy for what he had done. His estate was meager in comparison with the estate of some of his peers; it was valued for tax purposes at less than $77.5 million. The old Rockefeller commented, "And to think that he wasn't even a rich man." His magnificent art collections were only valued at some $20.5 million and were left in the hands of his son Jack, not to the Metropolitan Museum.

Too late, the Board of Estimate of New York City offered to appropriate the money to construct a new wing on the museum for the Morgan hoard. If this had been done while the old man was still alive, in all probability he would have given the museum everything on loan there. As it was, his son put the banks before the art works. His father's mania for collecting in his last years had stretched even the resources of J. P. Morgan and Company, from which the old man was said to have taken 51 percent of the profits for his personal use, sometimes in advance, to pay for his purchases.[2]

Although faced with taxes and little cash after paying out various bequests, Jack Morgan first allowed the whole of his father's collection to be displayed at the Metropolitan Museum; it was the greatest private collection of art yet put on view in the New World. Its splendor and range awed those who saw it, particularly Joseph Duveen's surviving clients. If Duveen was losing to death his three premier collectors, Morgan and Altman and Widener, he was replacing them with H. E. Huntington and Frick and Mellon and Kress and Bache. They could see at the Metropolitan how a collector "who wasn't even a rich man" might amass a show worthy of a Medici.

When Jack Morgan made his great mistake and allowed three fifths of the collection to be put on sale after the exhibition rather than remain as a permanent memorial to his father's taste and vigor, Duveen profited from the occasion, selling posterity to his clients along with his pictures because of the fate of the Morgan treasures. As he did not fail to point out to them, they could live forever and avoid taxes and death duties. All they had to do was to bequeath their collections to the nation as evidence of a life spent in appreciating more than mere money appreciating.

Incredibly, Morgan's son did not value highly enough his father's urge toward posthumous fame. Duveen moved in with the wealthy vultures. Five of Morgan's prized Fragonards went to Frick for $1.2 million to make up the most elegant room in his Fifth Avenue mansion and future museum. Other Morgan masterworks went to other dealers and Duveen clients. Belle da Costa Greene, taken to appreciate Jules Bache's collection in his Fifth Avenue house, hid her sadness at the loss of her beloved Morgan treasures by exclaiming, "How utterly duveen!" After some time, she did persuade Jack Morgan to support his father's Library and stop the sale of more treasures, two fifths of which were finally donated to the Metropolitan. Yet eventually the name of Morgan meant more as the provenance of a work of art than as a donation.

The damage had been done. If Jack Morgan was within his rights in breaking up the collection, his act was comparable "with that other great artistic tragedy, the dispersal by the Commonwealth of the carefully chosen treasures of King Charles the First."[3] The Chinese porcelain collection, the major tapestries, and the Bourbon decorative art works were all sold to English dealers for some three million pounds. Most of them were immediately resold at a profit by the Duveens. To some observers, the sale seemed almost to represent posthumous parricide, as if Jack Morgan had so long lived in his father's shadow that he wanted to make a public gesture against his father's extravagance.

He was very different in character, almost more English than the English, a huge couth gentleman of forty-six who had spent so long on the other side of the Atlantic that he seemed an aristocratic expatriate in his own country. He loved shooting grouse and playing squash and wearing tweeds and other activities symbolic of discreet British wealth. These foreign habits made him almost as unpopular as his father, another imagined conspirator within the financial paranoia of the American grass roots.

In fact, Jack Morgan's long stay in England as his father's representative was probably the old man's most important legacy to his second home. With the outbreak of the First World War, the house of Morgan became the banker of the Allied cause, initially arranging a gold loan of $100 million in 1914, and then another loan of $500 million a year later. During the war, the house of Morgan became the chief purchasing agent for the Allies and disposed of two billion dollars' worth of American securities held by the Europeans. Jack Morgan's involvement was so great that a German sympathizer tried to assassinate him at his home with revolvers and dynamite in 1915. After the war, the house of Morgan's role in the Allied victory and the anti-Bolshevik crusade was signaled by the explosion of a huge bomb outside the Morgan building, which shattered all its windows and decapitated one of its members, just sparing Pierpont Morgan's grandson, the young Junius.

In the 1920s, under Jack Morgan's unaggressive leadership, the firm lost influence as that of the Rockefellers and the Mellons and the Whitneys rose. Although the old Pierpont Morgan had backed much of the technology of the future, he had stayed largely out of chemicals, leaving the wealth there to the Du Ponts, and had preferred owning railroads to automobile companies. In 1908, a one-third share in the W. C. Durant automobile company had been refused for the sum of half a million dollars; it would become General Motors, and twenty years later, that stock would be worth $200 million. Morgan was not a clairvoyant about the prospects of new inventions, even though Evangeline Adams, the Carnegie Hall astrologer, claimed to have advised him on how the changing planets affected business and the stock markets.[4]

Unfortunately, Jack Morgan came out of his conservative banking practices just in time to help worsen the crash of 1929. He allowed the house of Morgan to promote the stock of three major holding companies: the United Corporation in electricity, the Allegheny Corporation in railroads, and Standard Brands in retail foods. The old devices of pyramiding stocks and allowing special share deals to influential people were resurrected from Pierpont Morgan's times. It was twenty years too late for such devices. Luckily, however, the opposition of a single Morgan partner prevented the house from joining other leading investment firms in backing the unscrupulous international swindles of the "Match King," Ivar Kreuger.

When the crash came, Jack Morgan did not have the power, the courage or the will to stand up persistently against the panic as his father had done in 1907. Yet as a consequence, he also had to appear before the congressional Committee on Banking and Currency in 1933 to explain the interlocking roles of deposit banking and stock promotion. Despite his declaration that a private banker was a national asset and not a national danger, his appearance before this new investigating committee was overplayed and unconvincing.[5] His public image was not helped when a press photographer dumped a lady midget in his lap and took the picture. The Franklin Roosevelt administration completed what Woodrow Wilson's had begun, passing laws to end the house of Morgan's double role as commercial bankers and stock promoters. No longer would it be possible for a trust or bank to sell itself its own corporate promotions under the pretense that its left hand did not know what its right hand was doing.

Morgan's direct legacy of works of art and of a private international investment bank did not preserve his reputation after his death so much as the legends about his life. He had deliberately become the Golden Calf of the gilded age of American capitalism. He had been worshipped and cast down by the mob. In the Depression, when Marxist economics became fashionable, he seemed the ultimate villain and the source of the exploitation of the American worker. He was the man who, above all, had concentrated the power of capital in a few hands and had ignored the effect on unemployment and low wages. He had not spread wealth, he had stolen it. In the words of one Socialist writer, the Morgan interests had always pursued "a cold-blooded, ruthless policy, robbing the working class in the typical capitalist fashion and holding down the workers with brute force when they dare to revolt."[6]

Although such a radical view of the Morgans' role was common chiefly in the 1930s, when the very rich were comfortable only in each other's company, it had been the chief complaint of Theodore Roosevelt against Pierpont himself. He had asserted that the financier's extravagance and ostentation increased radical propaganda. The concept of a class war seemed real when there was such an enormous difference between the private Pullman car and the wooden seats of a cheap railroad carriage, between the *Corsair* staterooms and the immigrants' steerage space, between the Morgan Library and the union organizer's little office, between the marble New York mansions and the steel trust's shacks for its workers in its company towns.

Morgan was often blind to the social abyss between the American rich and the American poor. In fact, he increased the gap and flaunted his wealth. Trying to explain Morgan's blinkers, his friend Bishop Lawrence wrote of him:

> The intensity of his life necessarily limited his thought and imagination. He did not have time and strength to give to many great and important interests of society and democracy; some of them rising in his day to vital issues. He did not always consider the public or the force of public opinion. . . . He did not have weighing upon him the sodden condition of the poor, living within two miles of his house in London and in New York, and yet when a physician in whose skill and judgment he trusted, put before him in vivid language, the pitiful condition of the women in reek-

> ing tenements during childbirth, his imagination could see them and he gave a great hospital like a great Prince; when his sympathies were touched and his confidence gained, few princes ever equalled him.[7]

Like the Medicis, who were also bankers, Morgan loved conspicuous charity and consumption for his pleasure and his prestige. He did not care whom he offended by his display of wealth and contempt for equality. Everybody was free, as far as he was concerned, to become a Morgan; but then, as he also knew, nobody else would. His example spread the idea in America that the very rich were different from the rest of mankind for other reasons than that they were very rich. He thought himself to be a God-given commander of mankind, both rich and poor. And most other men resented him for this, preferring in hard times the politics of envy to the normal politics of emulation.

If Morgan's talents for spending money on art and living had not equaled his talent for making money and myths about himself, he would have been thought as ordinary and dull as the elder Rockefeller and most of the other magnates of his old age. On the whole, they were a boorish lot without tongues or taste. Charles Francis Adams did not choose to meet them in this world or the next, while Theodore Roosevelt always preferred the company of historians and big-game hunters. The ability to acquire riches did not confer any other distinction. Only Morgan made it seem that it did.

That was through the extraordinary force of his character, his lust to accumulate and to excel. He was a driven man, driven initially by greed, later by the self-inflicted scourge of his own sense of responsibility. For most men, the making of one million dollars would be enough, while the pursuit of more and more money would be a meaningless diversion from the business of living. Yet for Morgan, with his gargantuan appetites for money, power, and beauty in art and women, any reasonable limit was an obstacle.

His early illness, his suppressed romanticism, his nasal deformity, his need to outdo and deny his father — all contributed to his failure to bridle his desires. But the chief motives for his restless ambition were explained by another multimillionaire financier, Russell Sage, who once confessed why he had flogged himself on to become richer than Morgan:

> What else can I go at that will do as much good and give as much satisfaction? Well, you can't answer it. Nobody can. I have thought it over. This is my trade. Another thing: every man likes to excel. He likes to

> prove to be worth as much as folks say he is worth. Hardly any man sold out suddenly would measure up to his reputation. Men take the same pleasure in accumulating that boys do in climbing trees, or winning a wrestling match.[8]

Morgan was driven to do what he knew he did well and thought would do good. He lived in an age when the ostentation of the rich was not considered a crime, and when the doctrine of class war seemed subterranean and alien. In terms of America's economic development, he did fulfill an important role, collecting the capital needed to finance and rationalize new technologies, consolidating inefficient and competitive railroads into the beginnings of a national transport system, and acting as the leading broker between the era of cutthroat cannibalism in finance and the age of complacent overconcentration. Ironically enough, he was the midwife of the bourgeois revolution, the necesary stage of accumulation before provoking state intervention. His work made possible the economic transition from the farm belt to the conveyor belt: he died as he became unnecessary.

The reason for his preeminence lay more in his person than his methods. From Dos Passos' *U.S.A.* to Doctorow's *Ragtime*, the re-creation of his supreme force and presence has testified to his image in urban folklore. Physically imposing, he could thrust his version of events upon lesser men through awe, fear and considered silences. Otherwise, he could buy compliance by the threat of economic sanctions. He spoke as if he were superior and acted as if preordained to be so. Only in the last year of his life, after the Pujo Committee interrogation, did he have to confront his self-illusion and the frailty of his fame.

In fact, the rise of Morgan was only possible at a curious period in the history of a new nation, exploding at the seams. He began his career discreditably during the Civil War, speculating in the weapons and the gold that braver men needed to end the strife. He was quite successful on Wall Street at the time of the original robber barons, an apprentice among greater pirates than his namesake. Then, like Jonathan Wild, he turned from operating sharply on the margins of the law to sustaining it. Instead of speculating in gold, he upheld its standard.

When the trusts emerged, he became a thief catcher, combining raffish speculators and ruinous competitors into cartels of great or questionable worth. At a time when there was little government or regulation, he set up his own rules for a few men like himself. Because he did what he wanted to do in the silence of the law, he felt himself above the law.

And because he had more wealth, he set himself over a mere Congress or a President of the United States, until he met his adversary, Theodore Roosevelt.

At the peak of his dominance, he became the first great American collector, succeeding the declining aristocrats whom he tried to emulate. By creating the fashion for looting European art, so that every billionaire might aim to turn his private museum into a Metropolitan one, he confused the avarice of personal show with the display of public service. Few dared to challenge such an autocratic spirit seeming to be a benefactor; but those who did — Theodore Roosevelt and Roger Fry and Samuel Untermyer — were to prove what Morgan admitted to very few and very rarely: that he was as other men, capable of all their weaknesses behind his masks of control and contribution and culture.

He did not have feet of clay, but a glittering carapace. He wore a helmet of mirrors that blinded all true sight of him and his own insight. This was not self-deception: before the age of psychiatry, the inner eye was blinkered. He was a plutocrat who protested, in the English fashion, that he was an aristocrat. He was believed because most men at that time believed that the fittest ruled, if not the best.

He demonstrated the odd moral fragmentation that enables the voracious to consider money one thing and its effect on other human lives another. In making himself and his partners too rich, he usually ignored the loses and sufferings of the millions of workers and investors in his combinations. He believed that he had the right to take as much income from other people as he judged fair. He clung to the bishops of the Episcopal Church as a proof on earth of the hierarchy of the good — and the limitation of good works. Those selected by the Almighty ruled, and charity was a private affair that should have nothing to do with good business.

Morgan did not make his age. He made what he did because of his age. And finally it was for the happiness of his mind, as Bishop Lawrence wrote, that he lived no longer.[9]

Chapter Notes
A Select Bibliography

Chapter Notes

AN ACCOUNTING

1. Morgan's testimony was given before a subcommittee of the House Committee on Banking and Currency, the so-called Pujo Committee (after the name of the chairman, Arsène Pujo, congressman from Louisiana). See *Hearings and Report of the Committee Appointed Pursuant to House Resolutions 429 and 504 to Investigate the Concentration of Control of Money and Credit*, 62d Cong., 2d and 3d Sess. (1913). There is an entertaining account of Samuel Untermyer in Henry F. Pringle, *Big Frogs*, 139–160.
2. W. S. Rainsford, *The Story of a Varied Life*, 291.

1. THE BALANCE SHEET OF YOUTH

The only major sources for J. Pierpont Morgan's youth are the approved memoirs written by his son-in-law Herbert L. Satterlee: *The Life of J. Pierpont Morgan* (privately printed, 1937), which he revised for his *J. Pierpont Morgan: An Intimate Portrait* (New York, 1939). He has exhaustively collected every memory and record from the family and friends, and yet he has failed to illuminate his subject's early character. I remain deeply grateful to his revised memoir for his dedicated and essential work in recording all he has done for future generations.

Conceptually, I have relied heavily on Francis J. Grund's *Aristocracy in America* (London, 1839; reprinted, New York, 1959). This remarkable and unique social reportage of Jacksonian democracy describes the conditions which allowed the rise of the Morgan family in the nineteenth century. It provokes thought into the nature of the American rich and "aristocracy," which have never been accepted to their own satisfaction. As Grund writes, "I assure you no people in the world are better satisfied of their superiority than the higher classes of Americans. If their pretensions were recognized by the people at large, there would be no happier set of men in the world. There is no species of perfection which they do not attribute to one another."

1. See A. Sinclair, *A Concise History of the United States* (New York, 1967), 75–81.
2. F. Grund, *Aristocracy in America*, 183.
3. L. Corey, *The House of Morgan*, 44. Although Corey's book is a socialist critique of the rise of the Morgan financial structure, it has some penetrating insights into the conditions that allowed the rise to occur.
4. J. S. Morgan to J. P. Morgan, London, May 30, 1850.
5. J. S. Morgan to J. P. Morgan, Boston, Mar. 1, 1851.
6. J. S. Morgan to J. P. Morgan, Boston, Mar. 22, 1851.
7. Grund, 63.
8. Ibid., 64.
9. Ibid., 73, 154, 158.
10. New York *Herald*, Mar. 10, 1853.
11. Grund, 52, 60.
12. James Schouler, *History of the United States of America Under the Constitution*, 6 vols. (rev. ed., New York, 1894–99), 5:384.

13. H. Satterlee, *J. Pierpont Morgan*, 99.
14. C. Hovey, *The Life Story of J. Pierpont Morgan*, 23. All biographers of J. P. Morgan are indebted to Hovey's pioneer work, which was published during Morgan's lifetime and elicited no response from Morgan at all despite the many legal means at his disposal. Hovey had access to documents that have since disappeared and to eyewitnesses who have since died. He is the most lucid and accurate of all Morgan's biographers, although with a liking for the dramatic.

2. GUNS, GOLD AND NO GLORY

1. J. S. Morgan to J. P. Morgan, London, Oct. 29, 1857.
2. J. S. Morgan to J. P. Morgan, London, Apr. 16, 1858.
3. H. Satterlee, *J. Pierpont Morgan*, 108. See also J. S. Morgan to J. P. Morgan, London, Mar. 15, 1859.
4. Quoted in M. Josephson, *The Robber Barons*, 59.
5. J. S. Morgan to J. P. Morgan, London, July 11, 1860.
6. R. G. Wasson's remarkable monograph *The Hall Carbine Affair* is a fascinating exercise in how to try and clear a man's reputation by scrupulous research — only to succeed in making matters worse by revealing more than was known before. J. P. Morgan's own policy and that of his heirs was silence and destruction of all evidence about him. Opposite page 43 of his book, Wasson reproduces without comment the statement of Ketchum's account with Stevens submitted to the House investigating committee, which shows that Morgan took $26,343.54 for his advance of $20,000 from the check paid over by Frémont, and also that two other sums were paid to him by Ketchum: a check to "J.P.M." on Sept. 9, 1861, for $3,797 and a "draft favor of J. P. Morgan" on Oct. 2, 1861, for $31.95. See also *Report and Testimony of the Select House Committee Appointed to Inquire into Government Contracts*, No. 2, 2 vols., 37th Cong., 2d Sess. (1861), 2:515.
7. This rare letter from Morgan to his father is preserved in the George Peabody papers, Essex Institute, Salem, Mass.
8. J. K. Medbery, *Men and Mysteries of Wall Street*, 241.
9. Quoted in F. L. Collins, *Money Town*, 216.

3. ROBBERY AMONG THE BARONS

1. Quoted in L. Corey, *The House of Morgan*, 80.
2. Quoted in A. Sinclair, *A Concise History of the United States*, 110.
3. A. D. H. Smith, *Commodore Vanderbilt*, 138.
4. M. Minnigerode, *Certain Rich Men*, 183.
5. M. H. Smith, *Twenty Years Among the Bulls and Bears of Wall Street*, 411.
6. A. Carnegie, *Autobiography*, 170.
7. F. Grund, *Aristocracy in America*, 210.
8. J. K. Medbery, *Men and Mysteries of Wall Street*, 261.
9. Quoted in W. W. Fowler, *Ten Years in Wall Street*, 517–518.
10. Medbery, 266.
11. Fowler, 525–528.
12. C. F. Adams, Jr., and H. Adams, *Chapters of Erie*, 94.
13. Ibid., 96.
14. Ibid., 97.

4. CURE BY ACQUISITION

1. C. Canfield, *The Incredible Pierpont Morgan*, 53.
2. The Crown Princess Victoria of Prussia to Queen Victoria, Mar. 29, 1872, quoted in *Darling Child*, edited by Roger Fulford (London, 1976), 37.

3. Quoted in John Pearson, *Edward the Rake* (New York, 1975), 45.
4. See Joseph Alsop's important article "How Did Art Collecting Begin?" in *New York Review of Books*, Dec. 21, 1978.
5. G. Reitlinger, *The Economics of Taste*, 30.
6. F. Grund, *Aristocracy in America*, 89.
7. J. K. Winkler, *Morgan the Magnificent*, 80–81.
8. C. Hovey, *The Life Story of J. Pierpont Morgan*, 80.
9. A. Carnegie, *Autobiography*, 170–175.
10. Hovey, 71–73.
11. H. Satterlee, *J. Pierpont Morgan*, 172.
12. J. Moody, *The Masters of Capital*, 20. Moody confirms that until 1879, Pierpont Morgan was "merely the son of his grim-mouthed father." Additional confirmation comes from Henry Clewes in his *Twenty-eight Years in Wall Street* (New York, 1888), 666. Among his profiles of all the leading financiers in Wall Street, he fails to mention J. P. Morgan, but he does write a profile of Anthony J. Drexel, calling him the successful head of Drexel, Morgan and Company.
13. See G. Wheeler, *Pierpont Morgan and Friends*, 134. Although this is an interesting examination of Morgan and his contemporaries, it is ruined by its intemperate and incredible attacks on people like Edward, Prince of Wales, who the author thinks should have been put in an institution at an early age along with Kaiser Wilhelm II. Because of judgments such as these, the author's views on Morgan himself are suspect.

5. A SYSTEM FOR SOCIETY

1. L. Corey, *The House of Morgan*, 138.
2. W. McAllister, *Society as I Have Found It*, 116.
3. Ibid., 170.
4. Ibid., 214.
5. C. Amory, *Who Killed Society?* 122. Amory remains the best and the brightest commentator on American society.
6. E. D. Lehr, *"King" Lehr and the Gilded Age*, 19.
7. J. K. Winkler, *Morgan the Magnificent*, 101.

6. BLACKMAIL, WATER AND ORDER

1. See H. Satterlee, *J. Pierpont Morgan*, 202–204.
2. J. K. Winkler, *Morgan the Magnificent*, 91.
3. M. Josephson, *The Robber Barons*, 294.
4. Ibid., 293–294.
5. See *Pennsylvania Railroad Co. and Others* vs. *The Commonwealth of Pennsylvania*, as reported in *Atlantic Reporter* (1886), 368–377.
6. Quoted in C. Hovey, *The Life Story of J. Pierpont Morgan*, 108–112.
7. Ibid., 113–115.
8. Satterlee, 231–232.
9. See n. 5.
10. J. S. Morgan to J. P. Morgan, Monte Carlo, Dec. 29, 1887.
11. Satterlee, 222.
12. E. D. Lehr, *"King" Lehr and the Gilded Age*, 77–78.
13. W. S. Rainsford, *A Preacher"s Story of His Work*, 120.
14. Ibid., 176–177.
15. W. S. Rainsford, *The Story of a Varied Life*, 280–285.

7. TRUST, OR A GENTLEMEN'S AGREEMENT

1. M. Josephson, *The Robber Barons*, 306.
2. See *Proceedings of Conference Between Presidents of Railroad Lines West of Chicago and St. Louis, and Representatives of Banking Houses, Held at 219 Madison Avenue, New York, January 8 & 10, 1889, passim.* See also C. Hovey, *The Life Story of J. Pierpont Morgan*, 129–145.
3. Quoted in G. Wheeler, *Morgan and Friends*, 180.
4. J. Grodinsky, *Jay Gould*, 563.
5. See G. Kennan, *Edward H. Harriman*, 1:76–81.
6. J. S. Morgan to J. P. Morgan, Monte Carlo, Jan. 19, 1888.
7. S. N. Behrman, *Duveen*, 53.
8. H. Satterlee, *J. Pierpont Morgan*, 247.
9. When Morgan bought George Washington's sword, the New York *World* ran a cartoon called "The New Commander," showing him with a checkbook in one hand and the sword in the other, standing in Washington's place on a pedestal. "The Father of His Country" was crossed out for "The Father of Wall Street."

8. THE ENEMY OF THE WEST

1. Finley Peter Dunne's pieces on Mr. Dooley remain indispensable for an understanding of the period.
2. L. M. Hacker, *The World of Andrew Carnegie*, 373–384. This work is excellent on the subject of the Homestead strike and its effect on Carnegie's philanthropic image.
3. See the revisionist work of Norman Pollack, *The Populist Response to Industrial America* (Cambridge, Mass., 1966), 54.
4. H. Adams, *Education*, 346.
5. H. Satterlee, *J. Pierpont Morgan*, 268.
6. George W. Childs to Archibald McLeod, as reported on Sept. 8, 1893, to C. W. Barron. See Barron's *More They Told Barron*, 125.
7. See H. L. Higginson to Robert Bacon, Nov. 23, 1894, quoted in J. B. Scott, *Robert Bacon*, 71.
8. A. R. Burr, *The Portrait of a Banker: James Stillman*, 115.
9. F. H. Prince to C. W. Barron on June 1, 1894, in Barron's *More They Told Barron*, 144.
10. A. R. Burr, 115.
11. Wilson G. Hunt in the *Wall Street Journal*, Jan. 3, 1894. Also quoted by E. G. Campbell in his penetrating *The Reorganization of the American Railroad System, 1893–1900*, still essential for an understanding of the methods behind the railroad mergers of the 1890s.
12. Quoted in G. Kennan, *Harriman*, 1:119.
13. H. Adams, *Education*, 347.

9. THE GOLD BUGS AND THE GOVERNMENT

1. A. R. Burr, *James Stillman*, 116–117.
2. J. A. Barnes, *John G. Carlisle*, 368.
3. Atlanta *Constitution*, quoted in *Public Opinion*, Feb. 7, 1895.
4. C. Hovey, *Life Story of J. Pierpont Morgan*, 165. Hovey had a great deal of private information on the Gold Crisis, probably from Robert Bacon.
5. F. L. Allen, *The Great Pierpont Morgan*, 111. This is the most dependable modern biography of Morgan, although reticent on many matters.
6. Allan Nevins, in his biography *Grover Cleveland: A Study in Courage*, ascribes the idea of using the 1862 law to the Assistant Secretary of the Treasury, William

E. Curtis, but fails to disprove Cleveland's own assertion that the idea came from Morgan, which was also confirmed by three other sources. Morgan would have known of the law from his own speculations in the Gold Room during the Civil War. The differing accounts of Nevins, Satterlee, Barnes and Hovey are the result of differing testimonies from those present at the various stages of the crisis. I have chosen to believe the witnesses who confirm one another.

7. Morgan's account of the story was told later to Bishop William Lawrence, whose unpublished memoir is in the Pierpont Morgan Library.
8. George F. Parker, *Recollections of Grover Cleveland* (New York, 1909), 325.
9. Allen, 122.
10. L. Corey, *House of Morgan*, 189.
11. See U.S. Senate, Committee on Finance, *Investigation of the Sale of Bonds*, 54th Cong., 2d Sess., 1886.
12. Barnes, 390.
13. Portland *Oregonian*, Dec. 18, 1895.
14. E. P. Hoyt, *The House of Morgan*, 210.
15. Henry Adams to Brooks Adams, Dec. 27, 1895, in *Letters of Henry Adams*, 92–93.
16. W. A. Swanberg, *Pulitzer*, 200–201.
17. Grover Cleveland to Senator Caffery, Jan. 5, 1896, quoted in R. McElroy, *Grover Cleveland*, 2:102.
18. New York *Tribune*, Jan. 6, 1896.
19. Henry Adams to Brooks Adams, Feb. 7, 1896, in *Letters*, 97.
20. See C. G. Dawes, *A Journal of the McKinley Years*, xii.
21. H. Satterlee, *J. Pierpont Morgan*, 314.
22. T. B. Mott, *Myron T. Herrick*, 69–70.
23. W. A. White, *Masks in a Pageant*, 170.
24. E. Campbell, *Reorganization of the American Railroad System*, 190–215.
25. Barnes, 415–416.

10. THE GRAND STYLE

1. J. Moody, *Masters of Capital*, 31–32.
2. B. J. Hendrick, *The Life of Andrew Carnegie*, 2:27.
3. J. G. Pyle, *The Life of James J. Hill*, 2:28.
4. See *Peter Power* vs. *Great Northern Railroad*, quoted in J. K. Winkler, *Morgan the Magnificent*, 168.
5. John Hay to Whitelaw Reid, Nov. 13, 1898, in W. R. Thayer, *The Life and Letters of John Hay*, 2:194.
6. L. Corey, *House of Morgan*, 228.
7. H. Satterlee, *J. Pierpont Morgan*, 324.
8. For reminiscences of Morgan's relationship with the New York Yacht Club, I am indebted to an engaging memoir, R. Welling's *As the Twig Is Bent*, 205–213. Photographs and plans of all the four *Corsairs* built by Morgan can be found in E. Hofman, *The Steam Yachts*.
9. J. H. Duveen, *Collections and Recollections*, 125.
10. Ibid., 123.
11. Ibid., 137.
12. S. N. Behrman, *Duveen*, 56.
13. From the unpublished memoir of Bishop William Lawrence, courtesy of the Pierpont Morgan Library.
14. Henry Adams to John Hay, Sept. 13, 1900, quoted in Adams's *Letters*, 296.
15. Satterlee, 353.
16. Crown Princess Victoria of Prussia to Queen Victoria, July 23, 1882 (Z36/37), Royal Archives, Windsor Castle.
17. Satterlee, 352.
18. L. Steffens, *Autobiography*, 188–189.
19. J. B. Scott, *Robert Bacon*, 72.

20. Justin Kaplan, *Lincoln Steffens: A Biography* (New York, 1974), 64.
21. New York *Times*, Jan. 1, 1900.
22. M. Josephson, *The Robber Barons*, 404. See also pages 405–417.
23. I. M. Tarbell, *The Life of Elbert H. Gary*, 72. See also pages 73–97.
24. See L. M. Hacker, *The World of Andrew Carnegie*, 401–408.
25. U.S. House of Representatives, *Hearings Before the Committee of Investigation of the United States Steel Corporation*, 62d Cong., 1st and 2d Sess. (1911–12), 30, 2513.
26. B. J. Hendrick, *The Training of an American: The Earlier Life and Letters of Walter H. Page, 1855–1913* (New York, 1928), 182–183. See also P. Lyon, *S. S. McClure*, 160–172.
27. A. D. Noyes, *The Market Place*, 182–183.
28. Quoted in H. F. Pringle, *Theodore Roosevelt*, 227.

11. STEEL, RAILS, RAIDS AND MURDER

1. C. W. Barron, *They Told Barron*, 85.
2. A. Cotter, *The Authentic History of the United States Steel Corporation*, 14.
3. See H. N. Casson, *The Romance of Steel*, 189–190.
4. U.S. House of Representatives, *Hearings Before the Committee of Investigation of the United States Steel Corporation*, 62d Cong., 1st and 2d Sess. (1911–12), 2380.
5. *Wall Street Journal*, Aug. 2, 1909.
6. A. R. Burr, *James Stillman*, 159.
7. I. M. Tarbell, *Elbert H. Gary*, 122–123. This biography of Gary remains the main source for the stories about Morgan and the steel trust. Tarbell was a former editor of *McClure's Magazine* and an expert at reportage. I am also grateful to B. J. Hendrick's excellent life of Andrew Carnegie, a model of its kind.
8. Ibid., 117.
9. E. P. Hoyt, *The House of Morgan*, 249.
10. B. Collier and D. Horowitz, *The Rockefellers: An American Dynasty* (New York, 1976), 55.
11. C. Hovey, *The Life Story of J. P. Morgan*, 214–216.
12. A. D. Noyes, *Forty Years of American Finance*, 300–301.
13. J. G. Pyle, *James J. Hill*, 2:116.
14. Ibid., 2:117.
15. J. A. Garraty, *Right-Hand Man*, 84–85. This biography of Perkins is an indispensable work for all students of the period.
16. C. W. Barron, *They Told Barron*, 58.
17. Burr, 124–125.
18. G. Kennan, *Harriman*, 1:303.
19. Pyle, 2:149.
20. See J. K. Winkler, *Morgan the Magnificent*, 193–194.
21. M. Josephson, *The Robber Barons*, 441.
22. Pyle, 2:154–155.
23. Ibid., 2:164.
24. W. A. White, *Masks in a Pageant*, 295.
25. New York *Times*, Sept. 8, 1901.
26. Tarbell, 161.
27. See H. F. Pringle, *Theodore Roosevelt*, 208.
28. Theodore Roosevelt to Douglas Robinson, Oct. 4, 1901, quoted in Pringle, 245.
29. Quoted in M. Sullivan, *Our Times*, 2:411.

12. AN UNCROWNED MONARCH

1. Quoted in G. Myers, *History of the Great American Fortunes*, 3:247.
2. T. Roosevelt, *Autobiography*, 439.

3. J. G. Pyle, *James J. Hill*, 2:171.
4. Henry Adams to Elizabeth Cameron, Feb. 23, 1902, in Adams's *Letters*, 374.
5. J. B. Bishop, *Theodore Roosevelt and His Times*, 1:184.
6. W. S. Rainsford, *Story of a Varied Life*, 291.
7. Bishop, 1:184–185.
8. H. Satterlee, *J. Pierpont Morgan*, 370.
9. C. Hovey, *The Life Story of J. Pierpont Morgan*, 253.
10. Satterlee, 373.
11. J. H. Duveen, *Collections and Recollections*, 127.
12. C. Canfield, *The Incredible Pierpont Morgan*, 117. This short memoir contains the best layman's account of Morgan as an art collector.
13. See Cleveland Amory's indispensable *The Last Resorts* for a description of the Jekyll Island resort (pp. 152–165).
14. Satterlee, 379.
15. B. H. Meyer, *A History of the Northern Securities Case*, 306.
16. M. Josephson, *The Robber Barons*, 450.
17. A. R. Burr, *James Stillman*, 202.
18. J. A. Garraty, *Right-Hand Man*, 99–100.
19. Henry Adams to Elizabeth Cameron, Apr. 8, 1901, in Adams's *Letters*, 324.
20. W. Lawrence, *Memories of a Happy Life*, 165.
21. C. W. Barron, *They Told Barron*, 322.
22. J. K. Winkler, *Morgan the Magnificent*, 199.
23. H. H. Kohlsaat, *From McKinley to Harding*, 120.
24. L. Corey, *The House of Morgan*, 213–214.
25. H. F. Pringle, *Theodore Roosevelt*, 267.
26. Ibid., 273.
27. T. Roosevelt to Senator Lodge, Oct. 17, 1902, quoted in Bishop, 1:214–215.
28. T. Roosevelt to J. P. Morgan, Oct. 16, 1902, quoted in Pringle, 264.
29. Bishop, 1:216.
30. F. L. Allen, *The Lords of Creation*, 70.
31. See New York *Times*, Mar. 31 and July 20, 1903.
32. Henry Clews, *Fifty Years in Wall Street*, 754. See also pp. 755–770.
33. Burr, 198.
34. Myers, 3:249.
35. Allen, *Lords*, 80. See also C. W. Barron, *More They Told Barron*, 150.
36. C. G. Dawes's journal, Nov. 23, 1902, in his *Journal of the McKinley Years*, 330–331, 337.
37. See Carl Sandburg, *Steichen: The Photographer* (New York, 1966), introduction.

13. ADVERSARIES IN HARNESS

1. Arthur W. Dunn, *Gridiron Nights* (New York, 1915), 134–136.
2. *Wall Street Journal*, Dec. 8, 1903.
3. Quoted in H. F. Pringle, *Theodore Roosevelt*, 351.
4. W. S. Rainsford, *The Story of a Varied Life*, 290.
5. O. Wister, *Roosevelt*, 194.
6. Ibid., 205–212.
7. C. W. Barron, *More They Told Barron*, 153.
8. Quoted in L. Corey, *The House of Morgan*, 313.
9. Henry Adams to Elizabeth Cameron, Apr. 12, 1903, in Adams's *Letters*, 404.
10. Quoted in Pringle, *Roosevelt*, 433.
11. Frederick P. Fisk, president of AT&T, to C. W. Barron, Nov. 21, 1903, in Barron's *More They Told Barron*, 13.
12. T. W. Lawson, *Frenzied Finance*, 2:546.
13. J. Moody, *The Truth About the Trusts*, 494.
14. J. A. Garraty, *Right-Hand Man*, 162.

15. *Hearings and Report of the Committee Appointed Pursuant to House Resolutions 429 and 504 to Investigate the Concentration of Control of Money and Credit*, 62d Cong., 2d and 3d Sess. (1913).
16. Garraty, 179.
17. New York *Evening World*, Sept. 16, 1905.
18. For a full account of the Panama Canal affair, see David McCullough's excellent *The Path Between the Seas*.
19. Herbert Croly's *Willard Straight* has an interesting discussion of the Chinese negotiations on behalf of the American government, Harriman and Morgan.
20. Garraty, 185.
21. P. C. Jessup, *Elihu Root*, 1:433.
22. Corey, 330.

14. PANIC, 1907

1. See J. B. Bishop, *Theodore Roosevelt and His Times*, 2:41.
2. T. Roosevelt to Henry L. Higginson, Mar. 28, 1907, in Bishop, 2:40.
3. T. Roosevelt to Hamlin Garland, Nov. 23, 1907, in Bishop, 2:49.
4. F. A. Vanderlip, *From Farm Boy to Financier*, 126.
5. W. Lawrence, *Memories of a Happy Life*, 251–252.
6. H. Satterlee, *J. Pierpont Morgan*, 463.
7. Vanderlip, 161.
8. A. R. Burr, *James Stillman*, 225.
9. Satterlee, 469.
10. Vanderlip, 168.
11. Satterlee, 473.
12. Ibid., 476, 477.
13. Vanderlip, 173.
14. J. A. Garraty, *Right-Hand Man*, 205.
15. Satterlee, 479.
16. New York *Times*, Oct. 28, 1907.
17. T. W. Lamont, *Henry P. Davison*, 85–87.
18. Garraty, 206.
19. T. W. Lamont, *Across World Frontiers*, 37.
20. Burr, 234–238.
21. Lamont, *Frontiers*, 39.
22. Elbert H. Gary to Elihu Root, Nov. 7, 1907, quoted in I. M. Tarbell, *Elbert H. Gary*, 202.
23. See H. F. Pringle, *Roosevelt*, 443.
24. W. A. White, *Autobiography*, 393.
25. Garraty, 212–213.
26. Vanderlip, 174–175.
27. F. L. Allen, *Lords of Creation*, 142.
28. Pringle, *Roosevelt*, 433.
29. Bishop, *Roosevelt*, 2:50.
30. Burr, 317.

15. A DISCRIMINATING COLLECTOR

1. C. Canfield, *The Incredible Pierpont Morgan*, 59.
2. Iona and Peter Opie, *The Lore and Language of Schoolchildren* (Oxford, 1959), 13.
3. E. Fowles, *Memories of Duveen Brothers*, 10–11.
4. J. H. Duveen, *Collections and Recollections*, 139–140.
5. Mary Anderson de Navarro, *A Few More Memories* (London, 1936), 123.

6. See C. Amory, *The Last Resorts*, 189.
7. Ibid., 292.
8. Duveen, *Collections*, 130.
9. J. K. Winkler, *Morgan the Magnificent*, 8.
10. D. Forbes-Robertson, *Maxine*, 178. This excellent biography has two intriguing chapters on Maxine Elliott's relationships with Morgan and King Edward VII.
11. L. Beebe, *The Big Spenders*, 101.
12. H. Satterlee, *J. Pierpont Morgan*, 526.
13. Winkler, 7–8.
14. Duveen, *Collections*, 141–142.
15. Lady V. Sackville, diary entries for July 8, 20, 30, 1911, and May 20, 22, 1912, in Susan Mary Alsop, *Lady Sackville: A Biography* (New York, 1978), 182–184. This is a stimulating and perceptive book.
16. J. H. Duveen, *Secrets of an Art Dealer*, 120–131.
17. S. N. Behrman, *Duveen*, 30.
18. Satterlee, 434.
19. Behrman, 69.
20. Francis Henry Taylor, *Pierpont Morgan as Collector and Patron, 1837–1913* (New York, 1970), 29. This monograph published by the Pierpont Morgan Library is excellent in its appraisal of Morgan's role as a collector and patron. See also Frederick B. Adams, Jr., *An Introduction to the Pierpont Morgan Library* (New York, 1974), and Gardner Teall, "An American Medici: J. Pierpont Morgan and His Various Collections," *Putnam's Magazine* (Nov., 1909).
21. This extract is taken from Bishop Lawrence's unpublished memoir on Morgan in the Pierpont Morgan Library.
22. Roger Fry to Helen Fry, Jan. 9, 11, 21, 1905, in Fry's *Letters*, 1:228–233.
23. Roger to Lady Fry, July 9, 1905 (?), in ibid., 1:241.
24. Quoted in Canfield, 127.
25. Roger Fry to Helen Fry, Feb. 18 and Mar. 2, 1906, in Fry's *Letters*, 1:250–251, 254–256.
26. See C. Tomkins, *Merchants and Masterpieces*, 109. For an appraisal of Morgan by an English art expert who admired him, see G. C. Williamson, *Stories of an Expert*.
27. W. Lawrence, *Memories of a Happy Life*, 262.

16. GOING DOWN AND GOING UP

1. H. Satterlee, *J. Pierpont Morgan*, 513–514.
2. C. Amory, *The Last Resorts*, 109.
3. A. R. Burr, *James Stillman*, 271.
4. F. L. Allen, *The Lords of Creation*, 175.
5. J. K. Winkler, *Morgan the Magnificent*, 280.
6. T. W. Lamont, *Across World Frontiers*, 41.
7. T. W. Lamont, *Henry P. Davison*, 122.
8. Ibid., 125–129.
9. See Thomas Lamont's statement to Frederick Lewis Allen, from an interview in 1947, quoted in J. A. Garraty, *Right-Hand Man*, 234.
10. Don C. Seitz, *Joseph Pulitzer: His Life and Letters* (New York, 1924), 426, 412.
11. F. Vanderlip, *From Farm Boy to Financier*, 190–196.
12. E. P. Mitchell, *Memoirs of an Editor*, 367–370.
13. Satterlee, 497.
14. W. Lawrence, *Memories of a Happy Life*, 283.
15. Satterlee, 506.
16. See the evidence of Salvatore Cortesi quoted in J. H. Duveen, *Collections and Recollections*, 141.
17. See M. Josephson, *The Robber Barons*, 320.
18. W. S. Rainsford, *The Story of a Varied Life*, 285.

17. DEATH IN ROME

1. W. R. Thayer, *The Life and Letters of John Hay*, 2:568.
2. L. Corey, *The House of Morgan*, 389.
3. W. S. Rainsford, *The Story of a Varied Life*, 289.
4. H. C. Brown, *In the Golden Nineties*, 262–263.
5. T. W. Lamont, *Henry P. Davison*, 137.
6. F. Vanderlip, *From Farm Boy to Financier*, 208–209.
7. Lamont, *Davison*, 134–135.
8. William Lawrence's unpublished memoir, Pierpont Morgan Library.
9. Quoted in E. P. Hoyt, *The House of Morgan*, 400.
10. Letter from Mssrs. J. P. Morgan & Co. in response to the invitation of the Sub-Committee (Hon. A. J. Pujo, Chairman) of the Committee on Banking and Currency of the House of Representatives, Feb. 25, 1913.
11. C. W. Barron, *More They Told Barron*, 157.
12. H. Satterlee, *J. Pierpont Morgan*, 568–569.
13. W. Lawrence, *Memories of a Happy Life*, 323.
14. London *Daily Mail*, Mar. 24, 1913.

18. THE RICH ARE DIFFERENT . . .

1. See the address of Senator Elihu Root in *Tributes to John Pierpont Morgan at the Meeting of the Chamber of Commerce of the State of New York, Held April 3, 1913* (privately printed).
2. George McFadden to Clarence W. Barron, Aug. 25, 1918, in Barron's *They Told Barron*, 62.
3. J. H. Duveen, *Secrets of an Art Dealer*, 114.
4. See Evangeline Adams, *The Bowl of Heaven* (New York, 1926).
5. See F. Pecora, *Wall Street Under Oath*, 1–31.
6. A. Rochester, *Rulers of America*, 46.
7. W. Lawrence, unpublished memoir, Pierpont Morgan Library.
8. W. A. Croffut, *An American Procession, 1855–1914*, 277.
9. See n. 7.

A Select Bibliography

Adams, Charles Francis, Jr. *An Autobiography*. Boston, 1916.
———, and Adams, Henry. *Chapters of Erie and Other Essays*. New York, 1871.
Adams, Frederick B., Jr. *An Introduction to the Pierpont Morgan Library*. New York, 1974.
Adams, Henry. *The Education of Henry Adams: An Autobiography*. Boston, 1918.
———. *The Letters of Henry Adams*. Edited by W. C. Ford. Boston, 1938.
Allen, Frederick Lewis. *The Great Pierpont Morgan*. New York, 1949.
———. *The Lords of Creation*. New York, 1935.
Amory, Cleveland. *The Last Resorts*. New York, 1952.
———. *Who Killed Society?* New York, 1960.
Andrews, Wayne. *The Vanderbilt Legend: The Story of the Vanderbilt Family, 1794–1940*. New York, 1941.
———. *Mr. Morgan and His Architect*. New York, 1957.
Anstice, Henry. *History of St. George's Church in the City of New York, 1752–1911*. New York, 1911.
Atkinson, Edward. *The Railway, the Farmer and the Public*. New York, 1885.
Azdy, A. C. M. *Signal 250: The Sea Fight off Santiago*. New York, 1964.
Barnes, James A. *John G. Carlisle: Financial Statesman*. New York, 1931.
Barnum, Mary Pierpont. *Genealogy of the Pierpont Family and Connections*. Edited by A. E. Boardman. Boston, 1928.
Barrett, Walter (Scoville, J. A.). *The Old Merchants of New York City*. 5 vols. Carleton, N.Y., 1862–63.
Barron, Clarence W. *They Told Barron*. New York, 1930.
———. *More They Told Barron*. New York, 1931.
Beard, Charles A. and Mary R. *The Rise of American Civilization*. 2 vols. New York, 1927.
Behrman, S. N. *Duveen*. New York, 1952.
Beebe, Lucius. *The Big Spenders*. New York, 1966.
Beer, Thomas. *The Mauve Decade*. New York, 1924.
Belmont, Eleanor R. *The Fabric of Memory*. New York, 1957.
Bishop, Joseph B. *Theodore Roosevelt and His Times*. 2 vols. New York, 1920.
Bourne, H. R. *Famous London Merchants*. New York, 1869.
Bowers, Claude G. *Beveridge and the Progressive Era*. New York, 1932.
Brandeis, Louis D. *Other People's Money and How the Bankers Used It*. New York, 1932.
Breen, Matthew P. *Thirty Years of New York Politics*. New York, 1899.
Bridge, James H. *The Inside Story of the Carnegie Steel Company*. New York, 1903.
Brooks, John. *The Seven Fat Years*. New York, 1954.
Brown, Henry C. *In the Golden Nineties*. Hastings-on-Hudson, N.Y., 1928.
Burlingame, Roger. *Backgrounds of Power*. New York, 1948.
Burr, Anna R. *The Portrait of a Banker: James Stillman, 1850–1918*. New York, 1927.
Campbell, Edward G. *The Reorganization of the American Railroad System, 1893–1900*. New York, 1938.
Canfield, Cass. *The Incredible Pierpont Morgan: Financier and Art Collector*. New York, 1974.
Carnegie, Andrew. *The Autobiography of Andrew Carnegie*. Boston, 1920.

———. *Miscellaneous Writings of Andrew Carnegie.* Edited by B. Hendrick. 2 vols. New York, 1933.

Carosso, Vincent P. *More Than a Century of Investment Banking: The Kidder Peabody Story.* New York, 1979.

Casson, Herbert N. *The Romance of Steel.* New York, 1907.

Chalmers, David M. *The Social and Political Ideas of the Muckrakers.* New York, 1964.

Churchill, Allen. *The Splendor Seekers.* New York, 1974.

Clews, Henry. *Fifty Years in Wall Street.* New York, 1908.

Collins, Frederick L. *Money Town.* New York, 1946.

Cornwallis, Kinahan. *The Gold Room.* New York, 1878.

Cortesi, Salvatore. *My Thirty Years of Friendships.* New York, 1927.

Corey, Lewis. *The House of Morgan.* New York, 1930.

Cotter, Arundel. *The Authentic History of the United States Steel Corporation.* New York, 1916.

Crockett, Albert S. *Peacocks on Parade.* New York, 1931.

Croffut, William A. *An American Procession, 1855–1914.* Boston, 1931.

Croly, Herbert A. *Marcus Alonzo Hanna.* New York, 1912.

———. *Willard Straight.* New York, 1925.

Daggett, Stuart. *Railroad Reorganization.* Cambridge, Mass., 1908.

Dawes, Charles G. *A Journal of the McKinley Years.* Chicago, 1950.

Depew, Chauncey M. *My Memories of Forty Years.* New York, 1924.

Dierks, J. C. *A Leap to Arms: The Cuban Campaign of 1898.* New York, 1970.

Dunn, Arthur W. *From Harrison to Harding.* New York, 1922.

Dunshee, Kenneth H. *As You Pass By.* New York, 1952.

Duveen, James H. *Collections and Recollections: A Century and a Half of Art Deals.* New York, 1936.

———. *Secrets of an Art Dealer.* New York, 1938.

———. *The Rise of the House of Duveen.* New York, 1957.

Faulkner, Harold U. *The Decline of Laissez-Faire, 1897–1917.* New York, 1951.

Flynn, John T. *God's Gold: The Story of Rockefeller and His Times.* New York, 1932.

———. *Men of Wealth.* New York, 1941.

Forbes-Robertson, Diana. *Maxine.* London, 1964.

Ford, Abbie A. *John Pierpont.* Boston, 1909.

Fowler, William W. *Ten Years in Wall Street.* Hartford, Conn., 1870.

Fowles, Edward. *Memories of Duveen Brothers.* New York, 1976.

Fry, Roger. *The Letters of Roger Fry.* Edited by D. Sutton. 2 vols. London, 1972.

Fuller R. H. *Jubilee Jim: The Life of Colonel James Fisk, Jr.* New York, 1928.

Garraty, John A. *Right-Hand Man: The Life of George W. Perkins.* New York, 1960.

George, Henry. *Progress and Poverty.* New York, 1879.

Glück, Elsie. *John Mitchell.* New York, 1929.

Grodinsky, Julius. *Jay Gould: His Business Career.* Philadelphia, 1957.

Grund, Francis J. *Aristocracy in America.* London, 1839.

Hacker, Louis M. *The World of Andrew Carnegie.* Philadelphia, 1968.

Hanaford, Phebe A. *The Life of George Peabody.* Boston, 1870.

Haney, Lewis H. *A Congressional History of Railways in the United States.* 2 vols. Madison, Wis., 1910.

Harris, Frank. *Latest Contemporary Portraits.* New York, 1927.

Harvey, George. *Henry Clay Frick, the Man.* New York, 1928.

Hendrick, Burton J. *The Age of Big Business.* New Haven, 1919.

———. *The Life of Andrew Carnegie.* 2 vols. New York, 1932.

———. *The Training of an American: The Earlier Life and Letters of Walter Hines Page.* New York, 1928.

Hicks, John D. *The Populist Revolt.* Minneapolis, 1931.

Hofman, Erik. *The Steam Yachts: An Era of Elegance.* Tuckahoe, N.Y., 1970.

Holbrook, Stewart H. *The Age of the Moguls.* New York, 1953.
Hovey, Carl. *The Life Story of J. Pierpont Morgan.* New York, 1911.
Hoyt, Edwin P. *The Guggenheims and the American Dream.* New York, 1977.
———. *The House of Morgan.* New York, 1967.
Hughes, Rupert. *The Real New York.* New York, 1904.
Jessup, Philip C. *Elihu Root.* 2 vols. New York, 1938.
Johnson, Robert U. *Remembered Yesterdays.* Boston, 1923.
Jones, Eliot. *The Trust Problem in the United States.* New York, 1921.
Josephson, Matthew. *The Robber Barons.* New York, 1962.
Kennan, George. *Edward H. Harriman: A Biography.* 2 vols. Cambridge, Mass. 1922.
Kirkland, Edward C. *Industry Comes of Age: Business, Labor and Public Policy, 1860–1897.* New York, 1961.
Knickerbocker, Jacob. *Then and Now.* New York, 1939.
Kohlsaat, Herman H. *From McKinley to Harding.* New York, 1923.
Lamont, Thomas W. *Across World Frontiers.* New York, 1951.
———. *Henry P. Davison: The Record of a Useful Life.* New York, 1933.
———. *My Boyhood in a Parsonage.* New York, 1946.
Larson, Henrietta M. *Jay Cooke, Private Banker.* Cambridge, Mass., 1936.
Lawrence, William. Memoir. Pierpont Morgan Library, New York.
———. *Memories of a Happy Life.* Boston, 1926.
Lawson, Thomas W. *Frenzied Finance.* 2 vols. New York, 1906. (Previously published as separate articles in *Everybody's Magazine*, Oct. 1904–Feb. 1906.)
Leech, Margaret. *In the Days of McKinley.* New York, 1959.
Lehr, Elizabeth Drexel. *"King" Lehr and the Gilded Age.* Philadelphia, 1935.
Levinson, Leonard L. *Wall Street: A Pictorial History.* New York, 1961.
Lindsay, Philip. *The Great Buccaneer.* New York, 1950.
Lord, Walter. *The Good Years.* New York, 1960.
Loucks, H. L. *The Great Conspiracy of the House of Morgan Exposed and How to Defeat It.* Privately printed, 1916.
Lundberg, Ferdinand. *America's 60 Families.* New York, 1937.
———. *The Rich and the Super-Rich.* New York, 1968.
Lynch, Denis T. *"Boss" Tweed: The Story of a Grim Generation.* New York, 1927.
Lyon, Peter. *Success Story: The Life and Times of S. S. McClure.* New York, 1963.
McAllister, Ward. *Society as I Have Found It.* New York, 1890.
McCarthy, James R. *Peacock Alley.* New York, 1931.
McCullough, David. *The Path Between the Seas: The Creation of the Panama Canal, 1870–1914.* New York, 1977.
McElroy, Robert. *Grover Cleveland: The Man and the Statesman.* 2 vols. New York, 1923.
Martin, F. T. *The Passing of the Idle Rich.* New York, 1912.
Medbery, J. K. *Men and Mysteries of Wall Street.* Boston, 1870.
Meyer, B. H. *A History of the Northern Securities Case.* Bulletin of the University of Wisconsin, No. 142. Madison, 1906.
Minnigerode, Meade. *Certain Rich Men.* New York, 1927.
Mirrors of Wall Street, The. New York, 1933.
Mitchell, Edward P. *Memoirs of an Editor.* New York, 1924.
Mitchell-Hedges, F. A. *Danger My Ally.* Boston, 1954.
Moody, John. *The Masters of Capital.* New Haven, 1919.
———. *The Railroad Builders.* New Haven, 1919.
———. *The Truth About the Trusts.* New York, 1904.
Morgan, J. P., & Co. *Morgan Papers.* New York, 1939.
Morgan, Junius Spencer. Letters to J. Pierpont Morgan, May 30, 1850–Jan. 19, 1888. Archives of the Pierpont Morgan Library, New York City.
Morgan, Nathaniel H. *Morgan Genealogy: A History of James Morgan of New London, Connecticut, and His Descendants from 1607 to 1869.* Hartford, 1869.
Morris, Lloyd. *Incredible New York.* New York, 1951.
Mott, T. B. *Myron T. Herrick, Friend of France.* New York, 1930.

Myers, Gustavus. *The Ending of Hereditary American Fortunes*. New York, 1939.
———. *History of the Great American Fortunes*. 3 vols. New York, 1909–11.
Nevins, Allan. *Grover Cleveland: A Study in Courage*. 2 vols. New York, 1932.
Nicolson, Harold. *Dwight Morrow*. New York, 1935.
Noyes, Alexander D. *Forty Years of American Finance*. New York, 1909.
———. *The Market Place: Reminiscences of a Financial Editor*. Boston, 1938.
Oberholtzer, E. P. *Jay Cooke, Financier of the Civil War*. 2 vols. New York, 1907.
O'Connor, Richard. *Gould's Millions*. New York, 1962.
Orth, Samuel P. *The Armies of Labor*. New Haven, 1919.
Paine, Ralph D. *The Corsair in the War Zone*. Boston, 1920.
Peck, H. T. *Twenty Years of the Republic, 1885–1905*. New York, 1907.
Pecora, Ferdinand. *Wall Street Under Oath*. New York, 1939.
Pitkin, Albert H. *The Morgan Collection*. Hartford, Conn., 1918.
Pringle, Henry F. *Big Frogs*. New York, 1928.
———. *Theodore Roosevelt: A Biography*. New York, 1931.
Pyle, James G. *The Life of James J. Hill*. 2 vols. New York, 1917.
Rainsford, W. S. *A Preacher's Story of His Work*. New York, 1904.
———. *The Story of a Varied Life*. New York, 1922.
Rawley, James A. *Edwin D. Morgan, 1811–1883: Merchant in Politics*. New York, 1955.
Reitlinger, Gerald. *The Economics of Taste: The Rise and Fall of the Picture Market, 1760–1960*. New York, 1964.
Ripley, William Z. *Railroads: Rates and Regulations*. New York, 1912.
———. *Trusts, Pools, and Corporations*. Rev. ed. New York, 1916.
Rochester, Anna. *Rulers of America: A Study of Finance Capital*. New York, 1936.
Rockefeller, John D. *Random Reminiscences of Men and Events*. New York, 1909.
Roosevelt, Theodore. *An Autobiography*. New York, 1920.
Saarinen, Aline. *The Proud Possessors*. New York, 1958.
Satterlee, Herbert L. *J. Pierpont Morgan: An Intimate Portrait*. New York, 1939.
———. *The Life of J. Pierpont Morgan*. Privately printed, 1937.
Scoville, J. A. *See* Barrett, Walter.
Scott, James B. *Robert Bacon: Life and Letters*. London, 1924.
Seldes, George. *One Thousand Americans*. New York, 1947.
Seligman, Germain. *Merchants of Art*. New York, 1961.
Seymour, Charles. *The Intimate Papers of Colonel House*. 2 vols. Boston, 1926.
Smalley, George W. *Anglo-American Memories*. New York, 1911.
Smith, Arthur D. H. *Commodore Vanderbilt: An Epic of American Achievement*. New York, 1927.
———. *Men Who Run America*. Indianapolis, 1935.
Smith, Matthew H. *Successful Folks*. Hartford, Conn., 1878.
———. *Sunshine and Shadow in New York*. Hartford, Conn., 1868.
———. *Twenty Years Among the Bulls and Bears of Wall Street*. Hartford, Conn., 1870.
Sobel, Robert. *The Curbstone Brokers*. New York, 1970.
———. *Panic on Wall Street*. New York, 1968.
Steffens, Lincoln. *The Autobiography of Lincoln Steffens*. New York, 1931.
Stevens, William S. *Industrial Combinations and Trusts*. New York, 1913.
Stoddard, Henry L. *As I Knew Them*. New York, 1927.
Sullivan, Mark. *Our Times*. 6 vols. New York, 1927.
Swanberg, W. A. *Pulitzer*. New York, 1967.
Tarbell, Ida M. *The Life of Elbert H. Gary: The Story of Steel*. New York, 1925.
Taylor, Francis Henry. *Pierpont Morgan as Collector and Patron, 1837–1913*. New York, 1970.
Taylor, John M. *Garfield of Ohio: The Available Man*. New York, 1970.
Teall, Gardner. "An American Medici: J. Pierpont Morgan and His Various Collections." *Putnam's Magazine* (Nov., 1909).
Thayer, William R. *The Life and Letters of John Hay*. 2 vols. Boston, 1915.

Thomas, Lately. *Delmonico's: A Century of Splendor.* Boston, 1967.
Tomkins, Calvin. *Merchants and Masterpieces: The Story of the Metropolitan Museum.* New York, 1970.
Untermyer, Samuel. *Is There a Money Trust?* New York, 1911.
Van Hise, C. R. *Concentration and Control.* New York, 1912.
Van Rensselaer, May, and Van de Water, F. F. *The Social Ladder.* New York, 1924.
Van Wyck, Frederick. *Recollections of an Old New Yorker.* New York, 1932.
Vanderlip, Frank. *From Farm Boy to Financier.* New York, 1935.
Wall, Joseph, F. *Andrew Carnegie.* New York, 1970.
Warshow, R. I. *The Story of Wall Street.* New York, 1929.
Wasson, R. Gordon. *The Hall Carbine Affair: A Study in Contemporary Folklore.* New York, 1948.
Wechsberg, Joseph. *The Mercant Bankers.* New York, 1968.
Wecter, Dixon. *The Saga of American Society.* New York, 1937.
Welling, Richard. *As the Twig Is Bent.* New York, 1942.
Wheeler, George. *Pierpont Morgan and Friends: The Anatomy of a Myth.* New York, 1973.
White, William Allen. *Autobiography.* New York, 1946.
———. *Masks in a Pageant.* New York, 1928.
Williamson, G. C. *Stories of an Expert.* London, 1925.
Winkler, John K. *The First Billion — The Stillmans and the National City Bank.* New York, 1934.
———. *Morgan the Magnificent.* New York, 1930.
Wister, Owen. *Roosevelt: The Story of a Friendship, 1880–1919.* New York, 1930.
Woolf, Virginia. *Roger Fry: A Biography.* New York, 1940.
Wyckoff, Richard D. *Wall Street Ventures and Adventures Through Forty Years.* New York, 1930.

Index

Index

Adams, Charles Francis, Jr., 36–38, 73, 81, 230, 235
Adams, Evangeline, 233
Adams, Henry, 36, 38, 86, 89–90, 98, 104; *The Education of Henry Adams*, 27; and gold crisis, 99, 100–101; and Paris Exhibition (1900), 113; on age of McKinley, 116; on Roosevelt's prosecution of Northern Securities, 141; on JPM's trip abroad, 148; on panic of 1903, 164
Adele (Countess of Essex), 151
Adriatic, 210, 227, 228
Aetna Fire Insurance Company, 4
Agnew and Company, 76, 113–114, 205
Albany & Susquehanna Railroad, 30–31, 32, 33, 52
Aldine Press (Venice), 112
Aldrich, Nelson W., 145, 189, 226, 227
Allegheny Valley Railroad, 29, 30, 45, 125
Allen, Frederick Lewis, 155; *The Lords of Creation*, 190
Alsop, Joseph, 42
Amalgamated Association of Iron, Steel and Tin Workers, 138
Amalgamated Copper, 155
America's Cup, 109–110
American Academy (Rome), 229
American Museum of Natural History, 41
American Railway Union, 84
American Steel and Wire Company, 118, 126
American Telephone and Telegraph Company, 145, 221
Annual Shipping Review, 143
Archbold, John D., 160
Armour, Philip, 25
Astor, John Jacob, IV, 222
Astor, Mrs. William B., 53–55, 82, 111, 195
Astor family, 9, 48, 89, 155
Atlantic, 121

Babcock family, 16
Bache, Jules, 231, 232
Bacon, Robert, 87, 94, 95, 116, 131, 212; and JPM's industrial consolidations, 118; and consolidation of steel industry, 124, 127, 133; and battle over control of Northern Pacific, 134, 135, 136; and Theodore Roosevelt, 138; and Northern Securities Company, 139; retirement of, 147; and coal strike, 153–154; appointed Assistant Secretary of State, 173
Badia and Vives textile collection, 113
Baer, George F., 152–154, 161
Baker, George A., 77
Baker, George F., 132, 134, 139, 146, 157; First National Bank under, 83, 117, 155, 176, 210; and panic of 1907, 179, 180, 181, 182, 184
Baker, Ray Stannard, 165
Ballinger, Richard A., 168
Baltimore & Ohio Railroad, 73, 76, 83
Bangs, Stetson, Tracy and McVeagh, 91
Bank of England, 10, 14, 85
Bank of France, 98
Baring Brothers, 4, 7, 11, 29, 44, 85
Barney, Charles T., 178
Baron textile collection, 113
Barron, Clarence W., 86, 88, 156, 165, 227
Bates, Joshua, 11
Beebe, James M., 7
Belden and Company, 35
Belmont, August, 11, 51, 89, 93–94, 95
Beni Souef (steamer), 48

Bennett collection of incunabula, 150
Berenson, Bernard, 150, 205
Bernhardt, Sarah, 197
Berkman, Alexander, 84
Bethlehem Steel Company, 125, 162–163
Bismarck, Otto von, 12, 38
Black Friday (September 24, 1869), 34–36, 45
Blaine, James G., 91
Blanc, Louis, 11
Blue Thursday (May 9, 1901), 129, 134–135
Bode, Wilhelm von, 150, 193–194, 202–203, 206
Bonheur, Rosa, 76
Bouguereau, Adolphe W., 56, 76
Bowdoin, George S., 16, 60, 62
Brandeis, Louis, 117
Brice, Senator, 89
Bryan, William Jennings, 80, 81, 93, 97–98; and election of 1896, 101, 102–104; and election of 1900, 122; and JPM's death, 230
Bunau-Varilla, Jean P., 169
Burlington Magazine, 144, 205, 206, 207
Burns, Mary Morgan (sister), 78, 205
Burns, Walter H., 60, 62, 112
Burr, Anna, 209
Byron, George Gordon, Lord, 113

Canning, George, 5
Canterbury, Archbishop of, 148, 177
Carlisle, John G., 93–94
Carnegie, Andrew, 25, 29–30, 45–46, 106, 164; and railroad wars, 62, 64, 66; and Homestead strike, 84, 102; and iron-ore and coke markets, 118; attempt to buy him out, 119–120; and consolidation of steel industry, 122, 124, 125–130; his bequest to United States Steel Corporation, 138; and dismissal of Schwab, 147; retirement of, 211
Carnegie Steel Company, 118, 125, 130
Cassidy (Pennsylvania state attorney), 65
Castle Erie, 34, 35, 40
Central Pacific Railroad, 30
Cervera, Pascual, 109
Charles I (of England), 43
Chase National Bank, 117, 210
Chesapeake & Ohio Railroad, 73
Chicago & Alton Railroad, 155
Chicago, Burlington & Quincy Railroad, 130; battle over control of, 132–134, 135
Chicago & Northwestern Railroad, 73
China Development Company, 171–172
Chinese Exclusion Act (1902), 172
Civil Rights Act (1875), 50
Clapp Committee, 222
Clarke, Sir Purdon, 205
Clayton Antitrust Act (1914), 226
Clearing House, 178, 182, 183, 184
Cleveland, Grover, 84, 91, 151; and gold crisis, 93–100, 104
Cleveland *Plain Dealer,* 147
Clews, Henry, 155–156
coal strike, 151–155
Cole, Dr., 10
Colombier, Marie, 40
Columbia, 110, 139
Committee on Banking and Currency, 233
Comstock, Anthony, 47, 207
Consolidated Steel and Wire Company, 117
Cooke, Jay, 23, 24, 30, 94; and bond issues during Civil War, 44–45; collapse of his empire, 45, 51
Cooper Union, 113
Corbin, Abel, 34
Corsair. See Morgan, John Pierpont, YACHTS AND BOATS
Corsair Club, 61, 111
Cortelyou, George B., 179–180, 181
Coster, Charles Henry, 62, 71, 75, 83, 106, 212; death of, 87, 116, 131, 162; and JPM's industrial consolidations, 117
Coxey's Army, 85
Cragston (JPM's country home), 43, 46–47, 60–61, 67
Crédit Mobilier bribery, 45
Crocker, Charles, 139
Cromwell, William Nelson, 169, 170
Cunard Line, 143, 163
Czolgosz, Leon, 137

Dabney, Charles H., 15, 25, 36
Dabney, Morgan and Company, 29, 30, 32, 34
Davison, Henry P., 145, 176, 189, 210–212, 223; and Pujo Committee, 220–221, 225–226
Dawes, Charles G., 101, 157
DeBeers diamond syndicate, 107
Debs, Eugene V., 84
Defender (American yacht), 109
de Forest collection of early French literature, 112
Degas, Hilaire, *Le Viol,* 207
Delaware & Hudson Canal Company, 32
Delaware, Lackawanna & Western Railroad, 29
Depew, Chauncey M., 63, 64
Deposit Act (1833), 4

Depression, The Great, 233, 234. *See also* panic(s)
Detaille, Édouard, 56
Deutsche Bank, 103, 107
Dewey, George, 109
Diamond Match Company, 119
Dickens, Charles, 77
Dill, James B., 116
Doubleday, Frank N., 120–121
Drew, Daniel, 12, 17, 28, 29, 82; and Albany & Susquehanna Railroad, 31, 32, 33
Drexel, Anthony J., 86, 87
Drexel, Elizabeth. *See* Lehr, Elizabeth Drexel
Drexel, Morgan and Company, 43–44, 46, 47, 48, 57; formation of, 36; aid to army and Treasury by, 51; and reorganization of American railroads, 52–53, 64, 86–87; and majority shareholding, 75
Drexel and Company, 30
Dubuque & Sioux City Railroad, 75–76
Duncan, Alexander, 13
Duncan, Sherman and Company, 13, 14, 17, 34
Dunne, Finley Peter, 155; *Mr. Dooley,* 139, 140, 159
Dunraven, Lord, 109–110
Durant, W. C., 233
Duveen, Henry, 77, 144; and JPM's art collection, 202–205
Duveen, James Henry, 111–112, 198; *Collections and Recollections,* 105, 192, 193; on JPM's women, 196; and JPM's art collection, 202
Duveen, Joseph (later Lord Duveen), 42, 76–77, 150; and JPM's art collection, 202–205, 231–232
Duveen Brothers, 149, 201

Eastman, Arthur M., 18–20
Economist, 103
Edison, Thomas A., 56–57, 107
Edison Company, 57
Edward VII, King, 15–16, 40, 147, 149; his coronation, 148, 150–151; his indiscretions, 194, 196, 198; and JPM's art collection, 203; his death, 218, 219
Elliott, Maxine, 149–150, 196–197, 198
Episcopal Church, Triennial Conventions of, 139, 177, 217
Equitable Life Insurance Company, 117, 167, 210
Erie Railroad, 17, 30, 42, 105; financial mismanagement of, 12, 28–29, 83; scandal involving board of directors of, 33–37; bankruptcy of (1893), 89; saved from bankruptcy (1908), 190
Everett, Edward, 5
Everybody's Magazine, 165

Fabbri, Egisto P., 87, 212
Farmers' Alliance, 80
Farmers' Loan and Trust, 210
Farragut, David G., 38
Federal Reserve Act (1913), 189–190, 226
Federal Reserve System, 145
Federal Steel Company, 118, 125
Field, Cyrus, 62
First National Bank of New York, 83, 117, 155, 176, 204, 210
Fisk, Jim, 25, 28–29; and Albany & Susquehanna Railroad, 31, 32, 33, 52; his attempt to corner gold, 34–36
Ford, Henry, 107, 110
Ford collection of early American documents, 112
Forest Service, U.S., 168
Four Hundred, 54, 55, 82
Fowles, Edward, 192–193
Fra Angelico, *Virgin and Child,* 207–208
Frémont, John C., 18–21
French Panama Canal Company, 107, 169–170
Frick, Henry C., 61–62, 106, 118, 124, 138; and Homestead strike, 84; his removal from Carnegie's companies, 119–120; George Harvey's biography of, 121; and consolidation of steel industry, 125, 128, 130; and Isthmian Canal Commission, 160; and panic of 1907, 179; and Tennessee Coal, 187; and JPM's art collection, 231, 232
Frick & Company, 125
Frick Museum, 144, 232
Fry, Roger, 205–208, 237

Gainsborough, Thomas, 76, 113–114; *Miss Linley,* 198, 199–200
Gallatin, A. E., 196
Garland, Hamlin, 176
Garland collection of Chinese ceramics, 144
Gary, Elbert, 65, 117–118, 138, 147, 220; and consolidation of steel industry, 126, 127–128; and Tennessee Coal, 187; and election of 1912, 222
Gates, John W., 117–118, 120, 142; and consolidation of steel industry, 124, 125, 126–127
General Electric Company, 117

General Motors, 233
Ghirlandaio, *Grandfather and Grandson,* 194, 206
Gilded Age, 56
Gloucester (gunboat), 108–109
gold crisis, 91–100, 104
Gold Room disaster, 24, 25, 26
Goodrich rubber company, 212
Goodwin, Jim (cousin), 7, 9, 12, 13, 22, 26
Gosford, Earl of, 112
Gould, Helen, 82
Gould, Jay, 25, 59, 66, 73, 105, 155; and Erie Railroad, 28–29; and Albany & Susquehanna Railroad, 30–31, 32, 33, 52; his attempt to corner gold, 33–36; and Missouri & Pacific Railroad, 53; and West Shore Railroad, 60–61; and Union Pacific Railroad, 81–82; death, 82
Gould family, 155
Grand Hotel (Rome), 228–229
Grange, 80
Grant, Ulysses S., 28, 33–34, 45, 48, 62
Great Northern Railroad, 103, 130, 132, 139
Green, Ashbel, 58
Greene, Belle da Costa, 77, 182, 185, 232
Gridiron Club, 159, 162
Grund, Francis J., 4, 31, 43; *Aristocracy in America,* 3, 8–9, 39, 50
Guaranty Trust Company, 210
Guggenheim, Benjamin, 222
Guggenheim family, 168, 173
Guiccioli, Teresa, 113
Gutman collection of antique silver and bronzes, 144

Hainauer, Oskar, 150, 202
Hall Carbine Affair, 18–21, 25, 26
Hamburg-American Line, 143, 150
Hand, Samuel, 32
Hanna, Mark, 101–102, 108, 122, 141, 159–160; on Theodore Roosevelt, 138; and coal strike, 152; death of, 160
Hanover Bank, 117
Harper and Brothers, 120–121
Harper's Weekly, 121, 227
Harriman, Edward H., 75–76, 105, 121, 145, 146; his reorganization of Union Pacific, 88–89, 103, 121; JPM's refusal to deal with, 130; and battle over control of Burlington and Northern Pacific, 132–137, 140, 147; and Chicago & Alton Railroad, 155; his donation to Roosevelt's campaign, 160; rivalry between Morgan and, in Far East, 170–172; and panic of 1907, 175, 177; Night and Day Bank of, 177; his saving of Erie Railroad from bankruptcy, 190; last years of, 209; death, 172, 210, 218
Harris, Frank, 78
Harvard Medical School, 215, 216
Harvard University, 216
Harvey, George, 121, 227
Hay, John, 107
Hayes, Rutherford, 50, 58
Heinze, F. Augustus, 178
Henry, Prince (of Prussia), 144
Hepburn Act (1906), 174
Herrick, Myron T., 101–102
Hertford, Lord, 201
Hill, James J., 105, 120, 145, 146, 155; and Great Northern Railroad, 103, 106; and battle over control of Burlington and Northern Pacific, 106, 130, 132–137; and Northern Securities Company, 139, 141
Hoffmann, Miss, 12, 13
Holmes, Oliver Wendell, 9
Homestead strike, 84, 102, 138
Hoyt, Colgate, 86
Hudson River Railroad, 29
Hughes, Charles Evans, 167, 223
Hugo, Victor, 11
Huntington, Collis P., 73
Huntington, H. E., 114, 133, 231
Huntington family, 155
Hyde, James Hazen, 167

Illinois Central Railroad, 75, 89
Illinois Steel Company, 118
Independent magazine, 140, 155
Indianapolis *News,* 170
International Banking Corporation, 170, 172
International Harvester Company, 147, 188, 221
International Mercantile Marine Company, 143, 150, 163, 219
Interstate Commerce Commission, 71, 83, 145, 174
Isthmian Canal Commission, 160
Ives, Henry S., 73

Jackson, Andrew, 13, 27, 31, 48; his destruction of the Second Bank of the U.S., 4, 81, 189–190
Jekyll Island Club, 144–145, 189, 195
Jersey Central Railroad, 147
Jones and Laughlin, 125
Judge, 164

Kaiser Friedrich Museum, 150
Kann, Rodolphe and Maurice, 150
Kansas Pacific Railroad, 30
Keats, John, *Endymion,* 77–78

Kessler, George, 149
Ketchum, Edward, 23–24, 25
Ketchum, Morris, 19, 20–21, 23
Ketchum, Son and Company, 19
Ketchum family, 16
King, Edward, 186
Kitchener, Lord, 227–228
Knickerbocker Trust Company, 178–179
Knox, Philander C., 140–142
Kohlsaat, Herman H., 151
Korda, Alexander, 70
Kreuger, Ivar, 233
Krupp steel plants, 125
Kuhn, Loeb and Company, 132, 134, 155, 190, 213; and JPM's reorganization of railroads, 89, 103

Laffan, William, 213–214
Lamont, Daniel S., 94
Lamont, Thomas W., 176, 184–185, 186, 211
Landis, K. M., 188
Landseer, Sir Edwin, 76
Lanier, Charles, 16, 61, 66, 83, 145
Lawrence, Bishop William, 139, 148, 228, 234–235, 237; quotes on Byron manuscripts, 113; and panic of 1907, 177–178; on JPM's character and way of living, 204–205, 208; and JPM's gift to Harvard Medical School, 215; and Pujo Committee, 224
Lawson, Thomas W., *Frenzied Finance*, 165–166
Leacock, Stephen, 70
Lehigh Valley Railroad, 88
Lehr, Elizabeth Drexel (Mrs. Harry "King" Lehr), 55–56
Lehr, Harry "King," 55
Leopold, King (of Belgium), 171, 173, 207
Leverhulme, Lord, 144
Leyland Company, 143
Liberty Bank, 117
Lincoln, Abraham, 23, 24, 27, 95, 139
Lincoln Trust Company, 180, 183, 188
Lindsay, Lord, 49
Lipton, Sir Thomas, 110
Little, Jacob, 12
London, Jack, 139
London *Daily Mail*, 229
London Stock Exchange, 74
Long Island Railroad, 52
Louisville & Nashville Railroad, 142
Lovett, Robert Scott, 132
Lowell, Abbott Lawrence, 216
Lusitania, 163, 188
Lythgoe, Albert, 216
McAllister, Ward, 53–55, 111
McClure, S. S., 120–121
McClure's Magazine, 120, 121, 165
McKim, Charles, 113, 144
McKinley, William, 103, 105, 136–137, 152; Henry Adams on, 100–101, 116; and currency issue, 102; his policy of American expansion abroad, 108; and election of 1900, 120, 122; assassination of, 123, 137, 138, 141; and Sherman Antitrust Law, 140
McLeod, Archibald, 71
Madison Square Garden, 47, 142, 215
Maine, 108, 109
Manhattan General Hospital, 111, 196
Mann, Colonel, 197
Mannheim collection of antiques, 144
Markoe, James, 111, 196
Markoe, Mrs. John, 177, 196
Mauretania, 163
Mazarin, Cardinal, 149, 151
Meissonier, Jean, 56
Mellen, Charles S., 163
Mellon, Andrew, 25, 231
Mellon, Thomas, 25
Mercantile National Bank, 178
Meteor (schooner), 144
Metropolitan Club, 88, 136
Metropolitan Museum of Art, 77, 203, 213–214, 222, 227; JPM becomes Patron of, 41; JPM's gifts to, 113, 144; and JPM's art collection, 204, 231, 232; JPM's presidency of, 205; and Roger Fry, 205–208
Metropolitan Opera House, 142
Michelangelo, 217
Millais, Sir John E., 76
Missouri & Pacific Railroad, 53
Mitchell, Edward, 214
Mitchell, John, 152–153, 154
Monarch (British ironclad), 38
Monroe Doctrine, 107, 170
Moody, John, 211; *The Truth About the Trusts*, 166
Moore Brothers, 119, 120, 125, 155
Moore and Schley, 186
Morgan, Amelia (Mimi) Sturges (first wife), 16, 17, 200, 213; JPM's marriage to, 21–22, 25; death of, 22, 26, 78
Morgan, Anne (daughter), 56, 148
Morgan, Frances Tracy (second wife), 29, 60, 82, 194–195; JPM's marriage to, 26
Morgan, Henry, 31, 79, 108
Morgan, John Pierpont: birth and early life, 3–12; family background, 3–4, 5–6, 13; education, 7–13; avoids serving in

Morgan, J. P. (cont.)
Civil War, 17, 21–22; marriages, 21–22, 26 (*see* Morgan, Amelia Sturges; Morgan, Frances Tracy); children (*see* Morgan, Anne; Morgan, John Pierpont, Jr.; Satterlee, Louisa Morgan); health, 10, 11, 12, 17, 25, 39, 48, 87–88, 219, 226–229; appearance, xi, 7, 10, 12, 57, 69, 121–122, 157–158, 192–194, 214, 215, 216; weight and physical strength, 110; his nasal deformity, 12, 17, 25, 48, 69, 158, 192–194; his cigars, 57, 189; his religious views and life, 6, 21, 26, 47–48, 67–69, 177, 217–218, 231, 237; his political views, 45, 91, 160, 173; threatened with assassination, 138; income, 25, 46; size of his estate, 231; his philanthropies, 111, 195, 196, 215, 234–235; hobbies of dog- and cattle-breeding, 215; as yachtsman, 88, 108, 109–111, 147; at the coronation of King Edward VII, 148–149, 150–151; audiences with Pope Pius X, 217; decorations and honorary degrees, 216, 219; his last years, 209–215, 226–230; death, 229, 230; will, 230, 231; funeral, 230–231; his character and achievements assessed, 234–237

EARLY CAREER: first venture, at age twelve, 7; as George Peabody's assistant, 13; in Duncan, Sherman and Company, 13, 14, 17, 34; learns bookkeeping, 15; as his father's eyes and ears in New York, 15–18, 23, 25, 38; his first speculation, 16–17; the Hall Carbine Affair, 18–21, 25, 26; founds J. P. Morgan and Company, 22; gold speculation, 23–24, 26; as partner in Dabney, Morgan and Company, 36, 44, 45, 48, 50–51, 52–53; defeats Drew and Gould in Albany & Susquehanna war, 32; purchases Carnegie's Allegheny Valley stock, 45–46; loses in Texas Pacific debacle, 46; guarantees soldiers' pay in Indian war, 51; and takeover of bond market, 51

1876–1898: consolidates railroads, 51–52, 105–106; purchases Long Island stock, 52; combines New York Central and Wabash, 52; settles trunk-line war between New York Central and Pennsylvania, 60–62, 63–66; reorganizes Philadelphia & Reading, 70–71, 73–74; tries to sell self-regulation to railroad magnates, 71–73, 74; puts Vandalia line out of business, 73; rescues B & O and C & O, 73; methods of reorganization, 75; loses to Harriman (Dubuque & Sioux City), 75–76; becomes his own man at his father's death, 79; bests Gould (Union Pacific), 81–82; acquires southern railroads, 83; helps alleviate panics of 1890 and 1893, 85–86; acquires Lehigh Valley, 88–89; acquires and reorganizes Erie, 89, 105; in the Gold Reserve crisis of 1895, 92–103; alliance with Hill to take over Northern Pacific, 103, 106; as scapegoat of Bryan Democrats, 102–104; loses Union Pacific to Harriman, 103; circumvents Sheman Antitrust Act, 103; his accomplishments as of 1898, 105; his attitude to his railroad trust, 106–107

1898–1913: his foreign transactions, 107–108; and creation of trusts and holding companies, 117; and creation of General Electric, 117; creates U.S. Steel, 117–120, 124–130; rescues Harper and Brothers, 120–121; battles Harriman over Chicago, Burlington & Quincy, 130–131, 132–135, 136–137; and McKinley's death, 137; breaks steel strike, 138; creates international shipping trust, 138, 139, 143–144, 147, 163; forms Northern Securities Company, 136; and T. Roosevelt's trust-busting, 140–142, 145–146, 160, 164; his power described as of 1901, 142–143; gains control of Jersey Central, 147; attempts to finance London subway system, 148; bails out T. Roosevelt, 151; and the anthracite miners' strike, 151, 152–155; as adviser to T. Roosevelt, 160; and the panic of 1903, 164–165; attacked by Lawson, 165–166; exposure of, 166–168; and the Equitable Life investigation, 167–168; and "the Second Purchase of Alaska," 168–169; and the taking of the Panama Canal, 169–170; his intervention in China, 170–173; and the panics of 1907, 177–190; and the creation of an alleged money trust, 210, 212, 223–227; rescues banks in trouble, 211–212; examined by the Pujo Committee, x, 223–227

THE BUSINESSMAN: his aims and philosophy, 31, 51–52, 70, 82–83, 85, 156–157; inability to delegate work, 22–23; compared to Drew and Gould, 31–32; attitude to new inventions, 56–57, 233; methods of doing business, 57, 65, 75, 86, 156–157; relations with his partners and employees, 62, 87, 115–116, 131–132, 147; as a scofflaw, 64–65; as a judge of men, 69, 120, 121; as a plunger, 86, 87–

88; described by Stillman, 87, 92; described by A. D. Noyes, 121–122; compared with Stillman, 121–122, 156–157; loss of reputation, 135, 136, 162–164; use of publicity, 156; compared with the Rockefellers, 156–157; hatred of, by the public, 162; refusal to admit defeat, 185; relations with business rivals, 209–210

CHARACTER AND PERSONALITY, xi–xiv, 87–88, 234–237; ability with figures, 9, 13, 15; arrogance, 25, 64–66, 81, 96, 97, 140; compartmentalizing, 68, 237; courtesy, 214; described by Bishop Lawrence, 208; described by Edward Mitchell, 214; generosity, 214–215; love of children, 26; love of the limelight, 195; lust to accumulate, 235; loyalty, gift for inspiring, 69; patriotism, 69; ruthlessness, 181; secretiveness, 15; self-doubts, 88; sentimentality, 215; sociability and charm, 26, 69; taciturnity, 11, 15, 44, 47, 57, 197, 198; tenacity, 57, 185

RELATIONS WITH OTHERS: his father, 15–17, 39, 43–44, 66, 78, 79; his son, 78, 148–149, 176, 213, 232; women, 60, 194–201; his attorneys, 65; the press, 215

THE COLLECTOR, 41–43, 49, 76–78, 195, 234; J. H. Duveen's opinion of, 111–112; methods of purchase, 112; his persistence, 113; purchases for institutions, 113; advisers (*see* Bode, Wilhelm von; Duveen, Henry; Duveen, William Henry); and forgeries, 112, 202; and alteration of customs regulations, 203. *See also* Fry, Roger; Metropolitan Museum of Art; Morgan Library

HIS COLLECTIONS, 111–115, 144–145, 201–205; of Bourbon decorative art, 232; catalogues of, 201–202, 204, 213; of Chinese ceramics, 144, 205, 232; display of after his death, 231; disposal of, 231–232; of Egyptian antiquities, 49; financing of, 201, 231; of Fragonard paintings, 232; housing of 112, 203, 222, 231 (*see also* Morgan Library); of manuscripts and books, 77–78, 112–113, 150; of miniatures, 201; statue of Ur-Engur, 214; of tapestries, 232; value of, 231; Washington's sword, 79; willed to his son, 222, 231

TRAVELS: to Europe, 10–11, 48, 147–151, 228–229; by rail in New York State, 12; to the West, 30; to Carlsbad, 39–41, 43; to Egypt, 41, 48–49, 216–217, 227–228; to the Holy Land, 60; his way of traveling, 144–145

HIS YACHTS AND BOATS: used for business conferences, 60, 64, 98, 101, 153; *Corsair*, 31, 60, 64, 72; *Corsair II*, 78–79, 88, 98, 101, 108–109; *Corsair III*, 109–111, 137, 147, 149–150, 153, 194–195, 219; *Khargeh*, 49, 228; *Louisa*, 60

HOMES: on East 40th Street, 41; Cragston, 43, 46–47, 60–61; at 219 Madison Ave., 53, 55–57, 76–77

Morgan, John Pierpont, Jr. (son), 29, 78, 148–149, 171, 176, 213; and JPM's art collections, 222–223, 231–232; and World War I, 232–233; and the stock market crash (1929), 233

Morgan, Joseph (grandfather), 3, 5, 6, 7, 43

Morgan, J. P., and Company (1862), 22

Morgan, J. P., and Company (1895), 86, 100; and consolidation of the steel industry, 127 (*see also* United States Steel Corporation); errors in effecting its reorganizations, 162–163; scandals associated with, 163, 167–168; and the "rich man's panic" of 1903, 164–165; as instrument of T. Roosevelt's and Taft's foreign policies, 170, 171–173; Joseph Pulitzer's view of the partners (1911), 212; and the Pujo Committee hearings, 223, 225; profits taken by JPM from 231. *See also* Morgan, John Pierpont

Morgan, J. S., and Company, 23, 25, 43, 85

Morgan, Juliet Pierpont (mother), 6, 66

Morgan, Junius Spencer (father), 6, 9, 10, 11; his dry goods store in Boston, 7; his correspondence with JPM, 7–8, 15; his partnership with George Peabody, 11–12; and Duncan, Sherman and Company, 13, 14; JPM's apprenticeship for, in New York, 15–18; and JPM's marriage to Mimi Sturges, 22; forms J. S. Morgan and Company, 23; and gold speculation, 24; and railroad bonds, 29–30; asked to join Erie board, 33; and formation of Drexel, Morgan and Company, 36; formation of syndicate by, 38; his loan to French government, 38, 39; JPM's resentment of, 39; his contributions to JPM's home and office, and Andrew Carnegie, 45–46, 125; estate in England, 46; and railroad wars, 60–61,

Morgan, Junius (cont.)
62, 66; portraits collected by, 76, 113, 222; death, 78; estate, 79; JPM's commemoration of, 215–216
Morgan, Junius (grandson), 233
Morgan, Louisa. *See* Satterlee, Louisa Morgan
Morgan Library, 78, 150, 153, 232; McKim's design of, 113, 144; conferences at, during panic of 1907, 178, 182, 185; collections displayed in, 204
Morse, Charles W., 176, 178
Morton, Levi P., 44–45, 51
Mutual Life Insurance Company, 117, 210
Myers, Gustavus, *History of the Great American Fortunes*, 20

Napoleon III, 38
Nashville (cruiser), 169
National Bank of America, 179
National Bank of Commerce, 117, 210, 212–213
National Biscuit Company, 119
National City Bank, 121, 155, 210, 213; James Stillman's presidency of, 87, 92, 121, 155, 176; and International Banking Corporation, 170
National Tube, 120, 125
Navarro, Mary Anderson de, 195
New York, New Haven & Hartford Railroad, 163, 221
New York *American*, 173
New York Cathedral, 142
New York Central Railroad, 52, 130; and JPM's reorganization of railroads, 60–66 *passim*
New York *Evening World*, 168
New York *Herald*, 13
New York *Journal*, 108
New York Life Insurance Company, 117, 131–132, 155, 223; resignation of Perkins from, 167–168
New York Public Library, 112
New York Society for the Suppression of Vice, 47, 207
New York Stock Exchange, 24, 110; and panic of 1907, 180, 181–182, 183, 184, 187
New York *Sun*, 213, 214
New York *Times*, 117, 230
New York *World*, 94, 98, 167, 170; on Jay Cooke, 44; on gold bonds, 99, 100; and Morgan partners, 212; on JPM's death, 230
New York Yacht Club, 88, 108, 109, 111
Nickel Plate Railroad, 61
Night and Day Bank, 179
Norris, Frank, 165
Northern Pacific Railroad, 30, 45, 103, 130, 132, 145; $50 million loan to, 53, 59; battle over control of, 130, 132–137, 140, 147; JPM's inspection of, 139
Northern Securities Company, 136, 139; government suit against, 140–141, 145–146, 147, 160
Noyes, Alexander Dana, 129–130

Oceanic (liner), 110, 151
Ohio Life and Trust Company, 14
Olney, Richard, 95
Olympia (warship), 109
Oregon (warship), 109
Owen, Robert Dale, 11

Page, Walter Hines, 121
Palace Car Company, 84
Panama Canal, taking of, 169–170
Panama Railroad, 107
Pandora (British steam yacht), 60
panic of 1837, 3–5
panic of 1857, 13–14, 15
panic of 1873, 45, 46, 51
panic of 1890, 85
panic of 1893, 83, 85–86
panic of 1901, 129, 134–135
panic of 1903, 156, 164–165
panic of 1907, 174; causes of, 175, 178; Roosevelt's role in, 175–176; events leading up to, 176–178; and trust companies, 178–188 *passim;* JPM's role in, 178–190 *passim;* and New York Stock Exchange, 180, 181–182, 183, 184, 187; and city of New York, 184; and Tennessee Coal, Iron and Railroad Company, 186–187, 188; effect of, 190
Paris Exhibition (1900), 113
Peabody, George, 4, 5, 7, 10, 29; characterized, 11; his partnership with Junius Morgan, 11–12; JPM his assistant, 13; his loan from Bank of England, 14; involvement in Civil War, 23; death, 38
Peabody, George, and Company, 5, 14, 17, 23
Pennsylvania Railroad, 30, 52, 70; and JPM's reorganization of railroads, 61–66 *passim*
Pennsylvania Turnpike, 62
Perkins, George W., 117, 131–132, 157, 176, 195, 220; and battle over control of Northern Pacific Railroad, 134, 135, 136; and Theodore Roosevelt, 138, 168; and International Harvester Company, 147, 188; and coal strike, 154; resignation of, from New York Life, 167–168; indictments against, 168; and Russian bond

issue, 171; and panic of 1907, 180, 181, 185, 187, 188; JPM's rift with, 212; and election of 1912, 222
Philadelphia & Reading Railroad, 61, 70–71, 73–74
Phipps, Henry, 130
Pierpont, John (grandfather), 6, 22
Pike's Opera House, 32, 40
Pinchot, Gifford, 168
Piombo, Sebastiano del, *Christopher Columbus*, 113
Pius X, Pope, 217
Platt, Orville H., 97
Platt, Thomas C., 138
Pluton (torpedo boat), 108–109
Poor's Manual, 59
Populist movement, 80, 92–93, 97
Porter, Horace, 60–61
Potter, Henry C., 47, 67
Prince, F. H., 227
Pujo Committee, 210, 221, 223–227, 236
Pulitzer, Joseph, 100, 195, 212; and New York *World*, 94, 98, 99, 167
Pullman, George M., 30, 61, 84
Pullman strike, 84–85

railroad(s), 81; wars, 30–33; JPM's reorganization of, 51–53, 59–66, 70–76, 88–89, 105–107, 130–131; JPM's control of comprehensive system of, 81–83; battle over control of Burlington and Northern Pacific, 130, 132–137; regulation of, 145–146. *See also names of individual railroads*
Rainsford, W. S., 67–69, 113, 121, 159, 191; and JPM's depressions, 87; on JPM's religious nature, 217–218
Ramsey, Joseph, 31, 32
Read, John, 192
Reid, Whitelaw, 107
Reynolds, Sir Joshua, 76
Rhodes, Cecil, 107
Richmond & West Point Terminal line, 83
Roberts, George Brooke, 61, 63, 64, 66, 72–73
Rockefeller, John D., 25, 83, 121, 128, 133; and exposé of Standard Oil, 165; and panic of 1907, 175, 181, 188; on JPM's estate, 231
Rockefeller, John D., Jr., 128
Rockefeller family, 64, 127–128, 155, 220; secrecy of, 156; effect of panic of 1907 on, 190
Romney, George, 76
Roosevelt, Franklin, 233
Roosevelt, Theodore, 122, 149, 212, 216, 218, 220; his relationship with JPM, 138–139, 140–142, 159–162, 173, 190, 234, 237; his prosecution of Northern Securities, 140–142, 146; and coal strike, 151–155; and election of 1904, 159–160; and Panama Canal, 169–170; and JPM's intervention in China, 171–172; dollar diplomacy of, 173; quoted, 174; public quarrel between Wall Street and, 174–176; and panic of 1907, 174–176, 183–184, 186–188; and election of 1912, 221, 222; company preferred by, 235
Root, Elihu, 153–154, 187, 230
Rothschild, Lord, 126, 147
Rothschild family, 4, 11, 43, 44, 51, 89
Russell, Lillian, 195
Russo-Japanese War, 170
Ryan, Thomas F., 210

Sackville, Lady Victoria, 198–201
Sackville, Lord, 198
Sackville-West, Lionel, 198
Sagamore (brigantine), 108
Sage, Russell, 235–236
Saint-Gaudens, Augustus, 88
Satterlee, Herbert, 115, 178, 183, 229
Satterlee, Louisa Morgan (daughter), 29, 77, 78, 137, 178, 229; marriage to Herbert Satterlee, 115
Schiff, Jacob H., 89, 155, 174, 190; and battle over control of Northern Pacific, 132, 133–134, 135
Schley, Grant B., 186
Schwab, Charles M., 118, 119, 120, 196; and consolidation of steel industry, 122–126; his Monte Carlo gambling spree, 147, 194; and Bethlehem Steel, 162–163
Scott, Sir John Murray, 198, 200
Second Bank of the United States, 4, 81, 190
Seligman, J. and W., 34, 51, 107
Shamrock II (yacht), 110, 139
Sherman Antitrust Act (1890), 83, 84, 103, 140, 164
Sherman Compromise Silver Act (1890), 85–86, 91
Sherry, Louis, 217
Sinclair, Upton, *The Jungle*, 165
Sitwell, Osbert, 203
Sloan, Samuel, 29, 30, 31
Smith, F. E., 200
Southern Pacific Railroad, 133
Southern Railway System, 83
South Pennsylvania Railroad, and JPM's reorganization of railroads, 61–66 *passim*
Spanish-American War, 108–109
Specie Circular, 4
Spencer, Samuel, 83

Speyers, Albert, 35
Standard Oil, 128, 133, 155, 156, 160; exposé of, 165; and International Banking Corporation, 170; and China Development Company, 171; fine levied on, 188; government's suit against, 220
Steele, Charles, 131, 176, 184–185
Steffens, Lincoln, 115–116, 124, 165
Steichen, Edward: his portrait of JPM, 157–158
Stephenson, George, 53
Stetson, Francis Lynde, 87, 91, 94, 127, 136, 184
Stevens, Henry, 18
Stevens, Simon, 18–21
Stevens, Sophia, 18
Stewart, Alexander T., 53
Stillman, James, 104, 126, 156, 157, 191; and National City Bank, 87, 92, 121, 155, 176; and George Perkins, 131; and battle over control of Northern Pacific, 133, 134; on dissolution of Northern Securities Company, 146; and coal strike, 151; and currency question, 160; and panic of 1907, 179–190 *passim;* last years of, 209–210; and election of 1912, 222
strikes: Homestead, 84, 102, 138; Pullman, 84–85; coal, 151–155
Studebaker Company, 212
Sturges, Mimi. *See* Morgan, Amelia Sturges
Sturges family, 16, 22

Taft, William Howard, 168, 172–173, 220, 221, 222
Tarbell, Ida, 165
Tate Gallery, 203
Tennessee Coal, Iron and Railroad Company, 186–187, 188
Tenth National Bank, 34
Texas Pacific Railroad, 46
Thackeray, William Makepeace, 77
Thomson, Frank, 63
Tilden, Samuel J., 28, 50
Titanic, 219; sinking of, 221
Toovey collection of books, 112
Tornabuoni, Giovanna, 194
Townsend, Miss, 177
Town Topics, 197
Tracy, Charles, 26, 32, 91
Tracy, Frances. *See* Morgan, Frances Tracy
trust companies, and panic of 1907, 178–188 *passim*
Trust Company of America, 180, 181, 183, 188
Tweed, William, 32
Tweeddale, Candida Lady, 151
Tyng, Stephen H., 16, 22, 48
Tz'u-hsi, Dowager Empress of China, 170, 171, 172

Uncle Tom's Cabin (Stowe), 165
Union Club, 32, 63, 153
Union Pacific Railroad, 30, 73, 81–82, 136, 145; reorganization of, by E. H. Harriman, 89, 103, 121, 132–133
United States Shipbuilding trust, 163
United States Steel Corporation, 138, 143, 163, 186, 212, 220; JPM's consolidation of steel industry into, 126–130; effect of Blue Thursday on, 135; Schwab's chairmanship of, 147; fall in common stock of, 163–164; and Tennessee Coal, 186, 187; seven-day workweek at, 220; suit brought to dissolve, 221
Untermyer, Samuel, 224–225, 226, 237
Ur-Engur, statue of, 214

Valkyrie III (yacht), 109
Van Buren, Martin, 4
Vanderbilt, Cornelius, 17, 28, 31, 32, 109, 155; and Hudson River Railroad, 29; death, 52
Vanderbilt, William H., 25, 52, 59, 105; Greek Renaissance blockhouses of, 53; press showing of his private art gallery, 56; and railroad wars, 60–66 *passim*
Vanderbilt, Mrs. William K., 55, 82, 111
Vanderbilt family, 9, 48, 155
Vanderlip, Frank, 176, 181, 210–211, 212–213, 223; on panic of 1907, 179, 182, 188–189
Vest, George G., 97
Victoria, Crown Princess of Prussia, 40, 114
Victoria, Queen, 10, 11, 38, 40, 46, 114; death, 148, 196; and Lady Victoria Sackville, 198
Victoria and Albert Museum, 202

Wabash, St. Louis & Pacific, 52
Wabash vs. *Illinois,* 71
Wadsworth Atheneum (Hartford), 113, 215
Wainwright, Richard, 109
Wallace, Lady, 198
Wallace, Sir Richard, 198, 201
Wall Street Journal, 88, 126, 160, 230
Ward and Grant, 62
Warren, Joseph, 6
Washington, George, 79
West, Benjamin, *The Raising of Lazarus,* 113, 215

"Western Blizzard," 14
Western Union, 221
Westinghouse Electric Company, 176
West Shore Railroad, and JPM's reorganization of railroads, 60–67 *passim*
Wharton, Edith, 195
Wheeler, Joseph, 8
White, Stanford, 88
White, William Allen, 102, 137, 188
White Star Line, 143, 147, 219
Widener, George, 222
Widener, P. A. B., 114, 222
Widener family, 155
Wilhelm I, Kaiser, 40, 147, 150, 202–203, 219–220; and JPM's death, 231
Williamson, George C., 201, 202
Wilson, Woodrow, 189, 221, 222, 226, 227, 233
Winkler, John, 197
Wister, Owen, 161–162
Woolf, Virginia, 205
Woollcott, Alexander, *While Rome Burns*, 197
Wright, J. Hood, 87

yachts. *See* Morgan, John Pierpont, YACHTS AND BOATS
Yale University, 216
Young, Brigham, 30
Young Men's Christian Association, 26